THE COURT OF JUSTICE OF THE EUROPEAN UNION

In 2017, the Court of Justice of the European Union (CJEU) celebrated 65 years and has thereby achieved retirement age in most EU Member States. If it were to retire, the Court would be able to look back at a fascinating journey, from its relatively humble beginning on 4 December 1952 as part of the then brand-new European Coal and Steel Community, to one of the most important and exciting judicial institutions in Europe, perhaps in the entire world.

The need to understand the CJEU has never been greater. This volume is dedicated to improving our understanding of the Court in relationship to other actors, including other EU institutions, the Member States, national courts, third countries, and international organisations. It is based on a conference arranged by the Swedish Network for European Legal Studies (SNELS) held at Stockholm University in December 2016, and includes contributions by both lawyers and researchers in other fields, as well as current members of the Court.

The Court of Justice of the European Union

Multidisciplinary Perspectives

Swedish Studies in European Law
Volume 10

Edited by
Mattias Derlén and Johan Lindholm

•HART•
OXFORD • LONDON • NEW YORK • NEW DELHI • SYDNEY

HART PUBLISHING

Bloomsbury Publishing Plc

Kemp House, Chawley Park, Cumnor Hill, Oxford, OX2 9PH, UK

HART PUBLISHING, the Hart/Stag logo, BLOOMSBURY and the Diana logo are
trademarks of Bloomsbury Publishing Plc

First published in Great Britain 2018

First published in hardback, 2018
Paperback edition, 2020

A catalogue record for this book is available from the British Library.

Library of Congress Cataloging-in-Publication Data

Names: Derlén, Mattias, editor. | Lindholm, Johan, editor.

Title: The Court of Justice of the European Union : multidisciplinary perspectives /
edited by Mattias Derlén and Johan Lindholm.

Description: Oxford ; Portland, Oregon : Hart Publishing, 2018. | Series: Swedish studies
in European law ; 10. | Includes bibliographical references and index.

Identifiers: LCCN 2017050985 (print) | LCCN 2017050495 (ebook) |
ISBN 9781509919093 (Epub) | ISBN 9781509919086 (hardback : alk. paper)

Subjects: LCSH: Court of Justice of the European Union. |
Courts—European Union countries. | Law—European Union countries.

Classification: LCC KJE5461 (print) | LCC KJE5461 .C679 2018 (ebook) | DDC 347.24/01—dc23

LC record available at https://lccn.loc.gov/2017050985

ISBN: HB: 978-1-50991-908-6
PB: 978-1-50993-827-8
ePDF: 978-1-50991-910-9
ePub: 978-1-50991-909-3

Typeset by Compuscript Ltd, Shannon

To find out more about our authors and books visit www.hartpublishing.co.uk. Here you will find
extracts, author information, details of forthcoming events and the option to sign up for our newsletters.

This volume is dedicated to the memory of Pernilla McAlevey

Preface

The Court of Justice of the European Union (CJEU) is sixty-five years old this year and has achieved retirement age in most EU Member States, including Luxembourg. If it were to retire, the Court would be able to look back at an exciting journey, from its relatively humble beginning on 4 December 1952 as part of the brand-new European Coal and Steel Community to one of the most important and exciting judicial institutions in Europe, perhaps in the entire world. The European Union is currently facing several challenges, but there are no indications that the Court will retire anytime soon. Instead, over time, the Court has accrued a maturity and wisdom that will allow it to perform a crucial role in facing these challenges—and any new challenges that the future will bring. The need to understand the CJEU has never been greater. This volume is dedicated to improving our understanding of the Court in relationship to other actors, including other EU institutions, the Member States, national courts, third countries, and international organisations. It is based on a conference arranged by the Swedish Network for European Legal Studies (SNELS) at Stockholm University in December 2016, with the same title as this volume. We were very fortunate to have an excellent group of speakers, with both diverse backgrounds and research interests. We are particularly happy that the speakers included both lawyers and researchers from other areas, but also current members of the Court. We believe that the different perspectives of the contributions greatly add to our understanding of the Court and its relationships to different actors.

We would like to take this opportunity to thank all the authors for the work that they have put into their contributions, the Swedish Network for European Legal Studies for supporting this volume and the conference on which it builds (and particularly network coordinators Cornelia Larsson and Parasto Taffazoli who assisted with much of the practical arrangements) as well as the conference audience who asked important questions and made helpful comments and thereby contributed to the conference and to this volume.

Mattias Derlén and Johan Lindholm

Table of Contents

List of Contributors

Mohamed Ali is a legal secretary to Ulf Öberg at the General Court of the European Union. In addition, he is an associate judge at the Svea Court of Appeal in Stockholm, where he adjudicated criminal and civil cases.

Anthony Arnull is Barber Professor of Jurisprudence at the University of Birmingham, UK. He is Consultant Editor of the European Law Review and has previously worked at the Court of Justice in Luxembourg as a référendaire in the chambers of Advocate General FG Jacobs.

Ulf Bernitz is Professor of European Law at the Faculty of Law, Stockholm University and Senior Research Fellow, St Hilda's College, Oxford. His research interests include European law and its relation to national law, competition and market law, consumer law and intellectual property law.

Ana Bobić is pursuing a DPhil in law at the Oxford Law Faculty and a lecturer in Constitutional and Administrative Law at Keble College, Oxford. Her research seeks to determine how the principle of primacy of EU law works in reality and whether the national constitutional jurisprudence supports this concept.

Graham Butler is Assistant Professor of Law at Aarhus University, Denmark.

Mattias Derlén is Professor of Law at the Department of Law at Umeå University, Sweden. His research interests include Law & Language, European Union Law, Constitutional Law and Empirical Legal Studies.

Angelica Ericson is a PhD candidate at Lund University and a legal secretary at the Court of Justice of the European Union.

Desmond Johnson is a Lecturer in Comparative Public Law and Governance at The Hague University of Applied Science. His research explores how public power is balanced within a constitutional order and he currently focuses on the constitutional and institutional structures and processes in place to limit and balance the exercise of public power with individual and political self-determination in the EU and the United States.

Olof Larsson is a Post-doc at the Department of Political Science and connected to the Centre for European Research (CERGU) at the University of Gothenburg. His research focus is Judicial Politics, the Court of Justice of the European Union, the politics surrounding the decisions of the Court, and European integration theory.

Johan Lindholm is Professor of Law at the Department of Law at Umeå University, Sweden. His research interests include European Union law, Comparative Law, Sports Law, and Empirical Legal Studies.

Daniel Naurin is Professor in Political Science at PluriCourts, University of Oslo and at the Department of Political Science, University of Gothenburg. His research interests include judicial politics, transparency, international negotiations, interest group politics and the European Union.

Pauline Sabouret is a legal assistant to Ulf Öberg at the General Court of the European Union.

Anna Wallerman is a Max Weber Fellow at the European University Institute and an associate senior lecturer at the University of Gothenburg. Her research interests include the europeanisation of civil procedure, judicial dialogue and decision-making, and empirical legal methods.

Anna Wetter Ryde is a doctor of law and a senior researcher at the Swedish Institute for European Policy Studies (SIEPS). Her research interest is in the field of the EU's constitutional development with emphasis on the legislative process and the transparency regime.

Marlene Wind is Professor of Political Science at the Department of Political Science and Professor at iCourts at the Faculty of Law, both University of Copenhagen.

Ulf Öberg is a Judge at the General Court of the European Union. He has previously been a practicing attorney, lecturer, researcher, legal adviser at the Swedish Ministry of Foreign Affairs, and a legal secretary at the Court of Justice.

1

The Court of Justice Then, Now and Tomorrow

ANTHONY ARNULL

1. INTRODUCTION

IT IS UNDENIABLE that for many years the Court of Justice played a major role in the development of what is now the European Union (EU). Through its case law, the Court crafted 'a new kind of legal order, the nature of which is peculiar to the EU ...'.[1] In what follows, I briefly sketch how, from modest beginnings, the Court of Justice came to occupy a place at the very heart of the EU; some of the problems to which its vertiginous ascent gave rise; and how those problems might be addressed.

2. THE COURT OF JUSTICE THEN

It is easy to forget that the Court of Justice has not always occupied such a central a position in the process of European integration. Indeed, the possibility that it might acquire that status would have seemed remote when the Paris conference opened on 21 June 1950, less than two months after the publication of the Schuman Declaration.[2] The centrepiece of that Declaration was a proposal to place Franco-German coal and steel production under a common High Authority. The Declaration stated: 'Appropriate measures will be provided for means of appeal against the decisions of the

---

[1] Opinion 2/13 on the accession of the EU to the European Convention on Human Rights EU:C:2014:2454, para 158.

[2] See A Boerger-De Smedt, 'La Cour de Justice dans les Négotiations du Traité de Paris Instituant la CECA' (2008) 14 *Journal of European Integration History* 7; A Boerger-De Smedt, 'Negotiating the Foundations of European Law, 1950–57: The Legal History of the Treaties of Paris and Rome' (2012) 21 *Contemporary European History* 339; M Rasmussen, 'Constructing and Deconstructing "Constitutional" European Law: Some Reflections on How to Study the History of European Law' in H Koch *et al* (eds), *Europe: The New Legal Realism* (DJØF, 2010) 639.

authority.' Wary of a 'gouvernement des juges', Jean Monnet, the chair of the conference, had to be persuaded that the new Community should have a permanent court with the power to review acts of the High Authority.

Having come round to the view that the inclusion of a court of limited jurisdiction might reinforce the High Authority, Monnet enlisted the help of Maurice Lagrange, a member of the Conseil d'Etat, France's highest court in administrative law matters. His task was to ensure that the new court would resemble an administrative court along French lines with the limited remit of ensuring that the High Authority acted within its powers. Lagrange played a key role in the drafting of the Treaty articles on the court and in defining its jurisdiction.[3] In performing that task, he took as his blueprint the Conseil d'Etat and French administrative law.

The French influence was evident in the grounds of review set out in Article 33 ECSC, as Lagrange himself, by then an Advocate General in the new Court of Justice, would recognise in *Assider v High Authority*.[4] It was evident in the nomination of a judge-rapporteur to shepherd each case through the Court's procedure and draw up the draft judgment.[5] Perhaps most significantly, it was evident in the very institution of the Advocate General, acknowledged by Lagrange on his retirement from the Court of Justice in 1964 to have been 'inspired by the example of the French Conseil d'Etat'.[6]

The case law of the ECSC Court of Justice fills just two slim volumes of the European Court Reports and attracted little attention outside a small specialist readership. The composition of that Court is, however, worth noting here. The ECSC Treaty did not originally require the Judges to be legally qualified, merely that they should be 'persons of recognised independence and competence'.[7] Two of the original members, Petrus Serrarens of the Netherlands and Jacques Rueff of France, were not qualified lawyers. The Convention on Common Institutions, signed in Rome in 1957 alongside the EEC and Euratom Treaties, amended the ECSC Treaty to bring it in line with the two new Treaties. These required Judges to 'be chosen from persons whose independence is beyond doubt and who possess the qualifications required for appointment to the highest judicial offices in their respective Member States or who are jurisconsults of recognised competence ...'.[8] Judge Serrarens stood down when the Court of Justice of the ECSC became

---

[3] See Boerger-De Smedt, above n 2 at 8.

[4] Case 3/54 [1954–56] ECR 63, EU:C:1955:2, 75.

[5] M Lasser, *Judicial Deliberations* (Oxford, Oxford University Press, 2004) 47–60 (concerning the Cour de Cassation).

[6] Discours de Maurice Lagrange (8 octobre 1964). Available at: www.cvce.eu/obj/discours_de_maurice_lagrange_8_octobre_1964-fr-f2f00c1c-2587-497f-ace0-6890bf0cb85f.html (accessed 30 March 2017).

[7] Art 32 ECSC.

[8] Art 167 EEC; Art 139 Euratom. This wording now appears in Art 253 TFEU.

the Court of Justice of the European Communities, but Judge Rueff served until 1962. His reappointment is unlikely to have involved any assessment of whether he satisified the more stringent membership criteria introduced by the Rome Treaties because those Treaties and the ECSC Treaty all said that retiring Judges were eligible for reappointment.[9] This loophole enabled potentially under-qualified Judges to become members of the Court of Justice of the European Communities.

It is difficult to say whether Rueff himself would have met the new criteria. He might have been considered to satisfy them because of his experience as a Judge of the ECSC Court. He might always have satisfied them if, for example, he was eligible for appointment to the highest judicial offices in France.[10] It is possible, however, that none of the Member States, collectively responsible under the Treaties for making appointments to the Court, objected to his nomination. This would suggest that the appointment process was not sufficiently rigorous, a concern that would later lead to the introduction at Lisbon of the so-called Article 255 panel to give an opinion on the suitability of candidates for appointment.[11] It remains the case, however, that the Treaties do not impose on Member States any requirements relating to the manner in which they identify their nominees for appointment to the Court.

France took a back seat in the discussions that would lead ultimately to the signature of the Rome Treaties, having become disenchanted with the common market and supranational governance after the rejection of the European Defence Community Treaty in 1954.[12] As far as the Court's jurisdiction was concerned, the picture that emerged was mixed. The infringement procedure was weakened by omitting from the Rome Treaties a power to impose sanctions on defaulting Member States comparable to that provided for in Article 88 ECSC. That omission would not be rectified until Maastricht and Lisbon (and then only partly).[13] In addition, the modified standing rules set out in the second paragraph of Article 173 EEC were intended to restrict, by comparison with Article 33 ECSC, the right of private applicants to bring annulment actions against Community acts.[14] This is an area where the Court of Justice has proved a willing accomplice of the Member States to the present day.[15]

---

[9] Art 167 EEC; Art 309 Euratom; Art 32 ECSC.

[10] See J Cotter, 'Extra-Legal Steadying Factors in the Article 267 TFEU Preliminary Reference Procedure' (PhD thesis, Trinity College Dublin, 2016) 86–93.

[11] See Art 255 TFEU.

[12] See Boerger-De Smedt above n 2 at 349.

[13] See now Art 260(2) and (3) TFEU.

[14] See, e.g., Case 3/54 *Assider v High Authority* [1954–56] ECR 63, EU:C:1955:2; Case 4/54 *ISA v High Authority* [1954–56] ECR 91, EU:C:1955:3; Joined Cases 7 and 9/54 *Industries Sidérurgiques Luxembourgeoises v High Authority* [1954–56] ECR 175, EU:C:1956:2.

[15] A Arnull, 'Judicial Review in the European Union' in A Arnull and D Chalmers (eds), *The Oxford Handbook of European Union Law* (Oxford, Oxford University Press, 2015) ch 15.

Perhaps the most significant innovation concerned the preliminary rulings procedure, then assumed to be confined under Article 41 ECSC to questions of validity.[16] The Italian Nicola Catalano, former legal adviser to the High Authority, a member of the *Groupe de rédaction* and later a Judge at the Court of Justice, produced a text proposing a preliminary rulings mechanism which also extended to questions of interpretation.[17] That proposal was reflected in the text of Article 177 EEC. It was to have momentous consequences, bringing before the Court of Justice a multitude of questions it might not otherwise have had a chance to address and enabling it to influence the application of the Treaties in the Member States.[18] It would allow the Court of Justice to emerge from the obscurity of the ECSC to become a major international legal institution.[19] Essentially, however, the new treaties left the judicial architecture of the Community unaltered, making it possible for agreement to be reached on the Convention on Common Institutions. This was a step France had initially resisted.[20]

The Court of Justice's big break came over a period of less than 18 months between 1963 and 1964.[21] It was during that period that the transformational doctrines of direct effect and primacy were laid down. Nearly 30 years later, they would be rounded off in the *Francovich* case[22] by the principle of State liability. The Court of Justice exploited the doctrines of direct effect and primacy with relish after the deadline for completing the common market was missed. Its case law of that time[23] fuelled a narrative of the Court of Justice as both saviour and architect of the integration process, compensating for the failings of weak and ineffectual Member States who could not be trusted to stick to the commitments they had made. One can go a long way with this narrative, but in truth it is hard to know what exactly would have happened if some of these cases had been decided differently.

---

[16] The Court would later read into Art 41 ECSC a jurisdiction to give preliminary rulings on interpretation as well as validity: Case C-221/88 *Busseni* [1990] ECR I-495, EU:C:1990:84.

[17] See Boerger-De Smedt above n 2 at 352; D Edward, '*CILFIT* and *Foto-Frost* in their Historical and Procedural Context' in M Maduro and L Azoulai (eds), *The Past and Future of EU Law* (Oxford, Hart, 2010) 173, 173–4.

[18] Significantly, Art 31 ECSC and Art 164 EEC from the outset required the Court to ensure observance of the law 'in the interpretation *and application*' of the respective Treaties (emphasis added).

[19] See Rasmussen, above n 2 at 642; M Rasmussen, 'From *Costa v ENEL* to the Treaties of Rome: A Brief History of a Legal Revolution' in Maduro and Azoulai, above n 17 at 69, 81–2.

[20] See Boerger-De Smedt, above n 2 at 349.

[21] A Arnull, 'The Effect of EU Law' in D Patterson and A Södersten (eds), *A Companion to European Law and International Law* (Chichester, John Wiley, 2016) 62.

[22] Joined Cases C–6/90 and C–9/90 *Francovich and Others* [1991] ECR I–5357, EU:C:1991:428.

[23] E.g., Case 2/74 *Reyners v Belgium* [1974] ECR 631, EU:C:1974:68; Case 33/74 *Van Binsbergen v Bedrijfsvereniging Metaalnijverheid* [1974] ECR 1299, EU:C:1974:131; Case 43/75 *Defrenne v SABENA* [1976] ECR 455, EU:C:1976:56.

If *Van Gend* and *Costa* had gone the other way, the Commission would doubtless have been forced to use more frequently the infringement procedure laid down in what was then Article 169 EEC. Political pressure would probably have been brought to bear on infringing states to comply with their obligations. If necessary, a treaty change might have been contemplated to encourage compliance, for example, by extending to the EEC the sanctions available under Article 88 ECSC. If the case law on freedom of movement[24] had gone the other way, the necessary directives would probably have been adopted in due course. By 1974, there had already been a flurry of legislation on the free movement of workers. Even in the area of establishment and services and equal treatment, the Community legislator had not been inactive. The scope of some of the measures adopted may have been limited, but it should not be forgotten that the EU still does not have a comprehensive internal market in services.

3. THE COURT OF JUSTICE NOW

3.1. The Legacy of *Van Gend* and *Costa*

So the substantive contribution of some of the cases mentioned above to the development of EU law should not be exaggerated. Moreover, the approach of the Court of Justice damaged its relationship with top national courts. Although direct effect and primacy are now by and large accepted by lower national courts, the beneficiaries of the inter-court competition generated by the preliminary rulings procedure,[25] absolute primacy has not been accepted by national constitutional and supreme courts.[26] For a long time direct clashes were avoided. It seemed at one stage that such a clash might occur in the *Gauweiler* case,[27] where the view taken by the Court of Justice following the first-ever reference for a preliminary ruling by the Bundesverfassungsgericht differed from the latter's own expressed views; ultimately the view of the Court of Justice was accepted.[28]

---

[24] See *Reyners* and *Van Binsbergen*, above n 23.

[25] See J Weiler, *The Constitution of Europe* (Cambridge, Cambridge University Press, 1999) 197; K Alter, 'Explaining National Court Acceptance of European Court Jurisprudence: A Critical Evaluation of Theories of Legal Integration' in A-M Slaughter, A Stone Sweet and J Weiler (eds), *The European Courts and National Courts—Doctrine and Jurisprudence* (Oxford, Hart, 1997) 227; K Alter, *Establishing the Supremacy of European Law* (Oxford, Oxford University Press, 2001) 47–52. A leading example is Case C-416/10 *Jozef Križan and Others v Slovenská inšpekcia životného prostredia* EU:C:2013:8.

[26] B de Witte, 'Direct Effect, Primacy, and the Nature of the Legal Order' in P Craig and G de Búrca (eds), *The Evolution of EU Law* 2nd edn (Oxford, Oxford University Press, 2011) 352.

[27] Case C-62/14 *Gauweiler and Others v Deutscher Bundestag* EU:C:2015:400.

[28] Judgment of 21 June 2016.

In the 'Slovak Pensions' case,[29] however, the Czech Constitutional Court described a decision of the Court of Justice[30] as 'ultra vires' on the basis that it exceeded the powers transferred to the EU under the Czech Constitution. It therefore declined to follow the decision, applying instead constitutional principles of domestic origin. More recently, the Supreme Court of Denmark[31] declined to follow the ruling of the Court of Justice in *Dansk Industri, acting on behalf of Ajos A/S v Estate of Karsten Eigil Rasmussen*.[32] The UK Supreme Court has also become increasingly outspoken in asserting that EU law takes effect in the UK only by virtue of an Act of Parliament passed on the occasion of UK accession, the European Communities Act 1972, and that it is for the UK courts to decide the scope of the 1972 Act. The issue has recently arisen in connection with the protection accorded by the Bill of Rights of 1689 to debates or proceedings in Parliament[33] and with national citizenship.[34]

Be that as it may, the lack of any serious political response to the growing case law of the Court of Justice before Maastricht in the early 1990s encouraged it to think that it held the solutions to many of the Community's problems and, what is more, that it was entitled to apply them. As suggested by the judgment in *Van Gend*, the wording of the Treaty was to be less important than its spirit and general scheme. This would create uncertainty about the meaning of the words agreed by the Member States and the EU legislature which would ultimately prove damaging to the Court's authority.[35]

Moreover, the 1970s was a period when the Court of Justice was unencumbered by a large body of previous case law or properly functioning political institutions.[36] That state of affairs could not last. In the following decade, particularly after the Single European Act, the institutions and the Member States began to play a more active role in the functioning of the EU. At the same time, the inexorable growth in the volume of case law presented the Court of Justice with new challenges.

---

[29] Pl. ÚS 5/12, 31 January 2012. See R Zbíral, 'A Legal Revolution or Negligible Episode? Court of Justice Decision Proclaimed *Ultra Vires*' (2012) 49 *Common Market Law Review* 1475.
[30] Case C-399/09 *Landtová v Česká správa sociálního zabezpečení* EU:C:2011:415.
[31] Judgment of the Supreme Court of Denmark, Case no 15/2014, 6 December 2016.
[32] Case C-441/14 EU:C:2016:278. See below at n 48.
[33] *R (HS2 Action Alliance Limited) v The Secretary of State for Transport* [2014] UKSC 3.
[34] *Pham v Secretary of State* [2015] UKSC 19. *Pham* was cited by Lord Reed (dissenting) in the 'Brexit' case, *R (Miller) v Secretary of State* [2017] UKSC 5, para 224.
[35] See the trenchant criticism of the approach of the Court of Justice to interpretation in *HS2*, n 33, joint judgment of Lord Neuberger and Lord Mance. For a notorious example of the Court's approach, see Joined Cases C-402/07 and C-432/07 *Sturgeon* [2009] ECR I-10923, EU:C:2009:716.
[36] See Arnull, above n 21 at 66.

3.2. The Coherence of the Case Law

One such challenge was to maintain the overall coherence of the case law.[37] A revolution appeared to have occurred in *HAG II*,[38] where the Court of Justice for the first time expressly overruled one of its own previous decisions. That case was followed by others where a similar approach was taken.[39] However, the Court's approach was uneven. In *Keck and Mithouard*,[40] a case on the free movement of goods, the Court said it was 'necessary to re-examine and clarify its case-law on this matter' and concluded, 'contrary to what has previously been decided', that certain types of national legislation, which might appear to hinder imports, were nonetheless compatible with the Treaty. Unfortunately, the Court did not make clear precisely what it was overruling.

Especially troubling were cases where the Court behaved as if it was entirely unconstrained by precedent, failing to acknowledge that it was breaking new ground or explaining the effect of a new decision on existing case law. The authorities on the direct effect of directives are replete with examples, making it difficult to avoid the conclusion that the Court of Justice regrets its decisions denying directives the capacity to produce horizontal direct effect,[41] but lacks the courage to overrule them.

A crack in the edifice was evident in the principle of consistent interpretation, which requires national courts to do their utmost to interpret their national law consistently with any overlapping provisions of EU law, particularly those contained in directives.[42] The principle has revealed a clash of cultures between the Court of Justice and some of its national interlocutors. While the approach of the former to matters of interpretation is famously creative, some of the latter, often working in a monolingual environment, consider themselves more constrained by the text.

Frustrated by the continuing failure of Member States to implement directives timeously and comprehensively and the inadequacy of its attempts to overcome that failure through its case law, the Court of Justice

---

[37] See generally J Bengoetxea, *The Legal Reasoning of the European Court of Justice* (Oxford, Clarendon Press, 1993); G Beck, *The Legal Reasoning of the Court of Justice of the EU* (Oxford, Hart, 2012); G Conway, *The Limits of Legal Reasoning and the European Court of Justice* (Cambridge, Cambridge University Press, 2012).

[38] Case C–10/89 *HAG GF* [1990] ECR I–3711, EU:C:1990:359.

[39] E.g., Case C–308/93 *Cabanis-Issarte* [1996] ECR I–2097, EU:C:1996:169; Case C–394/96 *Brown v Rentokil* [1998] ECR I–4185, EU:C:1998:331.

[40] Joined Cases C–267 and C–268/91 [1993] ECR I–6097, EU:C:1993:905.

[41] Case 152/84 *Marshall v Southampton and South-West Hampshire Area Health Authority* [1986] ECR 723, EU:C:1986:84; Case C–91/92 *Faccini Dori v Recreb* [1994] ECR I–3325, EU:C:1994:292.

[42] See e.g., Joined Cases C-378/07 to C-380/07 *Angelidaki* [2009] ECR I-3071, EU:C:2009:250.

in *Mangold*[43] took a radical new approach. *Mangold* concerned the effect of Directive 2000/78 establishing a general framework for equal treatment in employment and occupation.[44] The case was a horizontal one and the deadline for giving effect to the directive had not expired at the material time, so it could not be invoked directly. However, the Court of Justice achieved the same effect by ruling that it reflected a general principle enshrined in 'various [unspecified] international instruments and in the constitutional traditions [again unspecified] common to the Member States'.[45] The national court was responsible for guaranteeing that general principle 'full effectiveness'.[46] *Mangold* was later confirmed in *Kücükdeveci*.[47] Not only did this seem like a transparent attempt to circumvent further the no-horizontal-direct-effect rule, it also seemed to contradict Article 13 EC (now 19 TFEU), the legal basis of Directive 2000/78, which left it to the Council to decide whether, and if so to what extent, discrimination of the type in question (here on grounds of age) should be prohibited.

In 2016, the *Mangold* line of authority and the principle of consistent interpretation were at the heart of the clash, noted above, between the Court of Justice and the Supreme Court of Denmark. In *Ingeniørforeningen i Danmark*,[48] a vertical dispute decided in 2010, the Court of Justice held in preliminary reference proceedings that national legislation limiting the right of workers to claim a severance allowance, if they were eligible for an old-age pension from their employer under a pension scheme they had joined before reaching the age of 50, was incompatible with Directive 2000/78. In *Dansk Industri, acting on behalf of Ajos A/S v Estate of Karsten Eigil Rasmussen*,[49] a horizontal dispute, an employee who had been dismissed by his employer was refused a severance allowance on the basis of the national provision declared contrary to Directive 2000/78 in *Ingeniørforeningen i Danmark*. The Court of Justice said in response to a reference from the Supreme Court of Denmark that the principle of non-discrimination on grounds of age recognised in *Mangold* had to be applied by national courts in horizontal disputes where a result consistent with Directive 2000/78 could not be achieved through consistent interpretation. The Supreme Court took the view that such a result could only be achieved through a *contra legem* interpretation of the disputed national provisions but refused to apply the general principle directly.

It is evident that, following the judgment in *Ingeniørforeningen i Danmark*, Denmark should have taken steps to ensure that its national implementing

---

43 Case C–144/04 *Mangold v Helm* [2005] ECR I-9981, EU:C:2005:709.
44 OJ 2000 L 303/16.
45 Above n 43, para 74.
46 Ibid, para 78.
47 Case C-555/07 [2010] ECR I-365, EU:C:2010:21.
48 Case C-499/08 [2010] ECR I-9343, EU:C:2010:600.
49 Case C-441/14 EU:C:2016:278.

legislation was adequate to give effect to Directive 2000/78. However, the correct way to remedy Denmark's failure to do so was by means of enforcement proceedings by the Commission under Article 258 TFEU, not through recourse to a principle of dubious origin whose relationship with the no-horizontal-direct-effect rule has not been adequately explained. It is noteworthy that, in his Opinion in the *Rasmussen* case, Advocate General Bot confined himself to the principle of consistent interpretation.

Another attempt to mitigate some of the worst features of the no-horizontal-direct-effect rule was made in the case law on what is sometimes called 'incidental effect' beginning with *CIA Security v Signalson*.[50] That case law established that the failure of a Member State to comply with Directive 83/189 on national technical standards[51] could sometimes be invoked in disputes before national courts between private parties. The Court of Justice did not explain how this outcome could be reconciled with the no-horizontal-direct-effect rule. In subsequent case law,[52] the Court of Justice asserted that this rule remained valid, but did not offer a convincing rationale for the apparent inconsistency.

One suggestion was that a distinction should be drawn between reliance on a directive to *exclude* an incompatible national provision and reliance on a directive *in substitution* for an incompatible national provision. Only the latter, so the argument went, constituted true direct effect. The former was an application of the doctrine of primacy, not direct effect, and was not therefore subject to the no-horizontal-direct-effect rule. That suggestion involved a wholesale reassessment of the voluminous case law on the subject. To give just two simple examples, it would have meant that *Van Gend en Loos* and *Marshall*, both exclusion cases, were not about direct effect at all, but about primacy. This is impossible to reconcile with the judgments in those cases.

An opportunity for the Court of Justice to settle the matter arose in *Pfeiffer*,[53] a horizontal exclusion case. The Court of Justice accepted that the relevant provisions of the directive concerned (the Working Time Directive)[54] were clear enough to produce direct effect, but said that they could not do so in these circumstances because the dispute was between individuals. The national court was reminded of its duty to apply the principle

---

[50] Case C–194/94 *CIA Security v Signalson and Securitel* [1996] ECR I–2201, EU:C:1996:172.

[51] OJ 1983 L 109/8.

[52] See Case C–443/98 *Unilever Italia SpA v Central Food SpA* [2000] ECR I–7535, EU:C:2000:496, paras 50 and 51.

[53] Joined Cases C–397 & 403/01 *Pfeiffer and Others v Deutsches Rotes Creuz* [2004] ECR I–8835, EU:C:2004:584.

[54] Council Directive 93/104 concerning certain aspects of the organisation of working time, OJ 1993 L 307/18.

of consistent interpretation. This seemed to constitute a repudiation of the exclusion/substitution theory, but no alternative explanation for the *CIA Security* line of authority was forthcoming.

It is not, of course, suggested that all the Court's decisions are poorly reasoned, but simply that this is true of enough of them to be a problem that needs to be addressed. The basic flaw lies in the Court's judicial method. The form of the judgment remains a syllogistic one in which the conclusion is made to appear the inevitable consequence of the premises that precede it. There has been a growing reliance on formulaic judgments where original drafting is kept to a minimum and the priority seems to be linguistic consistency rather than clarity and persuasiveness.[55] The depersonalised form of the judgment allows the exercise to be presented as a mechanical one in which there is no room for personal opinions.[56] True, the Advocate General routinely reveals the possibility that a case might have several plausible solutions. Moreover, the Court of Justice's judgments have undoubtedly become more discursive than they used to be. However, they end by declaring what the law is. They do not make any serious attempt to persuade the reader of the rightness of the conclusion reached. It is the law because that is what the Court of Justice has decided. As Judge Prechal has admitted, 'as judges we do not really have debates with the outside world'.[57]

This is not appropriate in the current climate, where democracy requires a constant process of dialogue between citizens and the institutions of government, including the courts. This imperative was evident in the 'Brexit' case before the UK Supreme Court,[58] where the judgment of the majority began by explaining that the issue was a narrow legal one about the scope of the government's powers that it was appropriate for the courts to determine. In the EU legal order, the Court of Justice faces the additional challenge of maintaining a full and frank dialogue with the national courts, without which it risks losing their confidence.

The situation is exacerbated by the 'frequent' or 'fairly frequent'[59] use made by the Court of the possibility of proceeding without an Advocate General's Opinion (see table).[60]

---

[55] K McAuliffe, 'Language and Law in the European Union: The Multilingual Jurisprudence of the Court of Justice' in L Solan and P Tiersma, *The Oxford Handbook of Language and Law* (Oxford, Oxford University Press, 2012) 201; K McAuliffe, 'Hybrid Texts and Uniform Law? The Multilingual Case Law of the Court of Justice of the European Union' (2011) 24 *International Journal for the Semiotics of Law* 97.

[56] See Lasser, above n 5 at 33–34.

[57] See http://europeanlawblog.eu/?p=2115 (last accessed 30 March 2017).

[58] See n 34 above, para 3.

[59] One or other of those terms was used by the Court itself in several of its Annual Reports, eg 2004, 2006, 2008, 2010, 2012, 2013, 2014, 2015.

[60] See Statute, Art 20, para 5.

Table 1: Dispensing with an Advocate General's Opinion

Year	Judgments delivered without an Advocate General's Opinion (%)
2004	30
2005	35
2006	33
2007	43
2008	41
2009	52
2010	50
2011	46
2012	53
2013	48
2014	% not available*
2015	43
2016	34

Source: CJEU Annual Reports.
*The Annual Report for 2014 states (p.10): '208 judgments (in 228 cases when joinder is taken into account) were delivered in 2014 without an opinion.'

The UK Supreme Court has been critical of unconvincing judgments given without an Opinion[61] and of judgments which depart from the Opinion on the basis of flimsy reasoning which does not respond to the points the Advocate General has raised.[62] It is unlikely to be alone in holding these views. They matter because they undermine the standing of the Court of Justice and may discourage national courts from making references or applying the guidance they are given where they have done so.

The Court of Justice will know that in the UK there has for a long time been a strand of opinion which regards it as a political court with a mission of its own whose judgments can be hard to predict.[63] By the time of the

---

[61] There is, perhaps, evidence in the latest figures of waning enthusiasm for dispensing with an Opinion.

[62] See *Patmalniece v Secretary of State* [2011] UKSC 11; *Aimia Coalition Loyalty* [2013] UKSC 15; *R (HS2 Action Alliance Limited) v The Secretary of State for Transport* [2014] UKSC 3; *HMRC v Pendragon* [2015] UKSC 37; *Cavendish Square Holding v Talal El Makdessi* [2015] UKSC 67.

[63] E.g., P Neill, 'The European Court of Justice: A Case Study in Judicial Activism', Minutes of Evidence, House of Lords Sub-Committee on the 1996 IGC (Session 1994–95, 18th Report, HL Paper 88, 218–45); European Policy Forum, 1995; T Hartley, 'The European Court, Judicial Objectivity and the Constitution of the European Union' (1996) 112 *Law Quarterly Review* 95.

June 2016 referendum, that view had gained considerable political traction, so much so that extricating itself from the jurisdiction of the Court of Justice became one of the UK's objectives in the Brexit negotiations.[64] This view is not confined to the UK. It is evident in some of the case law of the Bundesverfassungsgericht and was evident in Ireland during its battle over the ratification of the Lisbon Treaty.[65]

3.3 Managing the Case Load

Another challenge confronting the Court of Justice has been the management of its growing case load. Although it welcomed the establishment of the Court of First Instance (now the General Court) in 1988, the relationship between the two has sometimes been frosty. It reached a nadir in 2014 when the Court of Justice submitted a request, now being implemented,[66] for the number of Judges at the General Court to be doubled by 2019.[67] This led to an unseemly public quarrel with members of the General Court, which favoured the creation of a further specialised court and an increase in support staff, including référendaires.[68] This failure of leadership, widely noted in the media, suceeded only in undermining the standing of both courts.

4. THE COURT OF JUSTICE TOMORROW?

In the remainder of this contribution, potential solutions to some of the problems now confronting the Court of Justice are tentatively suggested.

When the General Court was established, Article 168a EEC explicitly excluded certain categories of action from its jurisdiction, namely 'actions brought by Member States or by Community institutions or questions referred for a preliminary ruling under Article 177 [now 267 TFEU]'. The basic provision governing the jurisdiction of the General Court is now Article 256 TFEU, which is much more expansive. Article 256(1) provides:

> The General Court shall have jurisdiction to hear and determine at first instance actions or proceedings referred to in Articles 263, 265, 268, 270 and 272, with

[64] See, e.g., Prime Minister May's speech at Lancaster House on 17 January 2017 setting out the UK's negotiating objectives for exiting the EU; HM Government,' The United Kingdom's Exit From and New Partnership with the European Union' (Cm 9417) 13.
[65] See S Kingston, 'Ireland's Options after the Lisbon Referendum: Strategies, Implications and Competing Visions of Europe' (2009) 34 *European Law Review* 455 at 469–72.
[66] See Regulation 2015/2422 amending Protocol No 3 on the Statute of the Court of Justice of the European Union, OJ 2015 L 341/14.
[67] See U Öberg, M Ali and P Sabouret, Chapter 12 in this volume.
[68] See F Dehousse, 'The Reform of the EU Courts (II): Abandoning the Management Approach by Doubling the General Court' (Egmont Paper 83, March 2016) 28.

the exception of those assigned to a specialised court set up under Article 257 and those reserved in the Statute for the Court of Justice. The Statute may provide for the General Court to have jurisdiction for other classes of action or proceeding.

Article 256(3) goes on to provide:

> The General Court shall have jurisdiction to hear and determine questions referred for a preliminary ruling under Article 267, in specific areas laid down by the Statute.

Thus, Article 256 imposes only two limits on the jurisdiction of the General Court. The first is cases assigned to a specialised court. Following the abolition of the Civil Service Tribunal on 31 August 2016 as part of the reforms to the General Court referred to above,[69] there are no longer any specialised courts, though this could, of course, change in the future. The second is the extent to which jurisdiction to give preliminary rulings may be conferred on the General Court. A clear sign that the EU legislator now envisages the conferral of a preliminary rulings jurisdiction on the General Court was contained in Article 3(2) of the regulation[70] doubling the number of judges in that court. This requires the Court of Justice to draw up a report by the end of 2017 'on possible changes to the distribution of competence for preliminary rulings under Article 267 TFEU'. The report must 'be accompanied, where appropriate, by legislative requests'.

In 2016, preliminary rulings represented over 67 per cent of the new cases brought before the Court of Justice and over 64 per cent of those decided. It is therefore clear that there may shortly be an opportunity to reduce its case load significantly by transferring to the General Court responsibility for dealing with references from national courts. The mention in Article 256(3) of 'specific areas laid down by the Statute' appears to preclude the transfer to the General Court of all such references. What 'specific areas' might be laid down in the Statute?

The starting point should be to transfer as many references as possible. They should be identified by formal as opposed to substantive criteria since references commonly range over a number of areas and could not feasibly be divided between the General Court and the Court of Justice on substantive grounds. One option would be to exclude from the cases transferred references from national courts subject to the obligation to refer laid down in the third paragraph of Article 267 TFEU. Some such courts have shown considerable reluctance to refer cases to the Court of Justice.[71] Requiring

---

[69] See Regulation 2016/1192 on the transfer to the General Court of jurisdiction at first instance in disputes between the European Union and its servants, OJ 2016 L 200/137, Art 3.

[70] See n 66 above.

[71] The Spanish Tribunal Constitucional, the French Conseil Constitutionnel and the Bundesverfassungsgericht all waited some time before making their first references. See respectively Case C-399/11 *Melloni v Ministerio Fiscal* EU:C:2013:107; Case C-168/13 PPU *Jeremy F v Premier Ministre* EU:C:2013:358; Case C-62/14 *Gauweiler and Others v Deutscher Bundestag* EU:C:2015:400.

them to make references instead to a lower court would be unlikely to persuade them to overcome that reluctance more often. In addition, references on the validity of EU acts—or perhaps of legislative acts only—might also be excluded. Declaring an EU act invalid is a particularly serious step,[72] especially where it enjoys the enhanced democratic legitimacy conferred by a legislative procedure. It may therefore be considered appropriate that references in this area—including references on both validity and interpretation—should be reserved for the EU's highest court. All other references, described according to the Part and Title of the Treaties they concern, should be transferred to the General Court.

The result need not be to remove from the Court of Justice any capacity to supervise the way in which the General Court deals with references in the specific areas assigned to it. Article 256 TFEU goes on to provide:

> Decisions given by the General Court on questions referred for a preliminary ruling may exceptionally be subject to review by the Court of Justice, under the conditions and within the limits laid down by the Statute, where there is a serious risk of the unity or consistency of Union law being affected.

One possibility would be for the Statute to introduce a procedure similar to that contained in the old Title IV of Part III of the EC Treaty, which concerned visas, asylum, immigration and other policies related to the free movement of persons. Article 68(1) confined the right to refer questions to the Court of Justice concerning Title IV to national courts of last resort. To mitigate any adverse consequences of that provision for the flow of references, Article 68(3) provided:

> The Council, the Commission or a Member State may request the Court of Justice to give a ruling on a question of interpretation of this title or of acts of the institutions of the Community based on this title. The ruling given by the Court of Justice in response to such a request shall not apply to judgments of courts or tribunals of the Member States which have become *res judicata*.

A procedure of this sort could be adapted to provide for review by the Court of Justice of the exercise by the General Court of a preliminary rulings jurisdiction while at the same time avoiding additional delay and uncertainty for the referring court and the parties to the main action.

A further innovation might be to enable the Court of Justice to control its docket by selecting the cases brought before it that it wishes to consider. Régimes of this type are familiar in the common law and Nordic legal traditions.

The UK Supreme Court[73] grants permission to appeal only where it considers an application to raise 'an arguable point of law of general public

---

[72] See Case 314/85 *Foto-Frost v Hauptzollamt Lübeck-Ost* [1987] ECR 4199, EU:C:1987:452.

[73] See Practice Direction 3, para 3.3.3.

importance' which it is timely to consider 'bearing in mind that the matter will already have been the subject of judicial decision and may have already been reviewed on appeal'. Where permission is refused, brief reasons are given. It is expressly stated that those reasons 'should not be regarded as having any value as a precedent'.

In the US Supreme Court, most cases are brought on what is known as a writ of *certiorari* granted by the Justices. According to Rule 10 of the Rules of the Supreme Court '[a] petition for a writ of certiorari will be granted only for compelling reasons.' Rule 10 goes on to 'indicate the character of the reasons the Court considers'. Those listed include situations where lower courts have given conflicting decisions on important matters; where there has been a serious departure 'from the accepted and usual course of judicial proceedings' calling for the exercise of the Supreme Court's supervisory power; and where certain courts have 'decided an important question of federal law that has not been, but should be, settled by' the Supreme Court or 'in a way that conflicts with relevant decisions' of the Supreme Court. However, Rule 10 warns the reader that the list given neither controls nor fully measures the Supreme Court's discretion.

The approach of the Swedish Supreme Court was brought to the attention of a wider audience in *Lyckeskog*.[74] As Advocate General Tizzano explained in that case,[75] an appeal to the Swedish Supreme Court against a decision of one of Sweden's six Courts of Appeal could normally only be brought with the permission of the Supreme Court, which could grant permission in only two situations: (a) where it was 'important for the uniform application of the law that the appeal be heard by the Supreme Court'; or (b) that there were 'particular reasons for hearing the appeal, such as the existence of grounds for review on a point of law, a formal defect, or if the decision by the Court of Appeal manifestly rests on a serious omission or error'.

In the EU, systems of this sort are not excluded *a priori*. The joint discussion paper produced in 1999 by the Court of Justice and the Court of First Instance (as it then was)[76] contemplated the introduction of a so-called filtering system in two contexts: first, as a way of limiting the number of appeals to the Court from the CFI; and secondly, in preliminary references, to enable the Court to decide 'which of the questions referred needed to be answered by it on account of, for example, their novelty, complexity or importance'. A filtering system was also mooted in connection with the recent reforms to the General Court to help the Court of Justice cope with an anticipated increase in the volume of appeals.[77]

---

[74] Case C-99/00 [2002] ECR I-4839, EU:C:2002:329.

[75] [2002] ECR I-4839, EU:C:2002:108, paras 3–7.

[76] For the text of the paper, see A Dashwood and A Johnston, *The Future of the Judicial System of the European Union* (Oxford, Hart, 2001) 113, 127, 135–38.

[77] See Dehousse above n 68 at 28.

It is not suggested that the EU would necessarily want to follow precisely any of the examples given above. It might, for example, wish to impose stricter limits on the Court's discretion or to exclude certain categories of case from such a system. An obvious candidate for exclusion would be references from national courts (insofar as the Court of Justice retains a preliminary rulings jurisdiction). As the EU Courts acknowledged in their 1999 discussion paper, refusing to deal with a reference once made might prove fatal to the spirit of cooperation on which the preliminary rulings procedure depends.

If the Court of Justice had a reduced jurisdiction and some ability to control its docket, it would become possible realistically to contemplate other reforms. One might be to reduce its membership, which has now surely crossed 'the invisible boundary between a collegiate court and a deliberative assembly' which so preoccupied it in the run-up to the 1996 IGC.[78] A sensible approach would be to constitute a smaller court with a rotating membership of judges and Advocates General serving longer mandates. One could then envisage an Advocate General's Opinion in every case and longer majority judgments which engaged fully with the arguments of the parties, the underlying policy issues and the Advocate General's Opinion. It might also be worth revisiting the debate about whether dissenting judgments should be permitted.[79] There is a strong argument that the continuing absence of dissents is undermining the coherence of the Court's judgments by requiring them to reflect too wide a range of views.

The new dispensation might even, in due course, be reflected in a change of name. How does 'Supreme Court of the European Union' sound?

---

[78] Proceedings of the Court of Justice and Court of First Instance of the European Communities, 22–26 May 1995, No 15/95.

[79] See G Slynn, *Introducing a European Legal Order* (London, Stevens, 1992) 160–162; D Edward, 'How the Court of Justice Works' (1995) 20 *European Law Review* 539, 557–58; C Turner and R Muñoz, 'Revising the Judicial Architecture of the European Union' (1999–2000) 19 *Yearbook of European Law* 1, 85–86; J Weiler, 'Epilogue: The Judicial *Après Nice*' in G de Búrca and J Weiler (eds), *The European Court of Justice* (Oxford, Oxford University Press, 2001) 215, 225; F Jacobs, 'Approaches to Interpretation in a Plurilingual Legal System' in M Hoskins and W Robinson (eds), *A True European: Essays for Judge David Edward* (Oxford, Hart, 2003) 297; A Arnull, *The European Union and its Court of Justice* 2nd edn (Oxford, Oxford University Press, 2006) 9–14.

2

Preliminary Rulings to the CJEU and the Swedish Judiciary

Current Developments

ULF BERNITZ

1. INTRODUCTION

THE RELATIONSHIP BETWEEN the Swedish judiciary and the Court of Justice of the European Union (CJEU) is a matter of great importance. As is well known, the Swedish courts are not only the courts of the Kingdom of Sweden. They constitute the national arm of the European Union (EU) legal order, having independent responsibility for its full effect and correct application within Sweden. This gives Swedish courts a role which had no real counterpart before Sweden's entry into the European Economic Area (EEA) in 1994 and the EU in 1995.

The issue of how well the Swedish courts have been faring has been discussed on many occasions. It is a well-known fact that the European Commission started an infringement proceeding against Sweden in 2006, arguing that Swedish courts had been too restrictive in their application of the preliminary ruling procedure, thus, Sweden had failed to fulfill its Treaty obligations. I have discussed this case in a Report on Preliminary Rulings by the EU Court of Justice—The Attitude and Practice of Swedish Courts, covering the years 1995–2009.[1] An article in English, based on this Report and discussing the Commission's action against Sweden has been published in the first volume of this series of Swedish Studies in European Law.[2]

---

[1] U Bernitz, 'Förhandsavgöranden av EU-domstolen. Svenska domstolars hållning och praxis' (Sieps 2010: 2).
[2] U Bernitz, 'The Duty of Supreme Courts to Refer Cases to the ECJ: The Commission's Action Against Sweden' (2006) 1 Swedish Studies in European Law (eds. N Wahl and P Cramér) 37 ff., M Schmauch, 'Lack of Preliminary Rulings as an Infringement of Art. 234 EC? Commission Case COM 2003/2161, Procedure against Kingdom of Sweden' (2005) European Law Reporter 445 ff., M Broberg, 'National Courts of Last Instance Failing to Make a Preliminary Reference' (2016) European Public Law 243 ff.

The primary purpose of both publications was to clarify Swedish case law and the attitude of the courts when it comes to requesting preliminary rulings. In 2016, I published a new Report on preliminary references from Swedish courts dealing with the development of their attitudes and practice during 2010–2015.[3] That Report is primarily a follow-up of my previous study, although it also examines some additional issues. The primary purpose is to clarify Swedish case law and the attitude of the Swedish courts when it comes to requesting preliminary rulings and to look at any recent changes.

This chapter is based on my new Report of 2016 and can be characterised as a follow up to my article in Volume 1 of *Swedish Studies in European Law*. It is my point of departure that one can still observe a certain reluctance within the Swedish court system to ask the CJEU for preliminary rulings. The actual practice of the Swedish courts when it comes to requesting preliminary rulings is, of course, of core importance for the actual application and impact of EU law within the Swedish legal system. It constitutes the basis for the ongoing cooperation and dialogue between the national courts and the CJEU. As pointed out by the Court in the *Lyckeskog* case, a reference from a Swedish Court of Appeal, the obligation to refer cases 'is in particular designed to prevent a body of national case-law that is not in accordance with the rules of Community law from coming into existence in any Member State'.[4]

The chapter will focus primarily on the following topics. It will briefly mention the Commission's infringement action against Sweden. It will then discuss the duty to give reasons for decisions not to refer cases to the CJEU and Swedish practice in this regard. The next part deals with requests by Swedish courts for preliminary rulings during the period 2010–2015. This is followed by a section on the types of cases referred. The final part of the chapter deals with explanations of this restrictive attitude.

2. THE COMMISSION'S ACTION AGAINST SWEDEN—A BACKDROP

As already mentioned, in 2004 the Commission took the unique step of starting legal action against Sweden based on the observation that the Swedish courts of last resort, primarily the Supreme Court and (to a lesser extent) the Supreme Administrative Court, were too restrictive in their application of the preliminary ruling procedure. This reached the stage of a Reasoned Opinion, submitted to the Swedish Government. This has been made public in Sweden due to Swedish law on the transparency of public documents.[5]

---

[3] Förhandsavgöranden av EU-domstolen. Utvecklingen av svenska domstolars hållning och praxis 2010–2015, 2016 (Sieps 2016:9).
[4] Case C-99/00, *Public Procecutor v Lyckeskog*, EU:C:2002:329.
[5] Commission Docket No 2003/2161, C(2004) 3899, dated 13 October 2004.

The Commission mentioned specifically in its Reasoned Opinion that from 1995 until the end of 2002 the Supreme Court had only referred two cases to the CJEU while the Supreme Administrative Court had referred ten; in 2003, each court referred only one additional case. The Commission observed that the supreme courts had decided on the admissibility of a case without stating any reasons; they merely stated that admission (leave) was not granted. This made it impossible for the Commission to check if the court had observed its obligations under what is now Article 267(3) of the Treaty on the Functioning of the European Union (TFEU). The Commission required that Swedish courts, against whose decisions there is no judicial remedy under Swedish law (courts of last resort), should be obliged to give a statement of their reasons if they do not grant admission in cases involving the application of EU law.

The Swedish Government rejected any allegations about breach of EU law. However, it chose not to contest the Commission and possibly take a legal fight to the CJEU but to reach a compromise solution. It proposed special legislation requiring the courts of last resort to give reasons when deciding not grant admission in a case involving issues of EU law raised by a party to the case. The proposal was met with opposition from the Supreme Court and the Supreme Administrative Court, who regarded it as an unjustified intrusion. However, it was supported by the majority of the authorities and organisations heard by the government. A Government Bill based on the proposal was sent to Parliament where it was accepted without any difficulty, taking legal effect on 1 July 2006. After the legislative amendment had been approved by the Swedish Parliament, the Commission withdrew its case.

The case seems to have been unique in its kind.

3. THE DUTY TO GIVE REASONS FOR DECISIONS NOT TO REFER TO THE CJEU AND SWEDISH PRACTICE

The issue—whether the provision on the right to fair trial in Article 6(1) of the European Convention of Human Rights (ECHR) requires supreme courts to give a reason when they do not grant admission—was neither raised by the Commission in the legal action nor by Sweden in relation to the legislative amendment just mentioned. Obviously, the supreme courts, when opposing the legislative proposal, assumed there was no such requirement under the ECHR. Today, we know the European Court of Human Rights (ECtHR) has taken the opposite view in some very interesting cases. Perhaps somewhat surprisingly, the ECtHR has actively interpreted Article 267(3) TFEU in the light of Article 6 ECHR and requires courts against whose decisions there is no judicial remedy under national law to give sufficient reasons for a decision not to ask the CJEU for a preliminary ruling.

The position taken by the ECtHR adds a new dimension to the Commission's infringement action and the requirement to motivate a decision to refuse a request for a preliminary ruling.

A fundamental decision by the ECtHR was taken in 2011 in the case *Ullens de Schooten and Rezabek v Belgium*.[6] The case concerned tax fraud and was about a decision taken by a Belgian court of last resort (Cour de Cassation). According to the applicants, Belgian law was contrary to EU law on different points and, it was argued, the Cour de Cassation had set aside its duty to refer the case to the CJEU. In this case, the ECtHR found Article 6(1) ECHR required the Cour de Cassation to give reasons for its decision not to refer the case, but was satisfied by the reason given in this particular case.

The ECtHR expressed in paragraph 60 of its judgment that Article 6.1 ECHR 'imposes ... an obligation on domestic courts to give reasons, in the light of applicable law, for any decisions in which they refuse to refer a preliminary question, especially where the applicable law allows for such a refusal only on an exceptional basis'.

In paragraph 62 of the judgment, the ECtHR referred specifically to the criteria developed by the CJEU in the *CILFIT* case of 1982[7] to decide whether or not a referral to the CJEU is required. The ECtHR said:

> In the specific context of [Article 267.3 TFEU], this means that national courts against whose decisions there is no remedy under national law, which refuse to refer to the Court of Justice a preliminary question on the interpretation of Community law that has been raised before them, are obliged to give reasons for their refusal in the light of the exceptions provided for in the case-law of the Court of Justice. They will thus be required, in accordance with the above mentioned *Cilfit* case-law, to indicate the reasons why they have found that the question is irrelevant, that the European Union law provision in question has already been interpreted by the Court of Justice, or that the correct application of Community law is so obvious as to leave no scope for any reasonable doubt.

The ECtHR added a corresponding duty to give reasons could apply also to courts which do not decide in last resort. It expressed in paragraph 59:

> the [Court] does not rule out the possibility that, where a preliminary reference mechanism exists, refusal by a domestic court to grant a request for such a referral

---

[6] App Nos 3989/07 and 38353/07, judgment 20 Sept. 2011, M Schmauch 'The Preliminary Ruling Procedure and the Right to a Fair Trial: Strasbourg Demands Reasoned Decisions from National Courts when they Refuse to Refer A Case to the ECJ' (2011) *European Law Reporter* 362 ff., M Broberg and N Fenger, *Preliminary References to the European Court of Justice* 2nd edn (Oxford, Oxford University Press, 2014) 271 ff., C Lacchi, 'Multilevel Judicial Protection in the EU and Preliminary References' (2016) 53(3) *Common Market Law Review* 679–707, M Broberg and N Fenger, 'Preliminary References to the Court of Justice of the EU and the Right to a Fair Trial under Article 6 ECHR' (2016) 4(4) *European Law Review* 599–607; J Krommendijk, '"Open Sesame!" Improving Access to the ECJ by Requiring National Courts to Reason their Refusals to Refer' (2107) 1 *European Law Review* 46.

[7] Case 283/81, *CILFIT v Ministro della Sanità*, EU:C:1982:335.

may, in certain circumstances, infringe the fairness of proceedings—even if that court is not ruling in the last instance ... The same is true where the refusal proves arbitrary ... that is to say where there has been a refusal even though the applicable rules allow no exception to the principle of preliminary reference or no alternative thereto, where the refusal is based on reasons other than those provided for by the rules, and where the refusal has not been duly reasoned in accordance with those rules.

Recently, in 2014, the ECtHR has gone further in the case *Dhabi v Italy*.[8] It found the Italian Supreme Court had violated Article 6(1) ECHR by refusing to refer a case to the CJEU for a preliminary ruling without giving reasons. Dhabi was a Tunisian citizen. He was legally living in Italy and claimed he was entitled to social benefits under the Association Treaty between the EU and Tunisia. He argued the CJEU should be asked for a preliminary ruling on the interpretation of the relevant treaty provisions. The ECtHR noted the decision by the Italian Supreme Court was lacking reasons on this point and expressed in its decision (paras 33–34):

It is therefore not clear from the reasoning of the impugned judgment whether that question was considered not to be relevant or to relate to a provision which was clear or had already been interpreted by the CJEU, or whether it was simply ignored ... The Court observes in this connection that the reasoning of the Court of Cassation contains no reference to the case-law of the CJEU. That finding is sufficient for the Court to conclude that there has been a violation of Article 6 § 1 of the Convention.

There are also other judgments by the ECtHR supporting the duty to give reasons.[9] In a Grand Chamber judgment in May 2016, *Avotins*, the Court stated:

The Court observes that, in a different context, it has held that national courts against whose decisions no judicial remedy exists in national law are obliged to give reasons for refusing to refer a question to the CJEU for a preliminary ruling, in the light of the exceptions provided for by the case-law of the CJEU. The national courts must therefore state the reasons why they consider it unnecessary to seek a preliminary ruling (see Ullens de Schooten and Rezabek v. Belgium, nos. 3989/07 and 38353/07, § 62, 20 September 2011 and Dhahbi v. Italy, no. 17120/09, §§ 31–34, 8 April 2014). The Court emphasises that the purpose of the review it conducts in this regard is to ascertain whether the refusal to refer a question for a preliminary ruling constituted in itself a violation of Article 6 § 1 of the Convention; in so doing, it takes into account the approach already established by the case-law of the CJEU.[10]

---

[8] App No 17120/09, judgment 8 April 2014.
[9] Note App No 38369/09, *Schipani et al v Italy*, judgment 21 July 2015. This is another case in which the Italian Supreme Court had not given reasons for rejecting a request for a preliminary ruling by the CJEU. The ECtHR followed its reasoning in the *Dhabi* case.
[10] App No 17502/07, *Avotins v Latvia*, judgment 23 May 2016, para 110.

It can be concluded that it would be contrary to Article 6.1 ECHR if, for example, a Swedish court of last resort would refuse to ask for a preliminary ruling from the CJEU when a party to the case is requesting it without giving sufficient reasons. However, that Article does not comprise everything covered by EU law, as it is applicable only in criminal cases and those dealing with 'civil rights and obligations', albeit a concept interpreted broadly. Article 47 of the EU Charter on Fundamental Rights is based on Article 6(1) ECHR and is intended to be interpreted as such. The article in the Charter comprises EU law in its entirety. It should also follow from Article 47 of the Charter that national courts of last resort must give sufficient reasons why a case dealing with EU law is not referred to in the CJEU when a party to the case has requested a referral. So far, the CJEU has not expressed itself on the matter.

It follows from what the ECtHR has stated that the reasons given, in order to be satisfactory, should connect to the criteria the CJEU developed in the *CILFIT* case. This means that the national court has to indicate in its reasons:

(a) that the question is irrelevant because it does not concern EU law;
(b) that the EU law provision in question has already been interpreted by the CJEU (*acte éclairé*); or
(c) that the correct application of union law is so obvious as to leave no scope for any reasonable doubt (*acte clair*).

The *CILFIT* criteria have been criticised many times over the years as being too restrictive. However, they have recently been confirmed and somewhat refined in the *Ferreira da Silva e Brito* case of 2015.[11] In para 39, the CJEU clarified 'so obvious as to leave no scope for any reasonable doubt' as follows:

> The Court has also made clear that the existence of such a possibility must be assessed in the light of the specific characteristics of EU law, the particular difficulties to which the interpretation of the latter gives rise and the risk of divergences in judicial decisions with the European Union.

How does the practice of the Swedish courts of last resort relate to the developments in European law on the duty to give reasons? The legislation of 2006, which was the result of the Commission's action discussed in Section 2, above, only states that if a court of last resort refuses to ask for a preliminary ruling in a case where such a ruling has been requested, it should 'state the reasons for that' in its decision.[12]

The application of the duty to give reasons was studied in my Report of 2010. I could then partly rely on a 2009 article by Martin Johansson based on a study of the reasons given by the Swedish supreme courts in a substantial

---

[11] C-160/14, *Ferreira da Silva e Brito*, EU:C:2015:565.
[12] Statute 2006:502 with certain provisions about preliminary rulings from the CJEU, para 1.

number of cases involving EU law in which no admission had been granted.[13] He characterised the reform of 2006 as a 'paper tiger'. I reached the same conclusion in my Report. The reasons given were normally quite short and not very informative.

What is the present situation? We have had the important development by the ECtHR of the case law based on ECHR. Nowadays, the national courts of last instance are under a human rights obligation to present reasons why they refuse a request for a preliminary ruling. It is a minimum requirement according to case law these reasons fulfil the *CILFIT* criteria.

There are two kinds of situations to be observed, depending upon whether or not admission is granted. If a court of last resort decides not to grant admission to hear a case and the case does not involve EU law, the court would normally give no reason for its refusal in accordance with well-established legal practice. However, if the case does involve EU law and there is a request from one of the parties to refer the case for a preliminary ruling to the CJEU, the court must give reasons for not doing so when it decides not to grant admission. As these cases are not reported, it is not possible to base an assessment on a comprehensive study. That would have required the study of a very large number of unreported cases. However, based on a more limited number of such cases which I have come across, it seems the courts are still quite reluctant to give reasons of any real substance. Often the parties are only informed, in somewhat varying language that the court has not 'found reasons' to ask for a preliminary ruling. A standard phrase seems to be 'the case has not brought to the fore any issue of union law which would give cause for requesting a preliminary ruling from the EU Court'. Such empty phrases are obviously not fulfilling the requirements of Article 6(1) ECHR and Article 47 of the Charter.

If, however, a court of last resort grants admission and the case involves EU law, the court has two options when referring the case to the CJEU. It can decide either to refer the case or not in connection with its decision to grant admission or it can postpone the decision to a later stage, normally until the main proceedings have taken place. As these cases are normally reported, it is easier to make an assessment. In my Report of 2016, I studied all such cases from the Swedish Supreme Court from 2010 to 2015 inclusive. I found 17 such cases. In 12 cases, no real reasons were given why the Supreme Court had not found that EU law issues required a request for a preliminary ruling. In five of the cases the issue was discussed in the decision, but this was quite brief in three of them. Studying the decisions by the Swedish Supreme Administrative Court the result is similar. Different phrases are in use. Sometimes, the Supreme Court simply states the case does not involve any issue of EU law which obliges it to refer the case to the CJEU. In other cases,

[13] M Johansson and S Ahmed, De högsta domstolsinstansernas motiveringsskyldighet vid beslut att inhämta förhandsavgörande från EU-domstolen—en papperstiger, (2009) *Europarättslig Tidskrift* (*European Law Journal*) 769 ff.

it states there is sufficient EU case law available without giving clarifying references. The answer in its judgment to a request for a preliminary ruling can simply be: 'The Court finds the case can be decided based on existing union case law.' However, there are also some cases where the Swedish Supreme Court has given comprehensive information in its opinions about the case law of the CJEU and the court's assessment of that law and how it should be applied to the case at hand.

It is not possible to point at any judgment by the Swedish Supreme Court or the Supreme Administrative Court, in which the court has engaged itself in a discussion of the *CILFIT* criteria or any other issues of principle related to the obligation to refer cases to the CJEU.

To conclude, the legislation of 2006 on the duty for Swedish courts of last resort to give reasons when deciding not to grant admission in cases involving EU law has not changed the realities much. In particular, the practice of the Swedish courts of last resort is often not in line with the ECtHR requirements referring to the *CILFIT* criteria (e.g. it should not be sufficient for a court of last resort only to state it finds the relevant EU law clarified; it should also explain on what grounds it finds that to be the case). However, it would be welcome if the CJEU would express its own opinion on the scope and substance of the duty of courts of last resort to give reasons for rejecting requests for preliminary rulings.

4. REQUESTS BY SWEDISH COURTS FOR PRELIMINARY RULINGS 2010–2015. HOW DOES SWEDEN FARE?

It is of interest to clarify the scope and direction of Swedish case law in the field of preliminary references as viewed from a broader EU perspective and against the background of the criticism that has occurred. My Report covering the years 1995–2009 concluded there were 67 cases referred from Sweden and decided by the CJEU during that 15-year period. This represents less than five cases a year, when compared to the nearly 300 preliminary references decided by the CJEU every year at that time. The number of cases referred from Swedish courts stayed fairly constant over the years. The figures evidently demonstrated, there were essential differences in culture between the Member States. Sweden was among those states that, statistically, made the lowest number of requests for preliminary rulings (accompanied by Denmark, Finland, Ireland and Portugal). It was not possible to pinpoint any lasting change which could be connected to the Commission's infringement proceedings and the following Swedish legislative amendment in 2006.[14]

---

[14] See above n 2. For further statistical data related to the preliminary ruling procedure, see T de la Mare and C Donelly, 'Preliminary Rulings and EU Legal Integration: Evolution and Status' in P Craig and G de Búrca, *The Evolution of EU Law*, 2nd edn (Oxford, Oxford University Press, 2011) 363 ff.

By studying the 35 preliminary rulings that have been decided by the CJEU as requested by Swedish courts in the period between 2010 and 2015, the main purpose of the new Report has been to determine whether or not Swedish courts are still keeping a low profile in referring cases to the ECJ or whether a shift in attitude has taken place. It is possible to see a slight increase in the number of referrals from Swedish courts: approximately six referrals per year were made between 2010 and 2015.

However, there is no lack of cases in which lawyers litigating before Swedish courts request the Swedish court to refer the case to the CJEU, but it is a well-known fact that, in the overwhelming majority of those cases, the courts decide to reject the application for referral. To get a positive decision by a Swedish court to bring a legal matter before the CJEU is like passing a camel through the eye of a needle.

Of the 35 Swedish cases referred to and decided by the CJEU during the years 2010–2015, courts of last resort, primarily the Supreme Court and the Supreme Administrative Court, referred 13 cases and lower courts (courts of first instance and courts of appeal) referred 21 cases.[15] However, between 1995 and 2009, 34 cases were referred from courts of last resort and 28 from the lower courts. This indicates that it is primarily the general courts of first instance (in Swedish *tingsrätter*) that have become more active in asking for preliminary rulings. This development has brought Sweden more in line with the general pattern in most EU countries, where the large majority of cases referred to the CJEU emanate from lower courts.

A comparison can also be made between the number of references emanating from general courts versus administrative courts. The result is balanced: 18 cases versus 14 cases, although general courts make a few more requests. The remaining cases emanate from courts of special jurisdiction (i.e. the Labour Court and the Market Court). Four of the cases were referred from the Supreme Court and seven from the Supreme Administrative Court (of which four were concerned with VAT).

The general picture has not changed in 2016. There were five preliminary references from Swedish courts, of which two were from the Supreme Court. However, two of the cases have been dismissed on the request of the referring court.

It is interesting to look at the statistics for the different Member States. It is evident there are great differences in the attitudes towards requesting preliminary rulings. These are the figures:[16]

---

[15] One case was referred by an administrative body not regarded as a court or tribunal.
[16] The figures are derived from the statistics published in the Annual Report of the CJEU for 2015. Available at: www.curia.europa.eu.

Preliminary References from Member States´ Courts 2010–2015[17]		
	Total number of cases	*Inhabitants in millions*
Austria	122	8.7
Belgium	180	11.3
Bulgaria	74	7.2
Czech Republic	36	10.6
Cyprus	5	1.2
Denmark	47	5.6
Estonia	11	1.3
Finland	37	5.5
France	148	66.6
Germany	485	80.9
Greece	27	10.8
Hungary	94	9.9
Ireland	34	4.9
Italy	319	61.9
Latvia	39	2.0
Lithuania	29	2.9
Luxembourg	26	0.6
Malta	1	0.4
The Netherlands	206	16.9
Poland	65	38.6
Portugal	65	10.8
Romania	107	21.7
Slovakia	29	5.4
Slovenia	12	2.0
Spain	168	48.1
Sweden	40	9.8
United Kingdom	133	64.1

As this table shows, the number of references differs greatly between the different countries. Naturally, the large Member States generate more references, but quite visibly there are also different judicial cultures on this point.

---

[17] Croatia, which joined the EU in 2013, has been excluded.

Thus, there are more references from the older Member States, primarily the six founding States; those on the periphery of the EU tend to have fewer references. It is interesting to note the situation is quite similar in the three Scandinavian Member States, Denmark, Finland and Sweden, taking the population difference into account. Sweden is not faring particularly badly compared to its Scandinavian neighbours, Ireland and Portugal.[18] However, the number of references from Swedish courts has been consistently low.

However, comparing Austria and Belgium shows a different picture. Having a population somewhat smaller than Sweden and having entered the EU on the same date, Austria has generated three times more referrals. Belgium, also being of comparable size, has made more than four times as many referrals than Sweden. The situation is similar if Sweden is compared with the Netherlands. In these countries, as in Germany, the legal culture is definitely different when it comes to asking the CJEU. There seems to be a rather regular dialogue between the national courts and the CJEU.

Looking at the general picture, there should be scope for a substantial increase in the number of Swedish cases referred without cause for criticism for overburdening the CJEU. The statistics from the different Member States indicate that doubling the number of cases referred by Swedish courts would fit well within what can be considered as normal European practice and would strengthen the impact and correct application of union law in Sweden.

5. TYPES OF CASES REFERRED

What legal areas have been subject to preliminary rulings by Swedish courts? It is of interest to compare these with my previous Report to find out (a) if new types of cases have been referred to the CJEU and (b) if there are important types of cases in which referrals to the CJEU are not made.

The cases referred to the CJEU by Swedish courts have been systematised in my Report under the following headings: EU constitutional law including fundamental rights, general principles, EU international agreements, internal market law including, i.e., agricultural law, free movement of goods and services and freedom of establishment, Swedish legal monopolies, free movement of workers and employees and other labour law cases, social law, migration law, intellectual property law, marketing law, environmental law, competition law, tax law related to the free movement of services and capital, tax cases related to VAT and selective taxes, and, finally, freedom, security and justice.

---

[18] This aspect is stressed by M Broberg and N Fenger in their article' Förhandsavgöranden från svenska domstolar Är svenska domstolar väsentligt mindre benägnas att begära förhand-savgöranden än domstolar i andra medlemsstater?' (2015) *Europarättslig Tidskrift* 769 ff. The authors regard the Swedish situation as fairly satisfactory.

The large majority of cases have dealt with important legal issues of Union law which have either been unclear or not sufficiently clarified. There are one or two cases under most of the headings mentioned above. Once a Swedish court has taken the decision to refer a case to the CJEU, there has nearly always been good reason to do so. This indicates that Swedish courts have improved in their ability to identify central legal EU law issues. The CJEU has been able to deliver clarifying answers in its judgments which have been of fundamental importance for the final judgment in the case by the Swedish court.

In my previous Report, the conclusion could be drawn there were very few cases which had a connection to constitutional law. On this point, there has been a change. The *Åkerberg Fransson* case on *ne bis in idem* will be discussed below. In another case, the Supreme Court has asked the CJEU about the scope and applicability of the proportionality principle in relation to a heavy penalty for excess greenhouse gas emissions.[19] It is also worth noting that, for the first time, a Swedish court has asked the CJEU for an opinion on the validity of an EU legal act. That case, referred by an administrative court of first instance, concerned an antidumping regulation.[20]

Swedish courts have fully accepted the principles of the precedence and direct effects of EU law as well as the principle of interpretation in conformity with the treaties and directives. There are no Swedish cases in which Swedish courts have openly displayed a reluctance to accept the supremacy of EU law.

Certain legal areas have rarely been subject to a request for a preliminary ruling from Swedish courts (e.g. there are no cases in which Swedish courts have referred issues related to public procurement). This is surprising, as there are a large number of public procurement cases pending in the Swedish administrative courts and the CJEU is deciding a large number of such cases emanating from other jurisdictions. It could be argued that Sweden has developed a kind of silent practice not to refer public procurement cases. These are other areas in which there are no cases (e.g. state aid law). Also no Swedish court has referred the interpretation of provisions of Swedish law based on EU law but applied outside its ambit in accordance with the *Leur-Bloem* principle (e.g. competition law).[21]

Until recently Swedish courts had never used the urgent preliminary ruling proceeding (PPU). It was used for the first time in 2015, when a court of first instance (*tingsrätt*) asked for a preliminary ruling in a custody case, where the parents were living in different Member States.[22]

---

[19] Case C-203/12, *Billerud v Naturvårdsverket*, EU:C:2013:664.
[20] Case C-569/13, *Bricmate v Tullverket*, EU:C:2015:572.
[21] Case 28/95,130/95, *A Leur-Bloem v Inspecteur der Belastingdienst*, EU:C:1997:369.
[22] Case 455/15 PPU, *P v Q*, EU:C:2015:763.

The most important case during the period studied is the *Åkerberg Fransson* case[23] on *ne bis in idem*, in which the Court of Justice clarified the scope of the Charter. I have discussed this case and its implications in a previous volume of *Swedish Studies in European Law*.[24] The case was referred by the *Haparanda tingsrätt*, a small district court in the very north of Sweden.

I will only mention here two aspects of the *Åkerberg Fransson* case which relate directly to the law on preliminary references. The main issue in the case was whether or not the principle of *ne bis in idem* makes it possible to apply separate legal proceedings for tax surcharge and tax offences based on the same information in a tax return. The issue had been debated in Swedish legal circles for a long time. In 2002, the ECtHR had concluded in two cases that the Swedish system with tax surcharges was criminal in nature.[25] However, the decisions by the ECtHR did not cause the legislator to alter the Swedish legislation, nor did the courts change their practice. However, the sharpened definition of what constitutes *ne bis in idem*, introduced by the ECtHR in the *Zolotukhin* judgment[26] in 2009 made the problem acute. The Supreme Court ruled on the matter in two new decisions in 2010 and 2011. In the 2010 decision, which focused on the ECHR law, the majority of the justices took the view that the *Zolotukhin* judgment did not give 'clear support' to the need to change Swedish practice.[27] In the 2011 case,[28] the defendant invoked in particular the *ne bis in idem* principle in Article 50 of the Charter. The case dealt partly with tax surcharges for undeclared VAT. A Supreme Court majority, three Supreme Court justices, concluded that the Swedish legal provisions on tax offences and tax surcharges lay outside the scope of the Charter, thus a preliminary ruling was not required. Two dissenting justices took a different view and concluded with comprehensive reasons that the legal position was not clear as regards the possible application of the Charter and that a preliminary ruling should be requested. In reality, the Supreme Court voted on whether or not a preliminary ruling should be requested by the Court of Justice.

These decisions by the Supreme Court were much debated and some lower courts declined to follow them. The Haparanda Court decided to refer one such case to the CJEU, observing the undeclared tax was partly related to VAT.

---

[23] Case C-617/10, *Prosecutor v Hans Åkerberg Fransson*, EU:C:2013:105.
[24] U Bernitz, 'The Åkerberg Fransson Case. *Ne bis in Idem*: Double Procedures for Tax Surcharge and Tax Offences not Possible', *Swedish Studies in European Law Vol. 6: Human Rights in Contemporary European Law* (eds. J. Nergelius and E. Kristoffersson) (Oxford, Bloomsbury Publishing, 2015) 191 ff.
[25] App No 34619/97 *Janosevic v Sweden* and App No 36985/97 *Västberga Taxi and Vulk v Sweden*.
[26] App No 149393 *Sergey Zolotukin v Russia*, App No 149393.
[27] NJA 2010 p 168.
[28] NJA 2011 p 444.

In an effort to 'silence' the Haparanda Court, the Prosecutor appealed its decision to a stay of proceedings while waiting for the decision by the Court of Justice to the Court of Appeal on the grounds that the case was being delayed unnecessarily. However, the Court of Appeal rightly rejected the Prosecutor's request by referring to the *Cartesio* judgment of the Court of Justice.[29] According to that decision, it is important that each national court has the opportunity to decide independently and autonomously whether it finds that there is a need to request a preliminary ruling from the Court of Justice. The *Cartesio* judgment makes it clear that EU law does not accept that national courts of the higher instance, when issuing a ruling on an appeal, try to 'censor' a decision made by a court of the lower instance with regard to requesting a preliminary ruling. This applies even if the court of the higher instance takes the view that the decision made by the court of the lower instance is unjustified or would lead to an unwarranted delay in proceedings.

The developments in the *Åkerberg Fransson* case illustrate the importance of the *Cartesio* principle as established by the Court of Justice in securing the independence of the national court when requesting a preliminary ruling.[30] In its judgment in the case, the CJEU found it necessary to include a reminder—obviously addressed to the Supreme Court—about the duty to observe Article 267 TFEU as interpreted in the *CILFIT* case. As it turned out, the Haparanda district court, not the Supreme Court, had assessed the EU law correctly.

To conclude, Swedish courts have undergone a process of gestation in their relation to the preliminary ruling mechanism. This is reflected in the somewhat more frequent use of the preliminary ruling procedure, but also by the fact that more recent cases have dealt with central questions spanning a wide range of legal issues, including cases having a high degree of constitutional value. Nonetheless, I find the process of gestation has not yet finished, implying that there is still room for considerable progress.

6. EXPLANATIONS OF THE RESTRICTIVE ATTITUDE

What is the attitude of the Swedish courts towards requesting preliminary rulings from the CJEU? It seems possible to make the overall assessment the attitude would be more open today than during the first period of Swedish EU membership, but it is still possible, as the statistics clearly demonstrate, to observe a certain caution. New developments influencing

---

[29] Case 201/06, *Cartesio Oktató és Szolgátató*, EU:C:2008:723 paras 95–98. See my article, cited in n 22 above, for further details.

[30] M Broberg and N Fenger, 'Preliminary References as a Right: But for Whom? The Extent to Which Preliminary Reference Decisions can be Subject to Appeal' (2011) *European Law Review* 276 ff.

legal culture have a tendency not to penetrate so quickly and, as mentioned, the infringement proceedings brought by the Commission and the following legal amendments about the duty for the courts of last resort to give reasons have not had much effect. It would be difficult to regard the present situation as fully satisfactory. According to the overall picture, there is still a restrictiveness and in some instances probably a reluctance in Swedish courts about referring cases to Luxembourg. There is also scope to double the number of Swedish cases referred to the CJEU without attracting criticism for overburdening the latter.

What might be the reasons behind this restrictive attitude? In my view, the underlying explanations are to be found primarily in the differences in legal method and constitutional legal tradition between Swedish law, on the one hand, and European law on the other.

The Swedish legal method is often characterised as legal positivism.[31] Statutory law is the main source of law, although case law is the predominant source in certain fields. The *traveaux préparatoires* play a very important role. In the Government Bills to Parliament the intended interpretation and application of the proposed statutory rules is often explained in detail. These statements made in the preparatory works are not legally binding but normally the courts read them carefully and follow what they recommend, particularly when the legislation is fairly recent. General principles of law do exist, but they play a much lesser role than in EU law.[32] Also, there is no counterpart in Swedish law to the division in EU law between primary and secondary law. For Swedish lawyers, EU law represents a different type of legal system, applying other and less well-known methods of legal reasoning. In particular, there are distinctly different attitudes towards preparatory legislative material. Most likely, the majority of Swedish judges still regard EU law as a fairly unfamiliar and difficult legal system, which they approach with caution. They remain inclined to apply Swedish law if at all possible.

A particularly important feature of the differences in legal method is the different traditions in the field of constitutional law. Sweden has a centralised, non-federal governmental structure and there is no constitutional court or the like. When applying internal law, Swedish courts are only rarely involved in the application of constitutional legal issues—freedom of expression and transparency being the exceptions. In internal law, the constitutionality of statutes in force is normally taken for granted. Until 2011 the Swedish Constitution permitted the courts to disregard a statutory provision because it was considered to be unconstitutional only if the

---

[31] For an overview, see e.g., *Swedish Legal System* (ed. M Bogdan) (Stockholm, Norstedts Juridik 2010) Chapters 1–3.

[32] X Groussot, *General Principles of Community Law* (Groningen, Europa Law Publishing, 2006) 384 ff.

unconstitutionality was found to be manifest.[33] This was abolished by a revision of the text of the Constitution in 2010, but has not caused any important change in the practice of the courts. In the area of human rights, there is a steady increase in Swedish case law based on the application of the European Convention of Human Rights, but little such law is based on internal Swedish legal sources. However, on the whole, Swedish courts are not used to exercising judicial review and taking independent decisions on issues of constitutional law that are often sensitive in nature.

As mentioned in Part 4 above, the number of referrals from Danish and Finnish courts to the CJEU is largely of the same moderate size, taking into account the population difference between the countries. On this point, it is interesting to note that there are strong similarities between the Scandinavian countries in the areas of legal method and constitutional legal tradition. Austria and Belgium, countries having a federal structure, both generate many more references to Luxembourg.

The connection between the traditional lack of constitutional judicial review in the Nordic countries and the restrictive attitude towards referring cases to the CJEU for preliminary ruling have been observed by several authors in recent Scandinavian legal debate.[34] Behind the decision taken by a national court to refer a case to Luxembourg there is very often at least a suspicion that the internal law at issue is not fully in line with the requirements of EU law. By referring cases to the CJEU, national courts fulfill, to a large extent, a kind of judicial review. This seems to be quite a step for the Scandinavian judge trained in another legal tradition.

However, the situation seems to be changing slowly. The decisive role of the *traveaux préparatoires* is gradually loosening its grip on Swedish internal law and the Swedish courts have been given a wider scope for the application of constitutional law. The importance of the general principles of law seems to be more in evidence than before and the courts are gradually becoming more and more involved in human rights issues. In short, there is an ongoing 'Europeanisation' of Swedish law which should also have an effect on the attitudes towards referring cases to the CJEU for preliminary rulings, at least in the longer term. Recent research on trends in Swedish case law by the two European law professors at Umeå University Mattias Derlén and Johan Lindholm indicate a clear increase in recent years in

---

[33] Swedish Constitution, Chapter 11, Article 14.

[34] M Wind, 'The Nordics, the EU and the Reluctance towards Supranational Judicial Review' (2010) *Journal of Common Market Studies* 1039 ff., J Nergelius, 'Laval, Metock and the Recent Nordic Debate on Judicial Review, Europe' in *The New Legal Realism. Essays in Honour of Hjalte Rasmussen* (Copenhagen, DJOF Publishing 2010) 527 ff.

the number of cases in which Swedish courts cite European law in their judgments.[35] They have also observed a certain lingering insecurity in the courts' relationship with the characteristics of European law (e.g. Swedish courts are more inclined to refer to specific provisions of secondary law than to treaty articles or general principles of union law). They characterise this ongoing development using the Latin phrase *festina lente*: hurry slowly.

---

[35] M Derlén and J Lindholm, 'Festina lente—Europarättens genomslag i svensk rättspraxis 1995–2015' (2015) *Europarättslig tidskrift* 151 ff.

3

A Dynamic Analysis of Judicial Behaviour

The Auto-Correct Function of Constitutional Pluralism

ANA BOBIĆ*

1. INTRODUCTION TO THE AUTO-CORRECT FUNCTION

SINCE 1974, ACCORDING to the *Rheinmühlen I*[1] doctrine, national courts have been relieved of the obligation to be bound by rulings of superior national courts on points of law when dealing with questions of European Union (EU) law. Following the reasoning of AG Cruz Villalon in *Elchinov*,[2] *Rheinmühlen I* bestows upon national courts the right to set aside instructions of the superior court if they are contrary to EU law, encompassing the case law of constitutional courts as well,[3] a rule which was most recently confirmed in *Križan*.[4]

This doctrine resulted in different reactions on behalf of constitutional courts of the Member States, ranging from those that began referring preliminary questions to the European Court of Justice (ECJ) to others that explicitly rejected its case law as being *ultra vires*. National constitutional courts have also put forward identity-based limits to the principle of primacy

* The author would like to thank Angus Johnston, Petra Weingerl, Julian Nowag, Desmond Johnson and the participants of the Conference 'Understanding the European Court of Justice: Multidisciplinary Perspectives' on 8–9 December 2016 (Stockholm) for their useful comments on the earlier versions of this chapter.
[1] Case 166/73 *Rheinmühlen* [1974] ECLI:EU:C:1974:3, §4.
[2] Opinion of Advocate General Cruz Villalón in Case C-173/09 *Elchinov* [2010] ECLI:EU:C:2010:336, §21.
[3] The court dealt directly with this issue in the Case C-399/09 *Landtová* [2011] ECLI:EU:C:2011:415, §49. For the purposes of this work, reference to constitutional courts of Member States will encompass also national supreme jurisdictions performing binding constitutional review.
[4] Case C-416/10 *Križan* [2013] ECLI:EU:C:2013:8, §73. On this point, see also M Derlén and J Lindholm, 'Serving Two Masters: CJEU Case Law in Swedish First Instance Courts and National Courts of Precedence as Gatekeepers' in this volume, in particular Section 6 onwards.

of EU law, reasserting the untouchable character of the constitutional core.[5] This jurisprudence points to the parallel existence of competing claims to ultimate authority at the national level, thus illustrating the starting premise of the theory of constitutional pluralism.[6] Sovereignty claims at the national level are consistently put forward by constitutional adjudicators, in particular in situations of possible clashes in interpretation.[7] This, however, does not undermine the ability of constitutional pluralism to balance these opposing claims, and to place checks and balances among the courts involved through its auto-correct function.[8]

By way of introduction to the concept of the auto-correct function and how it works in the system of constitutional pluralism, it is first necessary to address another feature of a pluralist legal order—incrementalism. In particular, incrementalism accentuates the gradual development of the institutional interactions, but also substantively the creation of rules and principles.[9] Incrementalism may be regarded as stemming from an understanding of law as process, where the lines between *lex lata* and *lex ferenda* are becoming increasingly blurred, while the use of analogy and contextual interpretation take centre stage.[10] By looking at law in a dynamic fashion, legal norms on the resolution of constitutional conflict or an explicit clause on the final arbiter among national constitutional jurisdictions and the Court of Justice are unnecessary.

---

[5] For example, Czech *Ústavní Soud* Case Pl. ÚS 29/09 *Lisbon Treaty II*, Judgment of 3 November 2009, §150; French *Conseil Constitutionnel*, Case 2006-540 DC *Information Society*, Decision of 27 July 2006, §19; German *Bundesverfassungsgericht* 2 BVerfG 2/08 *Lisbon Treaty*, Judgment of 30 June 2009, §240 onwards; *Gauweiler*, Press Release No 9/2014 of 7 February 2014, §2.a; Italian *Corte costituzionale* Decision 183/73 *Frontini* of 27 December 1973, 2 [1974] CMLR 372; Latvian *Satversmes tiesa* Case 2008-35-01, Treaty of Lisbon, 7 April 2009, §§16.3, 17; Polish *Trybunał Konstytucyjny* K 32/09 Treaty of Lisbon, judgment of 24 November 2010, §1.1.2.

[6] For the purposes of the present work, I will subscribe to Neil Walker's definition of constitutional pluralism:

> [S]tates are no longer the sole locus of constitutional authority, but are now joined by other sites, or putative sites of constitutional authority, most prominently [...] those situated at the supra-state level, and that the relationship between state and non-state sites is better viewed as heterarchical rather than hierarchical.

N Walker, 'Late Sovereignty in the European Union' in N Walker (ed) *Sovereignty in Transition* (Hart, Oxford, 2003) 4. In addition, the present work relies on the following definition of heterarchy: 'the relation of elements to one another when they are unranked or when they possess the potential for being ranked in a number of different ways'. C L Crumley, 'Heterarchy and the Analysis of Complex Societies' (1995) 6 *Archaeological Papers of the American Anthropological Association* 1 at 3.

[7] For an analysis of the increasing frequency of state-centred claims by the *Bundesverfassungsgericht* see J Murkens, 'We Want Our Identity Back'—The Revival of National Sovereignty in the German Bundesverfassungsgericht's Decision on the Lisbon Treaty (2010) 25 PL 530.

[8] On how the national checks and balances influence judicial interactions in the EU, see A Wetter Ryde, 'Citizen Control through Judicial Review' Chapter 10 in this volume.

[9] N Krisch, *Beyond Constitutionalism—The Pluralist Structure of Postnational Law* (Oxford, Oxford University Press 2010), 247.

[10] R Higgins, *Problems and Process: International Law and How We Use It* (Oxford, Clarendon Press, 1995), 10.

Let us recall briefly the *Solange* saga to depict both how incrementalism influences intra-EU judicial interactions and also contributes more broadly to the development of EU constitutional law.[11] In its first *Solange* judgment,[12] the *Bundesverfassungsgericht* retained the right to exercise judicial review in matters of protection of fundamental rights, as long as the European integration process did not reach a level whereby it would guarantee a satisfactory level of protection. If we were to use the arguments of those criticising the lack of a final arbiter in constitutional pluralism[13] and apply them to the *Solange* situation, this judgment would probably be seen as the demise of the entire European project, while judicial interactions would be characterised at their absolute low. Conversely, subsequent events[14] demonstrated the gradual, step-by-step[15] development of the protection of fundamental rights at the EU level,[16] but also the contribution to the relationship between national constitutional jurisdictions and the Court of Justice.[17] It has also demonstrated how such a gradual development of institutional relations contributed to the avoidance of an outburst of conflict.

Keeping thus in mind that judicial interactions are to be regarded as a process, the auto-correct function of constitutional pluralism offers both a descriptive and a normative solution to the existence of competing claims to ultimate authority by apex courts in the European judicial space. The auto-correct functions in the following context: in the EU as we know it, issues prone to constitutional conflict arise regularly,[18] and both the Court of Justice and national constitutional jurisdictions are able, through their respective

---

[11] See also J Shaw, 'Process and Constitutional Discourse in the European Union' (2000) 27 *Journal of Law & Society* 4, 14, 19, 24; Z Bańkowski and E Christodoulidis, 'The European Union as an Essentially Contested Project' (1998) 4(4) *European Law Journal*, 341, 342.

[12] German *Bundesverfassungsgericht* case *Solange I* (BVerfGE 37, 271; English translation available at [1974] 2 CMLR 540).

[13] See, e.g., R D Kelemen, 'On the Unsustainability of Constitutional Pluralism. European Supremacy and the Survival of the Eurozone' (2016) 23 *Maastricht Journal of European and Comparative Law* 136, 140. Kelemen argues that the lack of a defined final arbiter in the EU is a sign of immaturity of the system and prevents it from being a 'constitutional' order.

[14] In its response, in Case 4/73 *Nold v Commission* [1974] ECLI:EU:C:1974:51, §13, the Court of Justice used the common constitutional traditions of Member States as the source of inspiration and the level of protection of fundamental rights that will be accorded on the EU level. Finally, the German Constitutional Court accepted such a level of protection in the *Solange II* judgment (BVerfGE 73, 339; English translation available at [1987] 3 CMLR 225).

[15] See Krisch above n 9 at 247 onwards.

[16] The area of fundamental rights is an excellent example of how the EU has evolved as a constitutional legal order not comparable to nation states. See, e.g., G de Búrca, 'After the EU Charter of Fundamental Rights: The Court of Justice as a Human Rights Adjudicator?' (2013) 20(2) *Maastricht Journal of European and Comparative Law* 168, 169.

[17] See also A Stone Sweet, 'The Structure of Constitutional Pluralism: Review of Nico Krisch, *Beyond Constitutionalism: The Pluralist Structure of Post-National Law*' (2013) 11(2) *International Journal of Constitutional Law* 491 at 500.

[18] Stone Sweet argues that the possibility of a conflict is a 'manifestation, probably permanent, of a pluralist structure of EU law'. A Stone Sweet, 'A Cosmopolitan Legal Order: Constitutional Pluralism and Rights Adjudication in Europe' (2012) 1(1) *Global Constitutionalism* 53 at 65.

procedural avenues,[19] to control the extent of the conflict. There are also two legal imperatives driving this dynamic in two opposite directions. On the one hand, the principle of primacy of EU law requires national courts to apply it in the spirit of sincere cooperation in order that it be uniformly applied throughout the EU. An explicit primacy clause that would serve as a resolution of this inherent conflict failed to come into force as part of the Constitutional Treaty after its signature in 2004, implying that the sentiment among Member States was and is against any such a conclusive provision.[20] Conversely, in the following Treaty amendment in 2007, the provision on the obligation of the EU to respect national identities of Member States was expanded in its wording, but it also henceforth fell under the jurisdiction of the Court of Justice.[21] Thus, the obligation to respect the national identities of Member States places an obligation on the EU and its institutions to take into account national particularities, including those enshrined in their constitutions.[22]

In such a setting, the auto-correct mechanism has the function of preventing conflict between either of the constitutional jurisdictions involved— in the EU judicial architecture, an awareness on the part of all the actors involved of the benefits of a pluralist setting results in conflict management and control. The result of a particular case will at some times favour national concerns,[23] and at others integration.[24] Such an outcome is in line with the definition of heterarchy,[25] according to which each of the courts involved can at times be the 'winner'.

---

[19] Interactions may take place through the preliminary reference procedure, but also in parallel cases concerning the same issue on both the EU and the national level. For a useful categorisation, see G Martinico, 'Judging in the Multilevel Legal Order: Exploring The Techniques Of 'Hidden Dialogue' (2010) 21 *King's College Law Journal* 257.

[20] This is not to diminish the importance of the principle of primacy in the case law of the Court of Justice, but rather to emphasise the importance of the 'political' in relation to the 'legal'. Moreover, it also serves to emphasise the importance the national constitutional setting has in its entirety, and its ability to constrain national constitutional courts. Admittedly, the focus of the present chapter is confined to courts. For an analysis of the institutional balance in the EU more generally, see D Johnson, Chapter 7 in this volume; for an analysis of the Scandinavian example of the influence of the domestic constitutional setting on judicial behaviour, see M Wind, Chapter 11 in this volume.

[21] B Guastaferro, 'Beyond the Exceptionalism of Constitutional Conflicts: The Ordinary Functions of the Identity Clause', Jean Monnet Working Paper 01/12, 4.

[22] The remainder of this chapter will, among other things, analyse how the Court of Justice and the *Bundesverfassungsgericht* regard the relationship and overlap between the concepts of 'national' and 'constitutional' identity.

[23] For instance, see: Case C-36/02 *Omega* [2004] ECLI:EU:C:2004:614; Case C-208/09 *Sayn-Wittgenstein* [2010] ECLI:EU:C:2010:806; Case C-391/09 *Runević-Vardyn* [2011] ECLI:EU:C:2011:291.

[24] See French *Conseil Constitutionnel* Case 2007-560 DC *Treaty of Lisbon*, decision of 20 December 2007; German *Bundesverfassungsgericht* case 2 B v R 2661/06 *Honeywell*, Order of 6 July 2010; Court of Justice Case C-62/14 *Gauweiler* [2015] ECLI:EU:C:2015:400.

[25] See above n 6.

In any event, the outcome will be reached after a careful balancing carried out by all the courts in the European judicial space, conducted through applying self-restraint and a strong will to avoid conflict.[26] In addition, national courts performing constitutional review apply an EU-friendly interpretation whenever possible, whereas the Court of Justice is bound to accommodate national identity claims put forward at the national level.[27] Over time, through the application of these different interpretative tools and principles, the pluralist setting will inherently work to auto-correct any imbalance.

This chapter will focus on a single area of constitutional review that constitutional courts of Member States have used to defy the principle of primacy—the interpretation and use of the national identity clause—to demonstrate the existence of the auto-correct function of constitutional pluralism. After looking in greater detail at the case law of Court of Justice on the national identity clause (section 2) and the German *Bundesverfassungsgericht* on constitutional identity (section 3), a pluralist interpretation of the national identity clause will be put forward (section 4). It will be argued that the auto-correct function of constitutional pluralism accommodates both the concerns of national constitutional courts, and the requirements of the principle of primacy of EU law. Should this exercise prove successful, the question of who is the final arbiter on matters of national and/or constitutional identity will not yield a single and clear winner, instead, more beneficially for a more general development of the EU's judicial architecture, it will render the question immaterial.[28]

The following sources will be used to test the viability of the auto-correct function: (1) judgments of the Court of Justice and national constitutional and supreme courts; (2) national reports drawn up by national constitutional courts in 2014 for the 26th Congress of European Constitutional Courts;[29] (3) interviews conducted with Judges and Advocates General of the Court of Justice;[30] and (4) public statements of members of all the judicial actors involved, by way of academic publications, talks, seminars and public interviews.

---

[26] See A Bobić, 'Constitutional Pluralism is Not Dead: An Analysis of Interactions between Constitutional Courts of Member States and the European Court of Justice' (2017) 18 *German Law Journal* (forthcoming). Available at: https://papers.ssrn.com/sol3/papers.cfm?abstract_id=2850589 (last accessed 1 April 2017). See also the Opinion of Advocate General Maduro in Joined cases C-402/05 P and C-415/05 P *Kadi* [2008] ECLI:EU:C:2008:11, §44.

[27] See Bobić above n 26 at 16 onwards.

[28] In this respect, Halberstam claims that the lack of a determined final authority is in fact 'an essential characteristic' of the system. D Halberstam, 'Constitutional Heterarchy: The Centrality of Conflict in the European Union and the United States', in, J L Dunoff and J P Trachtman (eds), *Ruling the World? Constitutionalism, International Law, and Global Governance* (Cambridge University Press, Cambridge, 2009), 331.

[29] All reports are available at www.confeuconstco.org/ (last accessed 4 March 2017). The advantage of the reports is that all constitutional/supreme courts answered the same questionnaire, thus ensuring that all the replies were given in the same context.

[30] The interviews were conducted as part of the research visit to the Court of Justice between February and May 2015, with seven Judges and Advocates General. To ensure the anonymity of the interviewees, they will be referred to as 'Interviewee 1', 'Interviewee 2', etc.

2. THE EU PERSPECTIVE IN THE ANALYSIS

Since its inclusion in the Treaty of Maastricht, the national identity clause has not found its way into a large number of judgments of the Court of Justice.[31] Initially, this was due to its exclusion from the jurisdiction of the Court.[32] Although the Lisbon Treaty eliminated this exclusion, the use of the clause still remains at a level that can hardly allow us to reach any serious conclusions as to its scope, meaning and use.[33] The small number of cases where the national identity clause has been invoked by national authorities has predominantly concerned the law of the internal market.

At the outset, it is important to emphasise the role that Advocates General have played in positioning the national identity clause in the wider architecture of EU law. Indeed, the Advocates General have repeatedly underlined the important position of the obligation of the EU to respect the national identities of the Member States,[34] but the first substantial contribution aimed at providing a further analysis of this duty was made by Advocate General Maduro. In *Marrosu*,[35] he took the position that national authorities and, in particular, national constitutional courts, are best placed to define the content of national identity, while the Court of Justice has the

---

[31] The Court has so far addressed the national identity claim in: Case 379/87 *Groener* [1989] ECLI:EU:C:1989:599, §18; Case C-473/93 *Commission v Luxembourg* [1996] ECLI:EU:C:1996:263, §§32, 35–36; See Case C-36/02 *Omega*, §32; Case C-208/09 *Sayn-Wittgenstein*, §92 ff; Case C-391/09 *Runevič-Vardyn*, §86 above n 26; Case C-393/10 *O'Brien* [2012] ECLI:EU:C:2012:110, §49; Case C-202/11 *Las* [2013] ECLI:EU:C:2013:239, §26; Case C-127/12 *Commission v Spain* [2014] ECLI:EU:C:2014:2130, §61; Case 151/12 *Commission v Spain* [2013] ECLI:EU:C:2013:690, §37; Joined Cases C-58/13 and C-59/13 *Torresi* [2014] ECLI:EU:C:2014:2088, §55; and Case 156/13 *Digibet* [2014] ECLI:EU:C:2014:1756, §34. Moreover, in only a few cases has the principle been elaborated upon in more detail, whereas the majority of the cases involved the Court's rejection of national authorities' invocation of the national identity clause.

[32] The exclusion was expressed in the pre-Lisbon Article 46 TEU.

[33] This trend is also confirmed in the recent judgment of the Court in Case C-62/14 *Gauweiler* (above n 24), where the Court omitted to address the claims of the German Constitutional Court concerning the difference between national identity as enshrined in Article 4(2) TEU and German constitutional identity.

[34] Opinion of Advocate General Tesauro in Case C-58/94 *Netherlands v Council* [1995] ECLI:EU:C:1995:409, §19; Opinion of Advocate General Maduro in Case C-160/03 *Spain v Eurojust* [2004] ECLI:EU:C:2004:817, §§24, 35–36; Opinion of Advocate General Maduro in Case C-53/04 *Marrosu* [2005] ECLI:EU:C:2005:569, §40; Opinion of Advocate General Stix-Hackl in Case C-193/05 *Commission v Luxembourg* [2006] ECLI:EU:C:2006:313, §52; Opinion of Advocate General Kokott in Joined Cases C-428/06 and C-434/06 *UGT-Rioja* [2008] ECLI:EU:C:2008:262, §54; Opinion of Advocate General Trstenjak in Case C-324/07 *Coditel* [2008] ECLI:EU:C:2008:317, §85; Opinion of Advocate General Maduro in Case C-213/07 *Michaniki* [2008] ECLI:EU:C:2008:544, §§31–33; Opinion of Advocate General Kokott in Case C-222/07 *UTECA* [2008] ECLI:EU:C:2008:468, §93; Opinion of Advocate General Ruiz-Jarabo Colomer in Case C-205/08 *Kärnten* [2009] ECLI:EU:C:2009:397, §47; Opinion of Advocate General Maduro in Case C-135/08 *Rottman* [2009] ECLI:EU:C:2009:588, §25; Opinion of Advocate General Bot in Case C-399/11 *Melloni* [2012] ECLI:EU:C:2012:600, §137; Opinion of Advocate General Cruz Villalón in Case C-62/14 *Gauweiler* [2015] ECLI:EU:C:2015:7, §59.

[35] Opinion of Advocate General Maduro in Case C-53/04 *Marrosu* (above n 34), §40.

role of determining how far Member States can go in derogating from EU law obligations on the basis of national identity.[36] In *Michaniki*, the role of the national identity clause is identified as a legitimate aim for derogating from the free movement rules.[37] *Michaniki* also shed some further light on the relationship between national and constitutional identity, finding the two concepts to be inherently overlapping due to the reference to fundamental constitutional structures in Article 4(2) TEU.[38]

Most recently, Advocate General Cruz Villalón had the opportunity to analyse the claim of the *Bundesverfassungsgericht* on the different scope of constitutional identity as opposed to national identity.[39] He shares Advocate General Maduro's understanding of the overlapping scope of constitutional and national identity and warns of the dangers that a different understanding of Article 4(2) TEU would have for the principle of primacy—rendering EU law automatically subordinate to 28 different legal systems.[40] It seems that the views of the Advocates General on the role and scope of the national identity clause broadly correspond to the most common understanding of the clause in scholarly writing.[41]

Before providing an argument on the pluralist interpretation of the national identity clause, I will address the limited case law thereon. The case law prior to the entry into force of the Lisbon Treaty reveals the tendency of Member States to put forward their national constitutional concerns as a justification for constraints that they have placed on the free movement rules. While the Court was willing to engage in the assessment of those claims in its interpretation of the limits of and acceptable derogations from the free movement rules, it has done so mainly through the public policy exception.

There is hardly any scholarly inquiry into the protection of national identity in EU law that does not refer to the Court's judgment in *Omega*,[42] where it

---

[36] ibid, §40. See also Opinion of Advocate General Maduro in Case C-213/07 *Michaniki* (above n 34), §33.

[37] Opinion of Advocate General Maduro in Case C-213/07 *Michaniki* (above n 34), §32.

[38] ibid, §31.

[39] Opinion of Advocate General Cruz Villalón in Case C-62/14 *Gauweiler* (above n 34). For a more detailed comparison of the Advocate General's Opinion and the judgment of the Court of Justice, see D Sarmiento, 'The Luxembourg "Double Look": The Advocate General's Opinion and the Judgment in the *Gauweiler* Case' (2016) 23(1) *Maastricht Journal of European and Comparative Law* 40.

[40] ibid, §60.

[41] A von Bogdandy and S Schill, 'Overcoming Absolute Primacy: Respect for National Identity under the Lisbon Treaty' (2011) 48 *CMLRev* 1417, 1452; M Wendel, 'Lisbon before the Courts: A Comparative Perspective' (2011) 7 *European Constitutional Law Review* 96, 137; L F M Besselink, 'National and Constitutional Identity Before and After Lisbon' (2010) 6(3) *Utrecht Law Review* 36, 45; and D Leczykiewicz, 'The 'National Identity Clause' in the EU Treaty: A Blow to Supremacy of Union law?' UK Constitutional Law Association Blog, http://ukconstitutionallaw.org/2012/06/21/dorota-leczykiewicz-the-national-identity-clause-in-the-eu-treaty-a-blow-to-supremacy-of-union-law/, accessed 8 June 2015.

[42] Case C-36/02 *Omega* (above n 31). In this case, the Court does not refer to the term national identity as such, but rather focuses on the public policy exception through which the German constitutional concern is framed.

stated that the special protection of human dignity in the German Constitution is a justified restriction on the free provision of services. Although the judgment makes no explicit reference to national identity, its relevance for research into the subject in the context of EU law results from the Court's treatment of a *national* constitutional concern from which a restriction of a fundamental freedom ensued. The facts of the case, in essence, dealt with the ban placed by the city of Bonn, Germany, on a laser game where players shoot at each other using laser guns, based on its violation of human dignity, a value of particular importance in the German Basic Law. The Court, therefore, employed the well-established practice on national measures restricting free movement, and applied the four-step proportionality test. The Court found that the German ban indeed restricted the free provision of services, and entered into an assessment of the aim that Germany was seeking to protect. Human dignity was recognised by the Court not only as a value of specific importance in Germany, but also as a part of general principles of *EU* law.[43]

Since the extended national identity clause entered into force, the Court first addressed it in *Sayn-Wittgenstein*, a case concerning Austria's ban on using reference to nobility in personal names, as a part of a wider abolition of nobility and a constitutional enforcement of the principle of equality.[44] The applicant in the case was an Austrian national, who was later adopted by a German national, and acquired his last name which entailed a nobility reference. Although several identity documents were issued in Austria under her new last name, the administrative authorities there informed her that her documents would be changed so as to exclude the reference to nobility.

She appealed, claiming that the mandatory change of her last name was contrary to the right to free movement and the right to provide services in the EU, as it would interfere with her luxury real estate business, carried out predominantly in Germany, but also in other Member States. The Court undertook the analysis of the measure, establishing the existence of a restriction on her right of free movement enshrined in Article 21 TFEU.[45] It subsequently turned to the question of justification, which was, according to Austria, the constitutional status of the abolition of nobility, as a more particular expression of the general principle of equal treatment, and as a part of the country's national identity.[46] The Court, faced with the need to accommodate the invocation of Article 4(2) TEU into its existing free movement case law stated that the national identity claim should be *'interpreted as reliance on public policy'*.[47] It proceeded by referring to the *Omega* reasoning, according to which the concept of public policy may vary

---

[43] Case C-36/02 *Omega* (n 31), §34.
[44] See Case C-208/09 *Sayn-Wittgenstein* above n 31.
[45] Ibid, §§71, 80.
[46] Ibid, §82.
[47] Ibid, §84.

across Member States and where Member States thus enjoy a certain margin of appreciation.[48] The subsequent examination of the justification seemed to follow the classic four-step proportionality test, whereby the Court did not leave any margin to the national court. It stated in clear terms that the national measure *was* proportionate to the '*fundamental constitutional objective pursued*'.[49]

There is a difference between *Omega* and *Sayn-Wittgenstein* that deserves brief attention, as it seems to have been overlooked in scholarly writings. The Court in *Omega* addressed the value of human dignity as a German specificity, but added that the protection of human dignity is a general principle that Community law strives to protect.[50] The Court concluded that the specific position of the protection of human dignity in Germany was *immaterial* as it coincided with the general principle of protection of human dignity, determined as a European value of high regard.[51] The wording of *Sayn-Wittgenstein* does not appear to follow the same logic as the Court includes a reference to the specificity of the abolition of nobility in the context of Austrian constitutional history.[52] While the abolition of nobility in Austria is, according to the Court, an expression of the principle of equality, which is also a general principle of EU law, it is precisely the Austrian *national* context that justifies the national provision. The difference becomes understandable when read in the wider context of EU primary law—*Omega* was a pre-Lisbon case, when the Court had no jurisdiction to interpret the national identity clause, and recourse to general principles of EU law was a safe harbour. *Sayn-Wittgenstein*, however, was a case where the Court was free to interpret and apply Article 4(2) TEU, and give some insight as to its future scope and application, regardless of the fact that the value invoked was confined to a single Member State.

There are, however, inherent similarities in the Court's reasoning in *Omega* and *Sayn-Wittgenstein* that might paint a broader picture on the use of Article 4(2) TEU in the area of free movement. First, the Court seems to take a unified approach in relation to Member State reliance on national identity, identifying it as an expression of public policy.[53] Second, Member States invoking 'national identity' as a legitimate aim benefit from a wider

---

[48] Ibid, §87.

[49] Ibid, §93.

[50] Case C-36/02 *Omega* (n 31), §34. The Opinion of Advocate General Stix-Hackl is even more telling in this regard, as she spends a major part of her Opinion determining the status of fundamental rights in the EU (§46–§73), human dignity as a legal concept (§74–§81), and its position in Community law (§82–§91). Opinion of Advocate General Stix-Hackl in Case C-36/02 *Omega* ECLI:EU:C:2004:162.

[51] Case C-36/02 *Omega* (n 31), §34. The status of human dignity in the EU is now highlighted in Article 2 TEU.

[52] Case C-208/09 *Sayn-Wittgenstein* (n 31), §§82–83.

[53] Case C-36/02 *Omega* (n 31), §28; Case C-208/09 *Sayn-Wittgenstein* (n 31), §84.

margin of discretion,[54] in particular as the Court stressed that the values protected need not to be uniform across Member States.[55] Finally, the Court clearly determined the division of tasks in the process of justification of a national measure, explaining that it is up to the national authorities to spell out the content of the national value, while the Court sets the limit regarding the application of such a value through the proportionality test. In both cases, the Court did not leave it to the national court to assess the proportionality of the measure in question, but undertook the evaluation itself.[56]

This approach to national identity in *Omega* and *Sayn-Wittgenstein* in fact represents a method that the Court employs in cases concerning public policy as a justification.[57] A brief look at the case law on public policy seems to reveal the pattern applicable in the cases relevant for the interpretation of Article 4(2) TEU. The Court's division of tasks in the application of the public policy exception is extremely useful in this regard—there is scope for discretion of national authorities in determining public policy requirements, which can also express national particularities. Once the national value is voiced as a justification, it is for the Court to perform control in accordance with the principle of proportionality.[58] While it would be misplaced to regard the national identity clause as merely an adjacent claim when Member States invoke the public policy exception, it would be equally wrong to ignore the Court's recurring application of the principles set out in the public policy jurisprudence on national identity cases.

3. THE MEMBER STATE PERSPECTIVE IN THE ANALYSIS

This section places the focus on the jurisprudence of the German *Bundesverfassungsgericht* concerning identity review, particularly in light of its recent interpretation of the Basic Law, underlining the difference between national and constitutional identity.[59] However, in order to draw a complete picture of the German court's understanding of constitutional identity and how it affects the primacy of EU law, it is necessary to take a step back and have a look at its older jurisprudence.

---

[54] Guastaferro advocates such a reading of the case law as well. B Guastaferro 'Beyond the Exceptionalism of Constitutional Conflicts: The Ordinary Functions of the Identity Clause', Jean Monnet Working Paper 01/12, 43.

[55] Case C-36/02 *Omega* above n 31, §31; Case C-208/09 *Sayn-Wittgenstein* above n 31, §87.

[56] Case C-36/02 *Omega* above n 31, §39; Case C-208/09 *Sayn-Wittgenstein* above n 31, §93.

[57] See in this respect, K Lenaerts, 'EU Values and Constitutional Pluralism: The EU System of Fundamental Rights Protection' (2014) 34 *Polish Yearbook of International Law* 135, 156.

[58] See, e.g., in the public policy case law: Case C-434/10 *Petar Aladzhov* [2011] ECLI:EU:C:2011:750, §34; Case C-33/07 *Jipa* [2008] ECLI:EU:C:2008:396, §23; and Case C-420/07 *Apostolides* [2009] ECLI:EU:C:2009:271, §57.

[59] German *Bundesverfassungsgericht*, 2 BvR 2728/13 *Gauweiler*, Order of 14 January 2014, §29.

The first mention of the notion of constitutional identity can be found in the famous *Solange I*[60] judgment, where the German court, apart from introducing the preferable standards for the review of fundamental rights protection at the Union level, also explained the limits to integration referring to the core of the German Basic Law as a basis for its identity.[61] Several decades later, a number of constitutional complaints against the ratification of the Lisbon Treaty proved an excellent opportunity for the German Court to present its coherent vision of identity review, added as a third head of review of EU acts, alongside the *ultra vires* and the fundamental rights reviews.[62] While the complaints were admitted based on an allegation of an infringement of the right to vote under Article 38(1) of the Basic Law, the German court engaged in a full review of the Treaty Amendment pending ratification. The identity review introduced in the judgment is defined in rather vague terms:

> [...] it must be possible within the German jurisdiction to assert the responsibility for integration if obvious transgressions of the boundaries occur when the European Union claims competences—this has also been emphasised by the agents of the German Bundestag and of the Federal Government in the oral hearing—and to preserve the inviolable core content of the Basic Law's constitutional identity by means of a identity review. [...][63]

The German court proceeded by giving examples of some core areas that are not subject to integration, listing criminal law (both substantive and procedural), the monopoly on the use of force by the police and by the military, fundamental fiscal decisions on public revenue and expenditure, the social state and the school and education system and the relationship with religious communities.[64]

The German court did not define or even give examples of what 'an obvious transgression' might entail. However, it underlined that undertaking the identity review needs to go hand-in-hand with the principle of sincere cooperation from Article 4(3) TEU, and should, furthermore, be performed while taking into account the Basic Law's openness towards EU law.[65] Wendel is pessimistic about the actual use of the principle of friendliness towards EU law when conducting identity review, considering it a trick by which the German Constitutional Court will use the national identity

---

[60] German *Bundesverfassungsgericht*, 37 BVerfGE 271 *Internationale Handelsgesellschaft (Solange I)* Judgment of 29 May 1974, (English translation available in [1974] 2 CMLR 540), §279).

[61] See also German *Bundesverfassungsgericht*, 73 BVerfGE 339 *Wünsche Handelsgesellschaft (Solange II)* Judgment of 22 October 1986, (English translation available at [1987] 3 CMLR 225), §§375–76.

[62] See German *Bundesverfassungsgericht*, *Lisbon Treaty* above n 5 at §§240–41.

[63] Ibid, §240.

[64] Ibid, §§252–60.

[65] Ibid, §240.

clause to place further limits on the applicability of EU law in Germany.[66] Pernice offers a more optimistic reading of the reference to the principle of friendliness towards European law, stating in particular that what is seemingly a contradictory statement is, in fact, in line with a 'non-hierarchical or pluralist' understanding of the relationship between European and national constitutional law.[67]

The wording of the German court can be read in support of a pluralist understanding of the European constitutional space. In particular, it refers to the *Kadi* judgment of the Court of Justice[68] as an example of a situation in which the identity claim overrides the EU's legal obligation.[69] In so doing, the German court refers to the 'contexts of political order which are not structured according to a strict hierarchy'[70] and subsequently applies the analogy to a hypothetical situation of a conflict between the German constitutional identity and the requirements of EU law.[71] Nevertheless, any pluralist understanding of the judgment should contain a dose of caution. Commentators have pointed out that the judgment holds a strong traditional view of State-centred sovereignty, which implies clear hierarchy and the superiority of the State constitution.[72]

Interestingly enough, the German court, in its analysis, states that the right to perform an identity review is 'rooted in constitutional law'[73] and exists because 'the guarantee of national constitutional identity under constitutional law and under Union law goes hand-in-hand in the European legal area'.[74] This point treats national and constitutional identity as synonyms,[75] and

---

[66] See Wendel above n 41 at 134. In general, it seems that the literature dealing with the judgment is mainly pessimistic as regards the use of the principle of openness to European law. See D Halberstam and C Möllers, 'The German Constitutional Court says "Ja zu Deutschland!"' (2009) 10(8) *German Law Journal* 1241; D Thym, 'From Ultra-Vires-Control to Constitutional Identity Review: The Lisbon Judgment of the German Constitutional Court', in J M Beneyto and I Pernice (eds) *Europe's Constitutional Challenges in the Light of the Recent Case Law of National Constitutional Courts—Lisbon and Beyond* (Baden Baden, Nomos Publishing, 2011); S Theil, 'What Red Lines, If Any, Do the Lisbon Judgments of European Constitutional Courts Draw for Future EU integration?' (2014) 15(4) *German Law Journal* 599.

[67] I Pernice, 'Motor or Brake for European Policies? Germany's New Role in the EU after the Lisbon-Judgment of Its Bundesverfassungsgericht' in Beneyto and Pernice (see n 66 above), 355, 385. See also D Thym, 'In the Name of the Sovereign Statehood: A Critical Introduction to the Lisbon Judgment of the German Constitutional Court' (2009) 46 *CMLRev* 1795, 1805.

[68] Court of Justice, Joined Cases C-402/05 P and C-415/05 P *Kadi* [2008] ECLI:EU:C:2008:461.

[69] See German *Bundesverfassungsgericht, Lisbon Treaty* n 5 above, §340.

[70] Ibid.

[71] Nicolaïdis argues that the *Bundesverfassungsgericht* in fact praises the heterarchical setting. See K Nicolaïdis, 'Germany as Europe: How the Constitutional Court Unwittingly Embraced EU Demoi-cracy. A comment on Franz Mayer' (2011) 9 (3–4) *International Journal of Constitutional Law* 786, 791.

[72] See Theil above n 66 at 603.

[73] See German *Bundesverfassungsgericht, Lisbon Treaty* above n 5 at §240.

[74] Ibid, Headnote 4 and §240.

[75] See Thym above n 67 at 41; See Halberstam and Möllers above n 66 at 1247.

therefore represents a reading of the identity clause similar to that employed by the Court of Justice, as well as the majority of the academic community.[76] In particular, Thym has, in his analysis of the *Lisbon* judgment, drawn a parallel between the case law of the Court of Justice on Article 4(2) TEU and the identity review put forward by the German Court.[77] In addition, he notes that the use of the expression 'hand in hand' for describing the relationship between national and constitutional identity might also serve as a subscription to the pluralist understanding of the EU constitutional framework.[78]

Somewhat surprisingly, in comparison to the reasoning of its judgment concerning the Lisbon Treaty, the *Bundesverfassungsgericht* set out a more detailed account of identity review in its first preliminary reference to the Court of Justice concerning the review of the Outright Monetary Transactions mechanism.[79] As regards the identity review, the German Court in its reference divides constitutional values into two categories: those underpinning national 'fundamental structures, political and constitutional' as set out in Article 4(2) TEU; and the core constitutional values that represent the national constitutional identity, and therefore lie beyond the reach of the primacy of EU law. The main difference between the two is that the latter values are not subject to the principle of primacy of EU law, and it is the exclusive jurisdiction of the German court to interpret them.[80] In consequence, it is apparent that the German court has abandoned its view from its *Lisbon Treaty* judgment that the term 'national identity' is synonymous with 'constitutional identity'. Furthermore, the court has stated that the values representing constitutional identity cannot be subject to any kind of balancing exercise, and must be unconditionally protected by the *Bundesverfassungsgericht*.[81]

The Court of Justice, in its reply to the preliminary reference, refrained from entering into any discussion on this point, and focused solely on the substantive questions concerning the ECB's mandate in relation to the OMT mechanism. The power relations in the context of this preliminary reference are complex and provide ample space for self-restraint on behalf of both courts, and serve as an excellent example of how the auto-correct function operates. It is argued that the Court of Justice was prudent not to enter into

---

[76] See Opinion of Advocate General Maduro in Case C-53/04 *Marrosu* above n 34 at §40. See also, Besselink, above n 41 at 37; S Rodin, 'National Identity and Market Freedoms after the Treaty of Lisbon' (2011) 7 *Croatian Yearbook of European Law and Policy* 11; See von Bogdandy and Schill above n 41 at 1435; G van der Schyff, 'The Constitutional Relationship Between the European Union and its Member States: The Role of National Identity in Article 4(2) TEU' (2012) 37(5) *ELRev* 563 at 568.

[77] See Thym above n 67 at 1811.

[78] Ibid.

[79] See German *Bundesverfassungsgericht, Gauweiler* above n 59.

[80] Ibid, §29.

[81] Ibid.

a discussion on this matter, and deferred to the *Bundesverfassungsgericht*.[82] In turn, the German Court also demonstrated mutual respect and self-restraint and did not dispute the interpretation on the validity of the OMT mechanism as given by the Court of Justice.[83]

Most recently, the *Bundesverfassungsgericht* decided not to refer a preliminary reference to the Court of Justice in a case where the European Arrest Warrant was to be applied to an American citizen, and he was to be extradited to Italy where he was sentenced *in absentia*.[84] The Düsseldorf Higher Regional Court allowed such an extradition, and the American citizen submitted a constitutional complaint to the German Constitutional Court claiming that he was sentenced *in absentia*, and would not have a chance of a new evidentiary hearing in Italy, as required by Article 5(1) of the Framework Decision on the European Arrest Warrant.[85]

The *Bundesverfassungsgericht* decided that the case was to be returned to the Higher Regional Court, but the Order is of interest as it gives some further information on the German Court's view of identity review. In particular, the Court reiterated the view introduced in *Gauweiler* on how the constitutional identity of Germany is a matter for it alone to interpret and protect, and is not open to European integration.[86] However, it continued by reiterating its stance from the Lisbon Treaty decision, that such an understanding of constitutional identity is inherent in the national identity clause from Article 4(2) TEU, and is in line with the principle of sincere cooperation in Article 4(3) TEU.[87] Nevertheless, the Court, taking into account the principle of openness to European integration, reserves solely for itself any possibility of declaring a provision of EU law inapplicable in Germany—underlining the exceptional nature of such a scenario.[88]

---

[82] M Claes and J-H Reestman, 'The Protection of National Constitutional Identity and the Limits of European Integration at the Occasion of the *Gauweiler* Case' (2015) 16(4) *German Law Journal* 917, 970.

[83] German *Bundesverfassungsgericht*, Decision of 21 June 2016, Case No 2 BvR 2728/13, 2 BvR 2729/13, 2 BvR 2730/13, 2 BvR 2731/13, 2 BvE 13/13 *Gauweiler II*.

[84] German *Bundesverfassungsgericht*, Order of 15 December 2015, 2 BvR 2735/14. For a more detailed analysis, see J Nowag, 'EU Law, Constitutional Identity, and Human Dignity: A Toxic Mix? *Bundesverfassungsgericht: Mr R*' (2016) 53(5) *CML Rev* 1441.

[85] Council Framework Decision 2002/584/JHA on the European arrest warrant and the surrender procedures between Member States, OJ L 190, 18/07/2002, 1–20.

[86] German *Bundesverfassungsgericht*, Order of 15 December 2015 (n 84), Key considerations §1. The case law of the United Kingdom Supreme Court might be interpreted as similar to the position of Germany. In a recent UK Supreme Court case, Lord Mance stated that should an unlikely situation of a constitutional conflict arise between the national and the EU constitutional order, it should be up to the Supreme Court itself to decide on the consistency of national constitutional requirements. He then went on to underline that such a situation would be unlikely, and should be treated with mutual respect and caution. UK Supreme Court case: *Pham* [2015] UKSC 19, §§90–1.

[87] See German *Bundesverfassungsgericht*, Order of 15 December 2015 above n 84, Key considerations §1.

[88] Ibid.

Such reasoning is perhaps best fit to serve as a conclusion to this review of the case law of the German Court on identity review—although it might come across as contrary to the principle of primacy, it in fact fits into the pluralist heterarchical scheme. In particular, the role of the national identity clause is precisely to underline differences between Member States and their constitutional values. However, national courts are not able to use this exception to circumvent the principle of primacy; the most extreme remedy is reserved solely for the Constitutional Court and only under strict conditions. It is argued that reference to these conditions will always be made taking into consideration the fact that Germany is a part of a pluralist system that functions on a heterarchical basis.

4. CONCLUSION

In the preceding sections, I have analysed the case law of the Court of Justice in relation to the interpretation of the national identity clause. The same was done in relation to the *Bundesverfassungsgericht* performing identity review. The aim of this concluding section is to propose a coherent interpretation grounded in the pluralist framework.

In a more general sense, it is possible to discern two different interpretations of the concepts of national and constitutional identity. According to the first interpretation, there are essentially two sets of constitutional values: those underpinning national 'fundamental structures, political and constitutional' as set out in Article 4(2) TEU; and the core constitutional values that represent the national constitutional identity and, therefore, in the view of some national constitutional courts,[89] lie beyond the reach of the primacy of EU law. The second line of interpretation endorses a more homogeneous understanding of the identity clause, according to which the concept of fundamental political and constitutional structures encompasses core constitutional values of Member States, leaving no national provision or principle outside its scope.

The first line of interpretation singles out national constitutional provisions that have a higher degree of constitutional entrenchment, such as provisions on the basic principles of state organisation, sovereignty, the principle of democracy, and human dignity.[90] In substantive terms, such a reading of the identity clause in relation to national constitutions creates an area of constitutional interpretation which appears to run counter to the principle of primacy of EU law. Interviews with Judges and Advocates General of the Court of Justice added further insight

---

[89] See above n 5.
[90] See von Bogdandy and Schill above n 41 at 1432.

to this point. Interviewee 5 stated that the scope of the national identity clause is broader in its content, and encompasses constitutional identity. The same interviewee stated that when it comes to constitutional identity as interpreted by the *Bundesverfassungsgericht*, there should be some areas of national constitutions that remain in the exclusive realm of national constitutional courts. Such a view opposes the Court's case law whereby Member States are bound by general principles of law even when exercising their exclusive competences.[91] From an institutional point of view, it represents an area of primacy for national constitutional courts, where their interpretative jurisdiction remains intact. However, constitutional courts that have introduced some form of identity review have also imposed limits to such review, grounded in the principles of EU-friendly interpretation and self-restraint.

It is difficult to imagine the Court of Justice subscribing to an understanding of the identity clause which would seriously undermine its decades-long jurisprudence on the principle of primacy of EU law over all sources of national law, including national constitutions, which are possibly in conflict with the provisions of EU law. At the same time, the Court of Justice has not shown much activity in interpreting the scope of the national identity clause in any greater depth. Advocates General have been more elaborate in proposing a comprehensive interpretation of the notion, which has only exceptionally found its way into the judgments of the Court.[92] In the view of Interviewee 6, since the national identity clause is contained in the Treaties, it is only natural that the Court of Justice treats it as an autonomous EU law concept, as it does with a large number of notions contained in primary and secondary sources of EU law.

In my opinion, contrary to the seemingly contrary approaches taken by the Court of Justice and national courts with a constitutional mandate that introduced identity review, the case law presented achieves coherence when viewed through the lens of incrementalism and constitutional pluralism. The underlying assumption of such an interpretation is that all the courts involved are aware of the need to preserve a peaceful relationship[93] in the European judicial space, without a clear or prior declaration of superiority or subordination. In consequence, the exhibition of self-restraint is key in a situation of potential constitutional conflict.

The argument of a pluralist interpretation of the identity clause is twofold: (1) the national identity clause is to serve as an exception to accommodate national particularities in the application of EU law at the

[91] Case C-267/06 *Maruko* [2008] ECLI:EU:C:2008:179, §59.
[92] See above n 34.
[93] The attitude can find its most explicit expression in the principle of sincere cooperation set out in Article 4(3) TEU, but also in different expressions of an EU-friendly interpretation relied upon by national constitutional jurisdictions (the principle was expressed in the case law of constitutional jurisdictions in Cyprus, Czech Republic, Germany, Hungary, Italy, Latvia, Lithuania, Poland and Portugal). See Bobić above n 26 at 16.

national level, while the role of the Court of Justice is to apply a uniform method in determining the limits to this exception through the application of the principle of proportionality;[94] and (2) the proportionality analysis will highlight the issues of jurisdictional and constitutional conflict, both between the EU and the national level, but potentially also conflicts within a Member State—the balancing of these issues will determine the extent of self-restraint that is to be applied in a particular case.[95] Interviewee 6 emphasised that the Court of Justice will, when taking into account national identity concerns, undertake a balancing exercise as it reaches its final judgment. The same interviewee also stated that the Court of Justice should carry out this balancing exercise carefully, taking into consideration the historical underpinnings of a particular national value, as was done in the case of *Sayn Wittgenstein*. Such a division of interpretative tasks between the national and EU judiciaries is inherently pluralist.

In order to understand the use of the proportionality analysis, and in particular the balancing exercise, it is necessary to distinguish between *institutional* and *substantive* balancing. In particular, institutional balancing is closely linked to the use of self-restraint, and is the step that follows when a particular national principle or value has been highlighted as an expression of national identity in a particular case. If the particular case is in the procedure before the Court of Justice, the use of institutional balancing will mean rendering a decision on which judicial instance is to take the final decision. Such an approach is well known in the case law of the Court and, as Tridimas explains, the Court of Justice employs it regularly in what he calls 'guidance' and 'deference' cases.[96] In particular, the Court either gives guidance to the national court that subsequently decides on the question of proportionality (guidance cases), or it leaves it entirely up to the national court to decide on proportionality (deference cases). In deciding whether to rule on a particular issue for itself, or leave it to the national court, I argue that the Court will be driven by the sensitivity of the case,[97] which will condition the extent of self-restraint that is to be applied. As was shown in section 2, the Court of Justice was mostly receptive to accommodating national identity claims, treating them as yet another legitimate aim for limiting the application of EU law at the national level.

In contrast, when a case is heard before a national constitutional jurisdiction, regardless of whether or not the national court has submitted

---

[94] See also Besselink above n 41 at 46; Wendel, above n 41 at 134–35.

[95] For an analysis of the Court's principle of proportionality in relation to Member States' margin of appreciation, see A Ericsson, Chapter 6 in this volume, in particular 5 onwards.

[96] T Tridimas, 'Constitutional Review of Member State Action: The Virtues and Vices of an Incomplete Jurisdiction', (2011) 9(3–4) *International Journal of Constitutional Law*, 737 at 739.

[97] A great majority of interviewees at the Court of Justice confirmed that they are taking particular care of national constitutional concerns when they arise in a case they are handling. See Bobić above n 27 at 18.

a preliminary reference, national instances will, in my opinion, be wary of the possible constitutional conflict that the protection of a particular national value might entail. The latest decision by the *Bundesverfassungsgericht* is an excellent example in this regard.[98] The German court did not refer a recent case to the Court of Justice for a further interpretation of the European Arrest Warrant (EAW), but has instead decided the case itself. Nevertheless, regardless of its statements concerning the protection of constitutional identity, the *Bundesverfassungsgericht* did not call into question the application of the EAW in the case in question. In addition, it stated that any constitutional conflict must be approached with great self-restraint, and in a manner open to European integration.[99] More importantly, it stated that any conflict which might arise would not undermine the uniform application of EU law in Germany as a whole, confirming incrementalism and the auto-correct function as one of the main features characterising a pluralist system.

The institutional balancing exercise (i.e. the determination of which instance will ultimately decide a case, as explained in the preceding paragraphs) is followed by the substantive balancing of values put forward as an expression of national identity. Surely, the result of the institutional balancing exercise will serve as a strong indicator regarding the extent of the substantive balancing act that a particular court is to exhibit. In essence, when the Court of Justice defers to a national court regarding the ultimate decision concerning the proportionality of a particular measure, this undoubtedly means an endorsement for that court to protect the national value in question.

The pluralist nature of the interpretation of Article 4(2) TEU presented stems from its intrinsically heterarchical nature, as it does not impose an overarching European value over specific national values, nor does it define the final arbiter in advance. On the contrary, it endorses an equal position of a variety of national specificity claims that are all subject to the same method applied by the Court of Justice through the proportionality test.[100] In essence, all the constitutional and supreme courts involved want both an assurance of national and constitutional identity, and the same is the case for the Court of Justice in relation to the autonomy of EU law. In parallel, all are aware of the need for a uniform interpretation and application of EU law, which is conditional upon the respect for the principle of primacy. Ultimately, it demonstrates the existence and value of the auto-correct function of constitutional pluralism, which serves to balance and resolve constitutional conflict in the EU in an incremental fashion.

---

[98] See German *Bundesverfassungsgericht*, Order of 15 December 2015 above n 84.

[99] Ibid, Key considerations §1.b.

[100] To quote the Polish *Trybunał Konstytucyjny*: 'confirming one's national identity in solidarity with other nations, and not against them'. See Case K 32/09 *Treaty of Lisbon* above n 5 at §2.1.

4

Pre-Ratification Judicial Review of International Agreements to be Concluded by the European Union

GRAHAM BUTLER

1. INTRODUCTION

THE COURT IS a curious judicial actor in EU external relations that continues to evolve with the passage of time. Whether it was the creation of the *ERTA* doctrine,[1] or the more recent Opinion 2/13 on Accession of the European EU to the European Convention on Human Rights in 2014,[2] the Court has been incrementally shaping the law of EU external relations and determining the manner in which the EU may enter into formal international relations. Understanding the Court's importance in this field has been done time and again, but yet, consideration of the pre-ratification judicial review option, available to certain actors for envisaged international agreements through Article 218(11) TFEU, is deserving of more attention to better understand the manner in which the Court has, does, and will continue to shape the external dimension of the EU through international agreements. Faced with difficult choices, and being forced to wade into institutional debates over competence and the autonomy of the EU's legal order, this chapter underlines the important role that the Court has played in external relations prior to international agreements being entered into, and seeks to carve out a formula for how *ex ante* judicial review can work in developing the EU into an even more enhanced global actor, through its own unique judicial order.

---

[1] Case C-22/70, *Commission v Council*, ECLI:EU:C:1971:32 (*European Agreement on Road Transport*).
[2] Opinion 2/13, *Accession of the European Union to the European Convention for the Protection of Human Rights and Fundamental Freedoms*, ECLI:EU:C:2014:2454.

2. THE EUROPEAN UNION AND INTERNATIONAL AGREEMENTS

The binding Opinions that the Court issues in Article 218(11) TFEU scenarios are there to offer the opportunity to map out the external dimension of the European Union (EU), whilst ensuring that international commitments to which it envisages agreeing to are in compliance with its constitutional law. Indeed they are the only *ex ante* procedure proposals for the Court to examine future legislative proposals.[3] Such Opinions can be utilised at the pre-ratification stage of international agreements to 'test' the extent of competences conferred upon the EU, and the ramifications and consequences they may have on its legal order. With the highly legal nature of the EU and its institutional framework, it comes with the organisation of an independent judicial arbiter overseeing the external nature of the EU and its international relations. The Article 218(11) TFEU procedure has been labelled as one of the 'miscellaneous functions of a constitutional nature' that the Court provides.[4] The traditional charges of disdain from certain quarters levelled against the Court as an integrationist institution no longer carries the significance that it used to, thus, the current era sends the clearest signal yet that the debate on its precise role has moved onto more legal matters. This development is welcome, as it allows a more deserving discussion on the role of the Court in external relations: what it can, or even what it should be. The global legal and political environment is a sphere in which the EU has consistently striven to achieve a greater role; consequently, it has had to avail itself of legal instruments to achieve these desired aims. Over time, as the EU's legal instruments have become more prominent and powerful, its institutions, particularly the Commission, have had to untie the straightjacket of the treaties that inhibited it, imposed by the EU Member States as High Contracting Parties to the treaties. Therefore, with a backbone, the role of the Court has been the ability to influence, from the bench, the international agreements the EU wishes to enter into.

The two different types of stages of an international agreement are *ex ante* and *ex post*. The Court's *ex ante* Opinions on envisaged international agreements have a remarkable role to play in the EU's external relations, despite not existing as an explicit actor in the political arena, but one confined to the legal scene. What has motivated the Court in delivering such wide-ranging Opinions when asked may puzzle the more casual observer of the EU's institutional dynamics, but from a judicial perspective, there is but an overarching aim—the prerogative for the maintenance and protection of the EU's legal order. In the Court's own words, it has ensured that, 'an

---

[3] See Anna Wetter Ryde, Chapter 10 in this volume.

[4] W Feld, *The Court of the European Communities: New Dimension in International Adjudication* (Martinus Nijhoff Publishers 1964) 63.

international agreement cannot have the effect of prejudicing the constitutional principles of the [treaties]'.[5] The Court has been called a '*laboratory of external law*',[6] as it continues to figuratively conceptualise the interaction of the EU legal order with other spheres, and how the mandate of the Court is to continue and protect the autonomy of the legal order. Accordingly, the EU's external relations are extremely Court-centric, given their potential to impinge upon the very heart of EU objectives set out in the treaties, thus making the principles, objectives, and values upon which the EU is founded, judicially contestable subjects of the Court.

The EU's capacity to act on the international stage, vis-à-vis its legal authority to do so, are sharply different notions. Right from the very beginning, albeit in a limited fashion, the precursors to the EU had the ability to form the basis for international agreements with actors beyond the EU itself. Without being specifically confined to law and rule-making internally within the EU, there existed the possibility to go further afield and, within the scope of the EU treaties, forge international agreements and resulting commitments with two types of third-parties: states, and other international organisations. The early days of EU law may be faint in modern lawyers' memory given those memories have largely been left to be cherished by previous generations, but understanding the Court in both an historical and modern context is important for elucidating its possible future direction. In discussions on the issues that were pertinent in the early days,[7] little was said of the Court adjudicating on international agreements or other treaties. This was despite the Court in those days acting as the judicial body for three entities: the European Coal and Steel Community; the European Economic Community; and the European Atomic Energy Community (EURATOM), three international treaties in themselves. The confidence of the Court to rule on international agreements, affirmatively, took time to develop, and along with it, a judicial legal order. Thus, this confidence has gone hand-in-hand with it being able to define itself, as a legal order in its own right,[8] and therefore, what its relationship to *other* legal orders would be.[9] Given the growth of globalism that has attempted to sweep the rug from

---

[5] Joined Cases C-402/05 and C-415/05 P, *Yassin Abdullah Kadi and Al Barakaat International Foundation v Council and Commission*, ECLI:EU:C:2008:461, para 285.

[6] P Eeckhout, 'A Panorama of Two Decades of EU External Relations Law' in A Arnull, P Eeckhout and T Tridimas (eds), *Continuity and Change in EU Law: Essays in Honour of Sir Francis Jacobs* (Oxford, Oxford University Press 2008) 337.

[7] For example, see the three lectures given in the United States in 1966 by a former President of the Court, whilst still on the Court, AM Donner, *The Role of the Lawyer in the European Communities* (Northwestern University Press 1968).

[8] Case C-26/62, *NV Algemene Transport- en Expeditie Onderneming van Gend en Loos v Netherlands Inland Revenue Administration*, ECLI:EU:C:1963:1.

[9] F Martines, 'Direct Effect of International Agreements of the European Union' (2014) 25 *European Journal of International Law* 129 at 130.

under the feet of nation states, the EU has been at the forefront of international developments, which have ultimately led to international agreements. Therefore, notwithstanding the internal ability of the EU to facilitate the development of economic integration through its own internal space,[10] it also had to progressively develop and amass an external arm.

Opinions of the Court on both the constitutional and intricate questions of international agreements and their position in the EU legal order rarely make the news headlines in the same way that popular or infamous cases do. Whether it be the issue of freedom of movement for football players previously,[11] or religious symbols in the workplace presently,[12] there are infrequent appearances of light-shining upon the Court, as it is usually tasked with much more mundane questions and issues. Most cases fail to capture the imagination of the EU's citizenry. The opportunities the Court is provided in an *ex ante* fashion on envisaged international agreements is but a tiny percentage of its caseload. And yet, it is monotonous *ex post* cases that keep the EU law show on the road, fleshing out the unclear primary and secondary law of the EU, with the occasional *ex ante* case through the Article 218(11) TFEU procedure thrown into the mix. That is not to say, however, that they have no meaning. In fact, it is cases of *external* nature, such as those entailing international agreements that touch upon the true essence of the ramifications of EU law.

The EU as an entity has extensive activities in areas of policy that have an external dimension. The various actors in such fields have an element of abidance to international agreements which the EU has concluded. Since the delivery of the Court's landmark *ERTA* doctrine,[13] there no longer exists the

---

[10] M Cremona, 'External Relations and External Competence of the European Union: The Emergence of an Integrated Policy' in P Craig and G De Búrca (eds), *The Evolution of EU Law* (Oxford, Oxford University Press 2011) 237.

[11] Case C-415/93, *Union royale belge des sociétés de football association ASBL v Jean-Marc Bosman, Royal club liégeois SA v Jean-Marc Bosman and others and Union des associations européennes de football (UEFA) v Jean-Marc Bosman*, ECLI:EU:C:1995:463. See M Derlén and J Lindholm, 'Bosman: A Legacy Beyond Sports' in A Duval and B Van Rompuy (eds), *The Legacy of Bosman: Revisiting the Relationship Between EU Law and Sport* (TMC Asser Press 2016).

[12] See Case C-157/15, *Samira Achbita and Centrum voor gelijkheid van kansen en voor racismebestrijding v G4S Secure Solutions NV*, ECLI:EU:C:2017:203, and, Case C-188/15, *Asma Bougnaoui and Association de défense des droits de l'homme (ADDH) v Micropole SA*, ECLI:EU:C:2017:204.

[13] Case C-22/70, *Commission v Council*, ECLI:EU:C:1971:32 ('*European Agreement on Road Transport*' or '*ERTA*'). See, *inter alia*, JT Lang, 'The ERTA Judgment and the Court's Case-Law on Competence and Conflict' (1986) 6 *Yearbook of European Law* 183; P Mengozzi, 'The EC External Competencies: From the ERTA Case to the Opinion in the Lugano Convention' in M Poiares Maduro and L Azoulai (eds), *The Past and Future of EU Law: The Classics of EU Law Revisited on the 50th Anniversary of the Rome Treaty* (Oxford, Hart Publishing 2010); P Eeckhout, 'Bold Constitutionalism and Beyond' in M Poiares Maduro and L Azoulai (eds), *The Past and Future of EU Law: The Classics of EU Law Revisited*

possibility for Member States to conclude international agreements if they come into conflict with commonly agreed rules of EU law. International agreements are entered into by the EU and its Member States to resolve issues that cannot be dealt with by other means. With the underlying rationale that an international agreement can provide the legal certainty required to achieve EU objectives that have been commonly agreed, they serve as one way of putting meat on the bones of a skeletal legal framework. Due to the fact that an international agreement exists, of which the EU is a guarantor, this implicitly decrees that the Court could potentially have a say, or at least, that is what can be construed. The general assumptions could be understood, in the pre-Lisbon area, at least at face-value, with the First Pillar seeing the Court having 'complete jurisdiction', the Second Pillar (Justice and Home Affairs (JHA)) having 'less extensive jurisdiction' for the Court, and finally in the Third Pillar (Common Foreign and Security Policy (CFSP)), the Court seeing *'no jurisdiction'*.[14] With this division of the areas of law internally within the law came the issue of determining complex questions about the necessary competence around international agreements when the external nature of policy fields was pursued.

Whereas Article 47 TEU now provides unequivocally that the EU has legal personality in the eyes of international law,[15] this was by no means certain before, despite general recognition that it did exist. Yet this legal personality pre-Lisbon only existed for the Community,[16] and furthermore, given its narrow basis, could not be considered a general legal basis for international agreements.[17] As the Court held in the *Kramer* judgment, the basis for legal personality for the purpose of external relations and international agreements is to only extend as far as, 'the whole field objectives

---

on the 50th Anniversary of the Rome Treaty (Oxford, Hart Publishing, 2010); C Hillion, 'ERTA, ECHR and Open Skies: Laying the Grounds of the EU System of External Relations' in M Poiares Maduro and L Azoulai (eds), *The Past and Future of EU Law: The Classics of EU Law Revisited on the 50th Anniversary of the Rome Treaty* (Oxford, Hart Publishing, 2010); R Post, 'Constructing the European Polity: ERTA and the Open Skies Judgments' in M Poiares Maduro and L Azoulai (eds), *The Past and Future of EU Law: The Classics of EU Law Revisited on the 50th Anniversary of the Rome Treaty* (Oxford, Hart Publishing 2010); J Klabbers, 'Case 22/70, Commission v Council (European Road Transport Agreement), Court of Justice of the EC [1971] ECR 263' in C Ryngaert *et al* (eds), *Judicial Decisions on the Law of International Organizations* (Oxford, Oxford University Press 2016).

[14] C Kaddous, 'Effects of International Agreements in the EU Legal Order' in M Cremona and B De Witte (eds), *EU Foreign Relations Law: Constitutional Fundamentals* (Oxford, Hart Publishing, 2008) 299.

[15] Article 47 TEU: 'The Union shall have legal personality.'

[16] Article 281 EC: 'The Community shall have legal personality.'

[17] G De Baere, 'The Basics of EU External Relations Law: An Overview of the Post-Lisbon Constitutional Framework for Developing the External Dimensions of EU Asylum and Migration Policy' in M Maes, MC Foblets and P De Bruycker (eds), *External Dimensions of European Migration and Asylum Law and Policy/Dimensions Externes du Droit et de la Politque d'Immigration et d'Asile de l'UE* (Bruylant 2011) 125.

defined …' in the treaties.[18] Thus, notwithstanding that there was at the time no explicit basis to enter into an international agreement, the basis to do so *may* have flown obliquely from provisions in the treaties.

The EU as a global actor is not alone, given that its time of expansion has been coupled with a proliferation of international courts, tribunals, and other global arbitral mechanisms for resolving disputes beyond the traditional nation state. Indeed, Europe has been where the *'foundations were laid'* for international courts,[19] and thus, has seen replication models for other regional entities. How the Court would interact *ex ante* with these other models of legal orders, before international agreements were entered into, was a test that was ultimately played out to suit the views of the EU legal order from the Court's perspective.

3. PRE-RATIFICATION JUDICIAL REVIEW

Therein lies a tension when international agreements are signed by the EU in that it poses a challenge for the autonomous nature of EU law. Defending this autonomy is a task which the Court has undertaken with a vengeful pedigree that can be demonstrated by looking at its approach from the *ex ante* vantage point—the pre-ratification judicial review of international agreements. Whereas the review of international agreements and their relationship with the legal order are deemed to be the normal practice in an *ex post* manner, the EU has a sophisticated model for judicial review on an international agreement to take place *ex ante*, during the pre-ratification stage. Within Article 218(11) TFEU in the context of the procedure surrounding an envisaged international agreement, it specifies that: 'A Member State, the European Parliament, the Council or the Commission may obtain the opinion of the Court of Justice as to whether an agreement envisaged is compatible with the Treaties. Where the opinion of the Court is adverse, the agreement envisaged may not enter into force unless it is amended or the Treaties are revised.' This judicial safety measure has been instrumental in ensuring that potential agreements, to which the EU could become a party, are compatible with its primary law. One of the EU Member States has within its own national judiciary a similar pre-ratification judicial review mechanism. The Constitutional Court of Hungary has the possibility to conduct *ex ante* reviews of international agreements

---

[18] Joined Cases C-3, C-4, and C-6/76, *Cornelius Kramer, Hendrik Van Den Berg, and Vennootschap Onder Firma (a partnership) Kramer En Bais*, ECLI:EU:C:1976:114, ('*Kramer*') paras 19–20.

[19] MR Madsen, 'Judicial Globalization: The Proliferation of International Courts' in S Cassese (ed), *Research Handbook on Global Administrative Law* (Cheltenham, Edward Elgar, 2016) 288.

regarding compatibility with its constitution,[20] and similarly, any international agreement by the Member State cannot be ratified until matters highlighted by the Constitutional Court are rectified.

Article 218(11) TFEU's entire *raison d'être* was to ensure an international agreement would not be concluded that would go against what is contained within the treaties. Furthermore, its purpose could even extend to ensuring that the internal EU procedure for an international agreement is done correctly.[21] In the course of issuing an Opinion, the Court has the possibility, *inter alia*, to determine if there is sufficient scope for the EU legal order to be undermined as a result of the EU entering into that international agreement. The procedure of asking the Court for an Opinion *ex ante* under Article 218(11) TFEU can also ensure that the correct legal basis is used from within the treaties. Another possible use of Article 218(11) TFEU is the potential for a listed entity within the article to extend a narrow institutional interest, to determine whether an individual institution of the EU can enter into an international agreement.[22] Equivalent to a constitutional check, the pre-ratification stage of an envisaged international agreement cannot proceed if the Court finds that it is not compliant with the treaties. Article 218(11) TFEU is an optional tool available to a limited number of parties, and there is no obligation to put questions on the compatibility of an international agreement to the Court for its binding opinion, *even* when there is doubt amongst the parties. Despite the non-obligation to refer an envisaged international agreement to the Court, it is nonetheless an extremely powerful tool when it is deployed, given its historical usage. Originally implanted as Article 228 of the Treaty of Rome in 1957,[23] it has been retained in substantive form, taking into account minor changes along the way,[24] from Rome to Lisbon.[25] The modern Article 218(11) TFEU

---

[20] D Shelton, 'Introduction' in D Shelton (ed), *International Law and Domestic Legal Systems: Incorporation, Transformation, and Persuasion* (Oxford, Oxford University Press, 2011) 8.

[21] Opinion 1/75 of the Court (*Understanding on a Local Cost Standard*) in *Opinion 1/75*, ECLI:EU:C:1975:145, p. 1361.

[22] Article 196(2): '*Written part of the procedure*'. 'L 265/1. Rules of Procedure of the Court of Justice'; 'L 173/65. Amendment to the Rules of Procedure of the Court of Justice'; 'L 217/69. Amendment of the Rules of Procedure of the Court of Justice'.

[23] Article 228(1): 'Where this Treaty provides for the conclusion of agreements between the Community and one or more States or an international organisation, such agreements shall be negotiated by the Commission. Subject to the powers vested in the Commission in this field, such agreements shall be concluded by the Council, after consulting the Assembly [European Parliament] where required by this Treaty. The Council, the Commission or a Member State may obtain beforehand the opinion of the Court of Justice as to whether an agreement envisaged is compatible with the provisions of this Treaty. Where the opinion of the Court of Justice is adverse, the agreement may enter into force only in accordance with Article 236.'

[24] The Parliament was originally not included in this list of institutions with the possibility of making a referral, but later attained it through litigation.

[25] Article 228(6) EC post-Maastricht, Article 300(6) EC post-Amsterdam, and Article 218(11) TFEU post-Lisbon.

is a rarely used mechanism for envisaged international agreements prior to their formal conclusion, but when the Opinion of the Court is sought in individual scenarios, its impact and importance is put on full display. How the Article 218(11) TFEU procedure manifested itself is in line with the overall constitutional structure of the EU is particularly intriguing as, despite the provision existing since 1957, it was not deployed until 1975 in Opinion 1/75.[26]

The lack of legal guidance for the Court for handling international agreements before it, either *ex ante* or *ex post*, has meant it has been an indigenous endeavour to embark upon for its Article 218(11) TFEU procedure. The guidance provided to the Court on the interpretation of how it fulfills its obligations, and furthermore, the international agreements into which the EU enters into, are few and far between. Article 19(1) TEU's light-touching nature notes that the Court, '... shall ensure that in the interpretation and application of the treaties the law is observed', providing a large margin of discretion for the Court to adopt sufficiently robust interpretations that are fitting with the types of cases before it, and affording it sufficient breadth to determine outcomes compatible with the EU's legal order. This legal imprecision stemming from the EU's primary law, deliberate or otherwise, can be traced right back to the original Communities, in which the Court, '... shall ensure the observance of law and justice in the interpretation and application of this Treaty', found in the Coal and Steel Community Treaty, the European Economic Community Treaty, and the Atomic Energy Community Treaty.[27]

4. *EX ANTE* OPINIONS IN ACTION: THE USE OF ARTICLE 218(11) TFEU

The *ex ante* procedure in and of itself is different from the normal cases expected to be before the Court. It deals with a question of law, which, before an international agreement is entered into, is answering a question that nearly amounts to a hypothetical one. However, the seriousness of the manner in which the Court can pre-emptively strike can defuse a dispute at a later juncture. Testing the approach of the Court and how it perceives the autonomy of the EU legal order, Article 218(11) TFEU presents it with encounters when determination must be made when the EU legal order intersects with other legal orders. Not all Opinions have been about the autonomy of the EU's legal order, yet they are tied to it in a heedful manner. Whilst it is assumed that the EU legal order 'interlocks' with that of its Member States,[28]

---

[26] Opinion 1/75 of the Court (Understanding on a Local Cost Standard) in Opinion 1/75, ECLI:EU:C:1975:145.

[27] Article 31, Article 164, and Article 136 respectively. As pointed to in Donner above n 7 at 22.

[28] See K Lenaerts, 'Interlocking Legal Orders in the European Union and Comparative Law' (2003) 52 *International and Comparative Law Quarterly* 873.

the approach by the Court to legal orders beyond the EU is a much more nuanced discussion it is having with itself. Over time, there has been a shift in the way the Court uses this Article 218(11) TFEU opportunity. As a result, it is possible to see tests being set for how far the competence of the EU can stretch. However, as time goes on, and the years roll by, an adapted measure for how the Court handles potential international agreements adjusts to becoming a test of compatibility with the EU legal order. In Opinion 1/75,[29] the case involved a draft understanding, drawn up under the auspices of the Organisation for Economic Co-operation and Development (OECD). This led to a question about how far the word 'agreement' could be stretched in accordance with its reference to the then Article 228(1). Giving a broad expansive view on what constituted an agreement within the context in which it can provide an Opinion on an agreement pre-ratification, the Court said it may 'indicate any undertaking entered into by entities subject to international law which has binding force, whatever its formal designation'.[30]

More substantively, the Opinion of the Court was sought by the Commission to determine the extent of the powers of Community competence. The question was two-fold: was the Community competent, and if so, did it have the exclusive competence to conclude the draft understanding? The reason for the case being brought to the Court in the first place was to settle a rumbling inter-institutional confrontation over the precise scope of the EU's Common Commercial Policy (CCP). Opinion 1/75 by no means settled the issue over the divergence of the Commission and Council positions regarding the scope of the CCP. When Opinion 1/78 was referred to the Court shortly thereafter on the draft international agreement surrounding Natural Rubber,[31] under the auspices of the United Nations Conference on Trade and Development (UNCTAD), the Court said that depending on the financing of the operations, it would determine whether the EU had the exclusive competence to deal with the issue, with full EU financing meaning exclusive competence, and financing by Member States to therefore mean shared competence. This is an important distinction, as the Court pushed the issue down the road of its own autonomy against other legal orders. The difference between Opinion 1/75 and Opinion 1/78 can be noted,[32] with the former not looking to whom is providing financial contributions, whilst affirming it is principal to the matter in the latter. However, these initial Opinions of the Court were just a stepping stone towards the continuous

---

[29] Opinion 1/75 of the Court (Understanding on a Local Cost Standard) in Opinion 1/75, ECLI:EU:C:1975:145.

[30] Opinion 1/75 of the Court (Understanding on a Local Cost Standard) in Opinion 1/75, ECLI:EU:C:1975:145, p. 1360.

[31] Opinion 1/78 of the Court (Natural Rubber), Opinion 1/78, ECLI:EU:C:1979:224.

[32] See, JHH Weiler, 'The External Legal Relations of Non-Unitary Actors: Mixity and the Federal Principle' in D O'Keeffe and HG Schermers (eds), *Mixed Agreements* (Kluwer Law and Taxation Publishers 1983).

build-up of law to facilitate the continued progress towards the objectives set out in the treaties to be achieved, *inter alia*, through the attainment of international agreements with relevant third parties.

It was not until some time later, but the case of Opinion 1/94 eventually reached the Court, this time on the WTO.[33] With Opinion 1/78 being the 'starting point' for Opinion 1/94,[34] therein came a bubbling case for the Court to handle. With the World Trade Organisation (WTO) seeking to strengthen the global trading system systematically through institutionalism, the liberalising effects of it on world trade, and the impact of it on the EU given its own competence, would be deeply felt. In Opinion 1/94, the Court found that the EU's CCP was a broad instrument, in line with previous Opinions, but nonetheless, that both the then Community and its Member States were competent to conclude the General Agreement on Trade in Services ('GATS') and the Agreement on Trade-Related Aspects of Intellectual Property Rights ('TRIPS').[35] There had been long disagreement between the Commission and the Council on the extent to which certain matters, namely services, came within the ambit of CCP. Thus, when it came to concluding the international agreement externally, the scope of CCP had to be settled internally between the institutions, and rather than negotiations and an agreed mutual settlement, the dispute was put through the Article 218(11) TFEU procedure.

With the establishment of the WTO came an enhanced legal order of its own. Given the previous expansive scope given to the CCP in Opinion 1/78 when there was no competing international legal framework for economic integration, Opinion 1/94 clearly demonstrates some hesitancy in providing the EU's CCP with such an expansive basis, so that the EU could conclude the international agreement alone. This Opinion was heavily criticised, including most notably by a former member of the Court, who accused his successors of focusing on 'fringe aspects of the vast field of trade' and having an 'inward-looking vision'.[36] The contents of Opinion 1/94 later found its way into the treaties at the next possible stage, the Treaty of Amsterdam, as Article 133(5) EC, and now post-Lisbon as Article 3(2) TFEU: '[t]he EU shall also have exclusive competence for the conclusion of an international agreement when its conclusion is provided for in a legislative act of the EU or is necessary to enable the EU to exercise its internal competence, or in so far as its conclusion may affect common rules or alter their scope.'

---

[33] Opinion 1/94 of the Court (WTO), Opinion 1/94.

[34] HW Micklitz and S Weatherill, *European Economic Law* (Ashgate Publishing 1997) 385.

[35] Opinion 1/94 of the Court, Competence of the Community to conclude international agreements concerning services and the protection of intellectual property, ECLI:EU:C:1994:384.

[36] P Pescatore, 'Opinion 1/94 on "Conclusion" of the WTO Agreement: Is There an Escape From a Programmed Disaster?' (1999) 36 *Common Market Law Review* 387 at 391.

Elsewhere in its *ex ante* Opinions, the Court has shown a willingness to be open to other international judicial mechanisms, but with some level of hesitation. Opinion 1/91 of the Court said that another judicial arbiter arriving on the international scene reaching across the aspects of EU law must be compliant with EU law.[37] Thus, the judicial mechanism proposed in the initial EEA Agreement, to extend the progressively developing internal market, by slightly derogating from the Court's principle position in the treaties as an institution, was a step too far. In the Court's view, it would have run contrary to the need for an institution to ultimately be an authoritative voice on EU law, and it was keen to point to the fact that despite the EU itself being premised upon the basis of an international agreement, it was more than that, as the treaties were the 'constitutional charter' of the EU.[38] The proposed system of an EEA Court, mixed with the Court itself, would in its view, undermine the autonomous nature of EU law. With that fear in the mind of the Court, it could have been asked, would any judicial mechanism to cater for non-Member States wanting to be close to the internal market be palpable to the Court? Accordingly, with some inventive thinking, the other parties invented a proposal for a new model, an EFTA Court, under a separate agreement between the EFTA States. Would this imaginative model be subject to similar objections of the Court? With the negotiating parties not taking any chances, a new Opinion was requested on the newly envisaged international agreement.

Opinion 1/92 of the Court said, *inter alia*, that with international agreements that the EU accedes inherently affecting the way in which the EU operates, it cannot alter what the Court must do by its very nature in accordance with the treaties.[39] Yet, it said the new agreement was permissible, 'as long as the principle that decisions taken by the Joint Committee are not to affect the case-law of the Court of Justice is laid down in a form binding on the Contracting Parties'. A traceable reading of the Court on international agreements that potentially undermine EU law is thus emergent. The use of EU law elsewhere for achieving the expansive aims of the treaties is permissible, but the exclusive use of EU law without recourse to an interpretation of EU law by the Court itself would be contrary to the EU legal order.

Questions about institutional competency and the autonomous legal order can also be seen more strongly. An ILO Convention and the EU's envisaged accession brought with it competency questions, and the nature of the EU's

---

[37] Opinion 1/91 of the Court (EEA Agreement I) in Opinion 1/91, ECLI:EU:C:1991:490, para 40.

[38] Opinion 1/91 of the Court (EEA Agreement I) in Opinion 1/91, ECLI:EU:C:1991:490, para 21.

[39] Opinion 1/92 of the Court (EEA Agreement II) in Opinion 1/92, ECLI:EU:C:1992:189, para 32.

autonomous legal order. The Convention was concerned with the safety
of individuals in employment, to protect them from hazardous chemicals.
Given the EU was not a member of the ILO, but rather a mere observer,
this posed questions as to how matters at the ILO were to be handled by
Member States when such competencies were within the ambit of EU law. The
ILO Convention fell into what is today Article 153 TFEU on social policy. In
Opinion 2/91,[40] it was acknowledged that the EU may not necessarily become
a member of international organisations in its own right, given the constraints
of membership imposed by the primary law of other international organisations. However, the Court, in assuring that the EU's own legal order was not
undermined by such external constraints, came up with a way around it.
Within the context of conventions moulded in the incubator of another
international organisation, the Court has said that in such situations where
the EU cannot be held to a resolution because it is not the competent authority, it was incumbent on the Member States of the EU to act 'jointly in the
[EU's] interest'.[41] This position, depending on the international organisation
in question, may have to be authorised by the EU, acting through a Decision
in the Council, should competence on the matter fall exclusively within
the EU's competence.[42] The Opinion is said to be in 'textbook fashion',[43]
laying down a set of principles to guide the executive and legislature in
future scenarios with similar situations arising.

  One the more touching and far-reaching uses of international agreements
by the Court in its case law has been the European Convention on Human
Rights (ECHR). Whilst the EU is not a party to this itself, its Member
States are, and contained within the EU's own treaties is an obligation for
the EU to accede,[44] once it is possible. The very existence of Article 6(2)
TEU, imposing an obligation on the EU to accede comes from the basis
that it formally attempted to accede once before, but was rejected on the
grounds that there was no legal basis within EU law to do so, according to
Opinion 2/94.[45] Whilst this is the reason why the ECHR is not yet an integral

---

[40] Opinion 2/91 of the Court (ILO Safety in the use of chemicals at work), Opinion 2/91,
ECLI:EU:C:1993:106.
[41] Opinion 2/91 of the Court (ILO Safety in the use of chemicals at work), *Opinion 2/91*,
ECLI:EU:C:1993:106, para 5. This was re-enforced at para 37: '... cooperation between the
Community and the Member States is all the more necessary in view of the fact that the former
cannot, as international law stands at present, itself conclude an ILO convention and must do
so through the medium of the Member States'.
[42] A Rosas, 'The Status in EU Law of International Agreements Concluded by EU Member
States' (2011) 34 *Fordham International Law Journal* 1304 at 1331.
[43] A Dashwood and J Heliskoski, 'The Classic Authorities Revisited' in A Dashwood and
C Hillion (eds), *The General Law of EC External Relations* (London, Sweet and Maxwell,
2000) 15.
[44] Article 6(2) TEU: 'The Union shall accede to the European Convention for the Protection
of Human Rights and Fundamental Freedoms ...'.
[45] Opinion 2/94 of the Court (Accession by the Community to the ECHR), Opinion 2/94,
ECLI:EU:C:1996:140.

formative part of the EU legal order, it has served as a means for guiding the Court on the interpretation of fundamental rights for many years, given the late arrival of the EU's Charter of Fundamental Rights (CFR).

Opinions of the Court through Article 218(11) TFEU, in an *ex ante* manner, are the pre-ratification method of challenging an envisaged international agreement to be concluded by the EU, but it is by no means the only manner in which it is judicially challengeable before the Court. An action for annulment is also possible *ex ante*, whilst an international agreement is being framed, such as was the situation in *MOU on EEC-US Government Procurement*,[46] and *Framework Agreement on Bananas*.[47] The latter followed the Opinion 3/94,[48] lodged by Germany to which the Court responded by declining to provide an Opinion given that the international agreement had already entered into force.[49] The pre-ratification issues that the Court faces demonstrates that the Court's approach to the issue of internal EU legal tools and their appropriate ramifications, inherently affect the external dimensions for the EU's potential actions. Not all the pre-ratification Opinions of the Court have delved into the issue of autonomy, as many have dealt with the extent of the competence of the institutions to conclude an international agreement, and to what extent the scope of EU competence is, including examination of whether an international agreement can be concluded exclusively, or on a mixed basis. Therefore, despite the Opinions mainly focusing on competence, the Court has found that where the competence for the conclusion of an international agreement is shared between the EU and its Member States, mixed agreements are to be the chosen manner of entering into that arrangement. Even in light of the post-Lisbon framework, which has significantly adapted to the modern manner in which the EU conducts its external relations, mixed agreements have been declared as 'here to stay',[50] despite the expansion of the EU's exclusive competency areas.

---

[46] Case C-360/93, *European Parliament v Council of the European Union*, ('*MOU on EEC-US Government Procurement*') ECLI:EU:C:1996:84. This concerned 'L 125/1. Council Decision of 10 May 1993 Concerning the Conclusion of an Agreement in the Form of a Memorandum of Understanding between the European Economic Community and the United States of America on Government Procurement (93/323/EEC)', and 'L 125/54. Council Decision of 10 May 1993 Concerning the Extension of the Benefit of the Provisions of Directive 90/531/EEC in Respect of the United States of America (93/324/EEC)'. See, M Cremona, 'Case C-360/93, European Parliament v. Council of the European Union, Judgment of 7 March 1996, [1996] ECR I-1195' (1997) 34 *Common Market Law Review* 389.

[47] Case C-122/95, *Federal Republic of Germany v Council of the European Union*, ('*Framework Agreement on Bananas*'), ECLI:EU:C:1998:94.

[48] Opinion 3/94 of the Court (Opinion on Framework Agreement on Bananas) in Opinion 3/94, ECLI:EU:C:1995:436.

[49] S Peers, 'Constitutional Principles and International Trade' (1999) 24 *European Law Review* 185 at 187.

[50] A Rosas, 'The Future of Mixity' in Christophe Hillion and Panos Koutrakos (eds), *Mixed Agreements Revisited: The EU and its Member States in the World* (Oxford, Hart Publishing, 2010) 367.

5. THE FAR SIDE OF AGREEMENTS: *EX POST*

The differences between the *ex ante* and *ex post* reviews greatly matter from the perspective of both EU law and international law. This is due to *ex ante* arrangements merely being an international agreement that has not yet been concluded, and thus, is a legal conundrum (to be had) within the EU legal order, without the formal involvement of third parties at that particular juncture. Once international agreements are concluded by the EU, they can be examined *ex post*, and can be determined to be incompatible with the treaties in the eyes of the Court, for which there can be adverse consequences. Such magnitudes are obviously detrimental to the EU's standing as a global actor, but also have ramifications for third-party entities with whom an agreement was concluded.

The Court has acknowledged that ultimately when it takes an issue with an international agreement on an *ex post* basis, the problem is compounded, in that 'international agreements cannot be amended unilaterally, without new negotiations being undertaken by the contracting parties'.[51] Even when internal acts are annulled, the *pacta sunt servanda* principle applies internationally, and within the EU legal order, the Court furthermore has the possibility to maintain the effects of the international agreement.[52] Many instances of this occurring leave the Court, when annulling the internal EU decisions, with little option other than to maintain the external effects of such international agreements.[53] Article 216(2) TFEU states, 'Agreements concluded by the Union are binding upon the institutions of the Union and on its Member States.'[54] Arising from this, it is mandatory for both the EU and its Member States to oblige with this obligation by fulfilling its side of commitments flowing for an international agreement. The Court has stated this in its case law, such as in *Kupferberg*, when it said, 'it is incumbent upon the ... institutions, as well as upon the Member States, to ensure compliance with the obligations arising from [international] agreements'.[55]

Given what could be perceived as a lack of flexibility from the EU's judiciary in ensuring that international agreements do not hinder the EU's ability

---

[51] Case C-211/01, *Commission v Council*, ECLI:EU:C:2003:452 ('*Carriage of goods by road and combined transport*'), para 55.

[52] Article 264 TFEU: '... the Court shall, if it considers this necessary, state which of the effects of the act which it has declared void shall be considered as definitive'.

[53] For more on these maintenance of effects instances, see, S Miettinen, 'Annulment in Action: How Does the Court of Justice of the European Union Explain Maintaining the Legal Effects of Annulled Instruments?' in J Petman (ed), *Finnish Yearbook of International Law 2012–2013: Volume 23* (Oxford, Hart Publishing 2016).

[54] Article 228(7) EC post-Maastricht, Article 300(7) EC post-Amsterdam, and Article 216(2) TFEU post-Lisbon.

[55] Case C-104/84, *Hauptzollamt Mainz v C.A. Kupferberg & Cie KG a.A.*, ECLI:EU:C:1982:362, para 11.

through the Article 218(11) TFEU *ex ante* procedure, other palpable options may in turn be explored, with an attempt to avoid the Court during the *ex ante* phase, and instead, for international agreements to be challenged later, *ex post*. Despite the role the Court holds in rectifying these issues when it is called upon to adjudicate matters of competence, there are also instances when the services of the Court have been deliberately avoided. However, despite this avoidance of the EU legal order, it has not meant the absence of the EU's judicial order. The *In 't Veld* cases,[56] amongst others, where individuals have sought access to documents for envisaged international agreements, with the institutions providing the documents in question to the Court, without disclosing them to the other parties to the proceedings. Moreover, in instances of international agreements associated with CFSP, it might not be possible for actors beyond the Council to know of the existence of an international agreement until it has been published in the *Official Journal*, and thereby, already concluded. In such instances, the possibility of asking the Court for an *ex ante* review through the Article 218(11) TFEU procedure of an international agreement concluded by the Council on a CFSP legal basis may not be possible. Thus, *ex post* scenarios may be the only option, for example, in the *Mauritius* and *Tanzania* cases brought by the Parliament, which successfully argued that its institutional right to be 'fully informed' under Article 218(10) TFEU were not respected.[57] However, given the 'specific rules and procedures' of CFSP,[58] it has been debated how Article 218(11) TFEU could be utilised in the context of that particular area of EU law.[59]

The existence of a 'disconnection clause',[60] where EU law applies between Member States, as opposed to putting obligations flowing from other

---

[56] Case T-529/09, *Sophie in't Veld v Council*, ECLI:EU:T:2012:215, and on appeal, Case C-350/12 P, *Council v Sophie in't Veld*, ECLI:EU:C:2014:2039. See, Deirdre Curtin, 'Official Secrets and the Negotiation of International Agreements: Is the EU Executive Unbound?' (2013) 50 *Common Market Law Review* 423 at 450.

[57] Case C-658/11, *Parliament v Council*, ECLI:EU:C:2014:2025 (*Mauritius*), and Case C-263/14, *Parliament v Council*, ECLI:EU:C:2016:435 (*Tanzania*). See, Graham Butler, 'Pinpointing the Appropriate Legal Basis for External Action' (2015) 6 *European Journal of Risk Regulation* 323; G Butler, 'Attacking or Defending? Jurisdiction of the Court of Justice in the EU's Common Foreign and Security Policy' (2016) 19 *Europarättslig Tidskrift* 671; R Passos, 'The External Powers of the European Parliament' in P Eeckhout and M López-Escudero (eds), *The European Union's External Action in Times of Crisis* (Oxford, Hart Publishing 2016).

[58] Article 24(1) TEU.

[59] C Hillion, 'A Powerless Court? The European Court of Justice and the Common Foreign and Security Policy' in Marise Cremona and Anne Thies (eds), *The European Court of Justice and External Relations Law: Constitutional Challenges* (Oxford, Hart Publishing, 2014) 56. G De Baere, *Constitutional Principles of EU External Relations* (Oxford, Oxford University Press, 2008) 190.

[60] See, M Cremona, 'Disconnection Clauses in EU Law and Practice' in C Hillion and P Koutrakos (eds), *Mixed Agreements Revisited: The EU and its Member States in the World* (Oxford, Hart Publishing, 2010).

international agreements first, may exist. In another form., that is to say that through this clause, international agreements do not encroach upon intra-Union matters. Such clauses are capable of being put in a number of different international agreements, ranging from EU-only agreements, mixed, and Member State-only scenarios. The effects may have become a way to prevent another *MOX Plant* saga.[61] Given the centrality of the Court protecting the EU legal order stemming from the treaties, it has even found itself ensuring that judicial proceedings outside its own remit involving two Member States must be cognisant of EU law and its interpretation. In *MOX Plant*, the Commission brought Ireland to the International Tribunal for the Law of the Sea (ITLOS) under the remit of the United Nations Convention on the Law of the Sea (UNCLOS) saying that, '[i]t is for the Court, should the need arise, to identify the elements of the dispute which relate to provisions of the international agreement in question which fall outside its jurisdiction.'[62] Thus, by proclaiming that it first had jurisdictional claim on issues relating to Member States, it prevented any other international courts from involving themselves with the interpretation of EU law.

6. ISSUES *IN POSTERUM*

It was the early days of the Court in the 1960s and 1970s that created the principles of EU law as it is known, with its various principles, landmark judgments, and doctrines which are accepted now, as they were then. Smidgeons of the Court seeing the EU legal order as being autonomous were traceable even back then,[63] in contrast to the international legal system which it may have been compared against, in addition to that of the legal systems of its Member States. The use of international agreements can be seen to elucidate the flappable but admirable values contained in the EU treaties. The assimilation of these international agreements can substantiate the provisions, which have not themselves been expounded upon by other EU legal instruments. Whilst the Court has had to determine the extent of EU competence, it latterly reoriented the instrument for ensuring international agreements where compatible with the legal order. This is demonstrative of how institutions of the EU are willing to adopt different and dynamic interpretations of EU primary law in order to extend, as far as possible, their own institution ends. To venture on this path, the key interlocutor has been the Court, which institutions and respective parties with legal standing

---

[61] Case C-459/03, *Commission v Ireland*, ECLI:EU:C:2006:345 ('*MOX Plant*').
[62] Case C-459/03, *Commission v Ireland*, ECLI:EU:C:2006:345 ('*MOX Plant*'), para 135.
[63] N Jääskinen, 'Constitutions in the European Union—Some Questions of Conflict and Convergence' (2011) 12 ERA Forum 205 at 211.

under Article 218(11) TFEU are respectively willing to ask for an Opinion to resolve competency disputes. The Court through its interpretation of international agreements, both pre- and post-ratification, has demonstrated the need to preserve the need for containing the EU's legal order within a controllable framework, in which it sits at the top.

It has been argued that if there had not been the existence of Article 218(11) TFEU in its current form, and its prior incarnations, that there might not have been as many external competence cases testing the limits of the treaties.[64] The deficiencies in the breadth of the EU's jurisdictional boundaries have been known for some time. The *ex ante* procedure does have blind spots, with no *locus standi* under this scheme for individuals who are ultimately impacted by EU law and its international agreement-making abilities. Furthermore, internally, the Member States and their own national courts do not have the possibility to ask the Court *ex ante* whether their own international agreements in their own areas of competence are in compliance with the EU's legal order. According to international law, once the EU becomes a party to an international agreement, it is part-and-parcel of its legal order. When an international agreement comes into force, the pre-ratification process has passed. Nonetheless, the possibility for challenges to occur post-ratification exists, but through a post-ratification, *ex post* process. Just like the *ex ante* Article 218(11) TFEU procedure, international agreements are justiciable by the Court, when relevant, to determine their compatibility with the treaties.

The Court's own doctrines for exercising judicial review over international agreements concluded with third-parties can, post-ratification, be treated by the Court as being equivalent to national legislation,[65] and thus, come within the scope of EU law, and must be in compliance with the lack of intention to undermine the EU legal order. Yet, this poses an issue in that the Court, 'in principle, [has] jurisdiction to interpret, in preliminary ruling proceedings, international agreements concluded between Member States and non-member countries'.[66] This determination for the first time by the Court, said that it could review the compatibility of an international agreement with the EU legal order, after the international agreement had

---

[64] P Eeckhout, *EU External Relations Law* 2nd edn, (Oxford, Oxford University Press, 2011) 14.

[65] R Schütze, 'EC Law and International Agreements of the Member States—An Ambivalent Relationship?' in C Barnard (ed), *Cambridge Yearbook of European Legal Studies 2006–2007: Volume 9* (Oxford, Hart Publishing, 2007) 432.

[66] Case C-533/08, *TNT Express Nederland BV v AXA Versicherung AG*, ECLI:EU:C:2010:243, para 61. This stems from, 'The Court has no jurisdiction under Article 177 of the EEC Treaty to give a ruling on the interpretation of provisions of international law which bind Member States outside the framework of Community law' in Case C-130/73, *Magdalena Vandeweghe and others v Berufsgenossenschaft für die chemische Industrie*, ECLI:EU:C:1973:131, para 2.

been concluded.[67] In practice, it is much more impenetrable to determine the legality of an international agreement once it has entered into force, and furthermore, the effects of an international agreement that the EU has entered into cannot be completely undone.

One of the prevailing matters in EU external actions in practice, as a whole, is to ultimately determine who the decision-maker is. The scope of international agreements and their potential reach, leading to the undermining of the EU's legal order may only interest the most conspicuous of lawyers, either in academic circles, the Legal Services of the respective EU institutions, or the Court itself. Yet, its significance extends far beyond this. Whereas the determination of the decision maker(s) can ultimately lead to internal EU legal basis contestation, given the lack of clarity of the law, or the potential taking advantage of an institutional position being challenged by another in *ex post* scenarios, it ultimately leads to the coherence of the EU being undermined. Accordingly, in *ex ante* situations, making use of Article 218(11) TFEU is a useful model for improving the nature of EU law and all that the EU has to offer in the world through international agreements. The Article 218(11) TFEU mechanism therefore, allows institutions to determine the compatibility of the agreement with the treaties *ex ante*, but it also has the possibility to ascertain the internal decision-maker, by probing questions about the legal basis of the external acts.

Article 218(11) TFEU and the procedure for the Court to provide a binding Opinion is only applicable to envisaged international agreements to which the EU wishes to accede in some form *externally*. However, the ability of the Court to provide a similar *ex ante* Opinion was once pondered for legal acts *internally* within the EU. In the run-up to the Treaty of Maastricht, consideration was put forward for it to be extended to internal review of legal acts on subsidiarity grounds,[68] although the proposal never had any real chance of progressing into a real substantive application.

It must be stated that the existence and use of Article 218(11) TFEU by any of the parties that may avail of it is by no means an ultimate remedy for alleviating and securing the EU's legal order. The number of legal actors who may avail of it remains restricted, and furthermore, the Court does not possess a crystal ball, despite its perceived wisdom. Even when an Article 218(11) TFEU procedure is used, and an answer is given in the affirmative that the EU either alone or with its Member States may conclude an international agreement, issues about its compatibility with the legal order can

---

[67] Case C-327/91, *French Republic v Commission of the European Communities*, ECLI:EU:C:1994:305.

[68] JP Jacqué and JHH Weiler, 'On the Road to European Union—A New Judicial Architecture: An Agenda for the Intergovernmental Conference' (1990) 27 *Common Market Law Review* 185 at 205.

later arise. This, *a posteriori* situation may involve an issue that was not raised during the course of the Article 218(11) TFEU procedure being utilised.[69] The establishment of the forthcoming Unified Patent Court (UPC) will be closely watched by the Court.[70] This new international court, whenever it is formed, will ultimately be to the detriment of the institution of the Court, given the General Court which has dealt with direct actions on intellectual property matters, will be freed largely of this responsibility, thus moving the interpretation of EU law outside of the Court's own judicial architecture. With the Court's own Opinion 1/09,[71] and no qualifying institution availing of the Article 218(11) TFEU procedure for the revised formulation of the forthcoming patent regime, the Court has to ask itself whether it has answered the right questions the first time around, or if it has deliberately avoided them *ex ante* the second time an attempt is made.

Notwithstanding the fact that the Court underlined the essential relationship it has with the national courts, the Court in Opinion 1/09 hinged upon the maintenance of a functioning EU judicial order. In part, the institution of the Court could itself be to blame for certain Member States willing to go ahead with enhanced cooperation, due to a lack of willingness to create specialised chambers within the General Court, and instead, proceeding with generalisation, and doubling the size of the General Court to handle its caseload.[72] With the Court's own ability to initiate reform of its own governing document, the Statute of the Court,[73] blame cannot be solely attributed elsewhere. Positives and negatives can arise from a non-referral to the Court of an EU institutional issue. To take the former, it can be said that the treaties are potentially no longer as ambiguous as they once were. Furthermore, EU institutions could be demonstrating signs of ageing maturity. However, failure to rectify external representation problems authoritatively can lead to future issues arising down the line, potentially undermining the EU legal order.

---

[69] T Tridimas and P Eeckhout, 'The External Competence of the Community and the Case-Law of the Court of Justice: Principle versus Pragmatism' (1994) 14 *Yearbook of European Law* 143 at 146.

[70] 'C 175/1. Agreement on a Unified Patent Court (2013/C 175/01)'.

[71] Opinion 1/09 of the Court (European and Community Patents Court), Opinion 1/09, ECLI:EU:C:2011:123. See, R Baratta, 'National Courts as "Guardians" and "Ordinary Courts" of EU Law: Opinion 1/09 of the ECJ' (2011) 38 *Legal Issues of Economic Integration* 297.

[72] For a critical viewpoint on these General Court reforms, see, A Alemanno and L Pech, 'Thinking Justice Outside the Docket: A Critical Assessment of the Reform of the EU's Court System' (2017) 54 *Common Market Law Review* 129.

[73] Article 281 TFEU: 'The Statute of the Court of Justice of the European Union shall be laid down in a separate Protocol. The European Parliament and the Council, acting in accordance with the ordinary legislative procedure, may amend the provisions of the Statute, with the exception of Title I and Article 64. The European Parliament and the Council shall act either at the request of the Court of Justice and after consultation of the Commission, or on a proposal from the Commission and after consultation of the Court of Justice.'

A further way of avoiding the Court altogether has been to adopt international agreements outside of the EU's legal order altogether. This form of differentiated integration has the ability to skew the effects of what the EU legal order is about in the first place. By proceeding with European integration outside the EU's legal framework creates problems for institutional balance, and the legitimacy of the EU from a democratic perspective.[74] The use of non-EU treaties by Member States to cater for new realms of law in Europe, to be later merged into the EU legal order, poses a significant threat, as the Court is no longer given its place as an *ex ante* judicial reviewer of envisaged international agreements if they are being conducted by Member States as actors in international law, as opposed to institutions negotiating an envisaged agreement. Thus, modern cases such as *Pringle*,[75] demonstrate attempts to legally question a non-EU international agreement, the Treaty establishing the European Stability Mechanism (ESM), yet in such a scenario, no *ex ante* procedure is available. Thus, an individual litigant like Mr Pringle was left with no choice but to challenge it in an *ex post* scenario, indirectly, through an Article 267 TFEU preliminary reference from a national court. The acceptance of non-EU treaties by the Court can be likened to, 'an act of judicial politics',[76] but yet non-EU treaties between Member States have long been permissible, as long as their purpose did not infringe upon EU matters. The Schengen Agreement, initially outside the EU framework before later being incorporated into EU law, meant that progress on European integration could occur, whilst later envisaging its ultimate compatibility with EU law by making it EU law itself. To have allowed the Schengen Agreement and all that it later entailed to fester outside the EU, in a sort of parallel system, would inevitably have brought it into conflict with the EU legal order, and its autonomy. With *Pringle*, the Court found that the ESM Treaty was compatible with the treaties, and similarly, that there continued to be effective judicial protection—a notion which the Court has long prided itself on. However, by stating this, the Court has recognised, and even confirmed that the two concepts of judicial review in the EU legal order; *ex ante* and *ex post*, can be reduced to just the latter to meet the overall principles of the treaties.

Questions on how exclusive the EU's competence is continues to be questioned through the use of Article 218(11) TFEU. Most recently, in

---

[74] A Łazowski and S Blockmans, 'Constitutional Foundations and EU Institutional Framework: Seven Years of Working with Lisbon Reform' in A Łazowski and S Blockmans (eds), *Research Handbook on EU Institutional Law* (Cheltenham, Edward Elgar, 2016) 45.

[75] Case C-370/12, *Thomas Pringle v Government of Ireland and Others*, ECLI:EU:C:2012:756.

[76] M Everson and C Joerges, 'Between Constitutional Command and Technocratic Rule: Post Crisis Governance and the Treaty on Stability, Coordination and Governance ("The Fiscal Compact")' in C Harlow, P Leino and G Della Cananea (eds), *Research Handbook on EU Administrative Law* (Cheltenham, Edward Elgar, 2017) 167.

Opinion 3/15,[77] the Court found that the EU had exclusive competence to conclude the Marrakesh Treaty to Facilitate Access to Published Works for Persons Who Are Blind, Visually Impaired or Otherwise Print Disabled. Pending are a number of important Opinions, which will clarify the scope of certain EU competences, and the respect that international agreements must have for the EU legal order, and its procedures. In Opinion 1/15,[78] the Parliament queried the legal bases used for a draft international agreement between the EU and Canada on data transfer of passenger names records. Furthermore, in Opinion 2/15 on the competences for who is to conclude the EU-Singapore Free Trade Agreement,[79] Advocate-General Sharpston in Opinion 2/15 issued an extensive Opinion attempting to fully categorise the competences and link them with their concluders.[80] Similarly, the Opinion of the Court teased out, based on the current treaties, case law post-Lisbon, and other established practice, what competences lie between the EU, the Member States, and ones that are of a shared nature. The implications of Article 218(11) TFEU Opinion's post-Lisbon are large ramifications for the practice of law at EU and national levels, as well as their political impact. In scenarios where the EU is found to be competent exclusively, an international agreement can be concluded through the EU process, including with the consent of the European Parliament. However, when an international agreement contains shared elements, it must be concluded in mixed format, thereby involving Member State ratification subject to their own respective constitutional requirements. Whilst the EU-Singapore Free Trade Agreement was found to be mixed, it did clarify many of the competences within the EU's CCP post-Lisbon, putting into question many of the Court's previous judgments and Opinion's on the extent of external competence.

In disguise however, Opinion 2/15 was sought by the Commission as a form of proxy question in anticipation of the future EU–US international agreement, known as the Transatlantic Trade and Investment Partnership (TTIP), which of course, many observers of EU affairs of multiple shades will have a stake in, given the discussion on the potential for investment courts to flow from such a far-reaching international agreement. International investment law and the modern dynamic of international trade and investment agreements continue to pose new encounters for the EU legal order and its autonomous nature. Beyond other courts that were to be established, the Court has also said that an international agreement can be

---

[77] Opinion 3/15 of the Court (Marrakesh Treaty), Opinion 3/15, ECLI:EU:C:2017:114.

[78] Opinion 1/15 of the Court (EU-Canada Passenger Name Record), Opinion 1/15, ECLI:EU:C:2017:592.

[79] Opinion 2/15 of the Court (EU–Singapore Free Trade Agreement), Opinion 2/15, ECLI:EU:C:2017:376.

[80] Opinion of Advocate-General Sharpston in Opinion 2/15 (EU-Singapore Free Trade Agreement), ECLI:EU:C:2016:992.

compatible with its own judicial character, and the autonomy of the EU's legal order as a whole.[81] Opinion 1/17 of the Court is awaiting, and the phenomenon of an investor-state dispute settlement (ISDS) and all that comes with it, has been argued, is difficult to fully reconcile with the Court's traditional notion of an autonomous EU legal order.[82]

The Tindemans Report of 1976, predicated on the question of what the EU would be in the future, remarked briefly on the role of the Court within the institutional setup. At this time, the *ex ante* Opinions through Article 218(11) TFEU's predecessor had not been utilised, but, whilst picturing a growing need for the EU, the future expansion stated, 'the Court must have powers identical to those which it has at present, so as to be able to interpret the law of the Union, to annul the acts of the institutions not in accordance with the Treaties ...'.[83] The moves from creating the 'new legal order' from *Van Gend En Loos* until then had gone hand-in-hand with the continued build-up of the EU's judicial order. Yet, one of the forgotten things about *Van Gend En Loos* is the fact that the 'new legal order' proclamation was followed by a small reservation, that is, 'for the benefit of which the states have limited their sovereign rights, albeit within limited fields'.[84] This limited fields notion stood for decades, until later the Court in Opinion 1/91 revised this even more expansively, to envisage it to be, 'for the benefit of which the States have limited their sovereign rights, in ever wider fields'.[85]

The developing line of case law in EU external relations continues. It is slow, and often non-controversial, at times it is possible to predict where a line of case law is heading in a particular direction,[86] notwithstanding ambiguities in the treaties requiring elucidation by the Court. Article 218(11) TFEU has been argued to have not yet reached its full potential, particularly as regards certain areas like the CFSP.[87] To prop up the EU's

---

[81] Opinion 1/00 of the Court (European Common Aviation Area), Opinion 1/00, ECLI:EU:C:2002:231, para 21. Recited in Opinion 1/09 of the Court (European and Community Patents Court), Opinion 1/09, ECLI:EU:C:2011:123, para 76.

[82] See H Lenk, 'Investment Arbitration under EU Investment Agreements: Is There a Role for an Autonomous EU Legal Order?' (2017) 28 *European Business Law Review* 135.

[83] 'European Union. Report' Mr Leo Tindemans, Prime Minister of Belgium, to the European Council. Bulletin of the European Communities, Supplement 1/76 (the 'Tindemans Report')' (Office for Official Publications of the European Communities 1976) p. 32.

[84] Case C-26/62, NV *Algemene Transport- en Expeditie Onderneming van Gend en Loos v Netherlands Inland Revenue Administration*, ECLI:EU:C:1963:1, para 3.

[85] Opinion 1/91 of the Court (EEA Agreement I) in *Opinion 1/91*, ECLI:EU:C:1991:490, para 21.

[86] For example, whether the Court can rule in the area of CFSP when it is brought to the Court through a preliminary reference, as opposed to a direct action. Case C-72/15, *PJSC Rosneft Oil Company, anciennement OJSC Rosneft Oil Company v Her Majesty's Treasury and Others*, ECLI:EU:C:2017:236. See, Graham Butler, 'A Question of Jurisdiction: Art. 267 TFEU Preliminary References of a CFSP Nature' (2017) 2 *European Papers*.

[87] See S Adam, *La procédure d'avis devant la Cour de justice de l'Union européenne* (Bruylant 2011).

judicial order, more substantiated reasons may slowly begin to emerge. One manner in which this may be elucidated is through the use of the provisions of the CFR, primarily relied upon in *ex post* scenarios. Despite the obvious fall-back option of resorting to phrasing the EU based upon the 'rule of law', the Court may also look beyond this, by selecting Article 47 CFR.[88] It has been highlighted that long-established case law that is nominally applied is 'fully defensible' when preserving the nature of the EU's judicial system.[89] Whatever role the Court has as regards its own judicial review arrangements, and the challenges therein as a result of new questions asked of it on a consistent basis, it is therefore to be had that, with some certainty, new envisaged international agreements will continue to come forward, posing new questions that have the potential for the Court to affirm the extent of competence, and question the compatibility of such draft agreements with the EU's legal order. The consistent building of an EU legal order necessitates sacrificing previously held positions. For effective external relations to work through the conclusion of international agreements, there has to be an EU legal order which is rigidly monitored. The Court has done this in both *ex ante* and *ex post* manners, with its cause rooted in both preserving existing practice, and continuing to adapt to new ways in which legal integration is occurring.

7. FORWARD THINKING

The nature of international agreements that the EU is a party to entails rights, obligations, and duties. Yet, as was the case decades ago,[90] and as it is now, the Court is far from reaching an absolutely affirmative theory on its approach to international agreements. With the Court existing in the first place, this alone can be considered significant for the international agreements that it enters into. Unlike most other international organisations which also have the ability to conduct external relations by accomplishing the successful conclusion of international agreements with third parties, most do not have their own independent judicial arbiter like the Union does, in the form of a strong Court. The legal space for Member States to enter into international agreements unilaterally, as opposed to through the prism of

---

[88] Article 47 CFR (Right to an effective remedy and to a fair trial): 'Everyone whose rights and freedoms guaranteed by the law of the Union are violated has the right to an effective remedy before a tribunal in compliance with the conditions laid down in this Article ...'.

[89] PJ Kuijper, 'The Changing Status of Private International Law Treaties of the Member States in Relation to Regulation No. 44/2001—Case No. C-533/08, TNT Express Nederland BV v. AXA Versicherung AG' (2011) 38 *Legal Issues of Economic Integration* 89 at 102.

[90] JHJ Bourgeois, 'Effects of International Agreements in European Community Law: Are the Dice Cast?' (1984) 82 *Michigan Law Review* 1250 at 1256.

EU law, continues to lessen as EU law continues to become a more-encompassing legal order. Accordingly, international agreements to which the EU is a party have been carefully negotiated to ensure their compliance with EU primary law, and reaching the objective for which they were intended. Given the Court's interpretative methods of other legal orders is systematically sceptical, certainly in more recent Opinions, the non-committal approach to other legal orders in its *ex ante* phase demonstrates the fluidity of the way in which international agreements are framed and how molten the EU's legal order is to accepting them, as the EU continues to integrate itself. International agreements continue to form an integral part of the EU's legal order.[91] The sincere cooperation (loyalty) obligations specified on both the EU and its Member States,[92] to work cooperatively to execute the fulfil obligations flowing from the treaties, extends to the execution of obligations of international agreements.

In earlier times with the predecessor of the Article 218(11) TFEU Opinion, the views or opinions of the Advocates-General acting as a whole were not made public. Only the Opinion of the Court was delivered after all the Advocates-General had been heard in private. Previously, some national courts have been critical of cases at the Court which have been delivered without the Opinion of an Advocate-General.[93] That practice has changed. A single Advocate-General is now assigned to deliver a view or opinion in the Article 218(11) TFEU procedure, just like in any normal case before the Court, and it is made public. This development is most certainly welcome, as it is now possible to see different interpretations at play between the non-binding view or Opinion of the Advocate-General, vis-à-vis that of the binding Opinion of the Court. Thus, with future Article 218(11) TFEU Opinions being delivered by the Court, this will pre-emptively halt this line of questioning by national courts, and other critics.

Whether Article 218(11) TFEU has been misused as a tool for determining the legality of international agreements concerning the EU's legal order is a thought that has yet to be conclusively answered. The role of the Court in clarifying the nature of international agreements regarding their ramifications on the legal order continues in the present, in stark contrast to another system like that of the United States, in which its Supreme Court has not elucidated certain matters of 'foreign' nature for some time.[94] It is easy to forget that the Court has continuously wrestled with itself over

---

[91] Case C-181/73, *R & V Haegeman v Belgian State*, ECLI:EU:C:1974:41, para 5.

[92] Article 4(3) TEU.

[93] See A Arnull, Chapter 2 in this volume.

[94] See generally, L Henkin, *Foreign Affairs and the United States Constitution* 2nd edn, (Oxford, Clarendon Press 1996). For concurrence with this view, H Jefferson Powell, *The President's Authority over Foreign Affairs: An Essay in Constitutional Interpretation* (Carolina Academic Press, 2002) 22.

the effect that international agreements and treaties can have within the EU legal order. The part-reluctance to provide direct effect to such measures is illustrative of the self-protection which it argues is the bedrock for a judicial legal order to effectively support an EU legal order. The *ex ante* Opinions from time-to-time can reflect the mood and prevailing political circumstances that are palpable in a particular climate,[95] but the EU's infant and teenage growing pains for creating its own unique identity are over. With the EU fledging into adulthood,[96] it has now branded itself as standing for its own decisions and ultimate destiny. Notwithstanding the Court's caution towards international agreements of any kind which inherently affect the EU's autonomy to effectively execute external relations, it is wise for it to constantly recall that it itself is merely an international court, set up by international agreements. Nonetheless, Article 218(11) TFEU and its *ex ante* nature, coupled with the ramifications of its Opinions, affirms the underlining theory and narrative that the Court is a constitutional adjudicator. A self-confessed insider has said the Court has shown 'remarkable ingenuity' in handling delicate Article 218(11) TFEU Opinions.[97] Hence, with the Court's spirited intentions of having much to offer in terms of giving the EU a strong external foundation for international agreements, the EU legal order is given prime status. The new standard of international agreements, particularly free trade agreements, is that it takes a considerable period of time for the negotiating directives to be agreed, followed by the negotiation of an international agreement themselves with a third party. With Article 218(11) TFEU having so much to offer the EU in terms of the legal certainty that it can provide, it is a wonder why it has not been used more frequently by pro-integration institutions than has been the case to date.

---

[95] For example, regarding the nature of Opinion 1/94, see, N Emiliou, 'The Death of Exclusive Competence?' (1996) 21 *European Law Review* 294.
[96] C Timmermans, 'The EU and International Public Law' (1999) 4 *European Foreign Affairs Review* 181 at 184.
[97] GF Mancini, 'The European Court of Justice and the External Competences of the Community' in Giuseppe Federico Mancini (ed), *Democracy and Constitutionalism in the European Union: Collected Essays* (Oxford, Hart Publishing 2000) 235.

5

Serving Two Masters

CJEU Case Law in Swedish First Instance Courts and National Courts of Precedent as Gatekeepers

MATTIAS DERLÉN AND JOHAN LINDHOLM

1. INTRODUCTION: CJEU JURISPRUDENCE AND UNION COURTS OF ORDINARY JURISDICTION

W E HAVE COME to accept as natural the fact that the judicial enforcement of European Union (EU) law involves both national and EU courts. Twenty years ago, Temple Lang confidently declared that '[e]very national court in the European Community is now a Community law court'.[1]

The division of labour between national and European courts is in theory quite straightforward: the EU courts are primarily responsible for interpreting what EU law mandates and it is primarily the national courts' responsibility to apply and enforce EU law in 'ordinary cases', disputes between individuals and Member States, and between individuals.[2] This is, for example, clearly expressed in the Court of Justice of the European Union's (CJEU) judgment in *Zwartfeld* where the Court declared that it is 'the judicial body responsible for ensuring that both the Member States and the [Union] institutions comply with the law' and that it is 'the judicial

---

[1] J Temple Lang, 'The Duties of National Courts under Community Constitutional Law', (1997) 22 *European Law Review* 3 at 3.

[2] See, e.g., R Barents, 'The Rule of Law in the European Union', in R Jansen et al (eds), *European Ambitions of the National Judiciary* (The Hague, Kluwer Law, 1997) 67; Advocate General Léger's opinion in Case C-224/01 *Köbler v Austria*, EU:C:2003:207, para 66 ('It can easily be inferred from all this case law that the Court confers on the national courts an essential role in the implementation of Community law and in the protection of the rights derived from it for individuals. Indeed people like to call the national courts, according to an expression commonly employed, Community courts of ordinary jurisdiction.'); S Prechal, 'National Courts in EU Judicial Structures' (2006) 25 *Yearbook of European Law* 429 at 432.

authorities of the Member States, who are responsible for ensuring that [Union] law is applied and respected in the national legal system.'[3] In the words of the General Court in *Tetra Pak*, 'national courts are acting as [Union] courts of general jurisdiction' whose role is to 'merely be applying' Union law.[4] National courts are the 'first-in-line' courts in the Union judiciary.[5]

There are good reasons for this division of labour between the EU courts and the national courts. Much of it dates back to what can be described as the twin values on which much of the judicial enforcement of EU law rests: the uniform and effective application of Union law. A system where Union courts are primarily responsible for the interpretation of Union law helps ensure that EU law is the same in every Member State compared to a system where national courts participate and possibly adopt diverging interpretations. Similarly, a system where EU law is effectively enforced at the national level is dependent on the cooperation of the national courts.[6]

The opportunities for legal and physical individuals to reach the EU courts are in practice extremely slim; only a handful of cases reach the EU courts and consequently and in practice the judicial enforcement of EU law largely occurs at the national level. Even if the EU courts had broader jurisdiction that would allow them to hear more cases, their workloads would not permit it. For this reason, loyal cooperation between the EU courts and the national courts is essential for a full, uniform, and effective application of EU law in its day-to-day implementation. Consistent with this division of labour, national courts have a right and sometimes an obligation to request preliminary rulings from the CJEU regarding the interpretation and validity of EU law, and, consistent with this division of labour, the majority of the CJEU's caseload consists of such preliminary rulings.[7] It is also the national courts that are capable of providing the remedies and procedures through which EU law can be realised, therefore they are under an obligation to do so.[8] Another benefit of the national courts applying and enforcing EU law

---

[3] Case C-2/88 *Zwartfeld*, EU:C:1990:440, paras 16 and 18 respectively.

[4] Case T-51/89 *Tetra Pak Rausing SA v Commission*, EU:T:1990:41, para 42 (discussing, more specifically, the role of national courts in the field of competition law). See also, e.g., Advocate General Bot's Opinion in Case C-555/07 *Kücükdeveci v Swedex GmbH & Co KG*, EU:C:2009:429, para 55; Advocate General Cosmas's Opinion in Case C-83/98 P *France v Ladbroke Racing Ltd & Commission*, EU:C:1999:577, para 92.

[5] M Claes, *The National Courts' Mandate in the European Constitution* (Oxford, Hart Publishing, 2006) 59.

[6] See T Tridimas, 'The ECJ and the National Courts: Dialogue, Cooperation, and Instability' in A Arnull and D Chalmers (eds), *The Oxford Handbook of European Union Law* (Oxford, Oxford University Press, 2015) 404.

[7] See, e.g., M Derlén and J Lindholm, 'Characteristics of Precedent: The Case Law of the European Court of Justice in Three Dimensions' (2015) 16 *German Law Journal* 1073. Most direct actions are infringement proceedings against Member States that have failed their obligations under Union law, most commonly to implement Union law correctly and in time.

[8] See, e.g., C-50/00 P *Unión de Pequeños Agricultores v Council*, EU:C:2002:462, para 41.

against individuals and Member States is that these are assumed to respect the national courts more than the EU courts.[9]

This does not mean that the relationship between the EU courts and the national courts is simple or static. Tridimas aptly describes their interaction as 'dialectical, full of circumspection and deference, albeit occasionally tense, and based on an incomplete and somewhat unstable political bargain'.[10] National courts wield considerable power as the effective application and enforcement of Union law depends on their continued and loyal cooperation.[11]

The fact that national courts are Union courts of general jurisdiction has multiple consequences and can, and should, be examined from multiple perspectives. One well-studied aspect is that it changes the national courts' relationship with the national political bodies that are responsible for their very existence. To use a well-worn expression, Member State courts are servants of two masters: the EU and the Member State.[12]

This chapter will focus on a different aspect, namely the relationship between the national and EU courts within the EU judiciary. This relationship has also been discussed extensively in the literature at hand, most frequently by focusing on the preliminary rulings institute.[13] That national courts request preliminary rulings and that the CJEU hands them down is important, even vital, for the division of labour between the EU and national courts to function well.[14] It is not, however, sufficient for the uniform and effective application and enforcement of Union law by national courts in all Member States. The unifying function of centralised interpretation depends on the ability and willingness of national courts to consider and loyally apply the EU courts' body of jurisprudence. This is the focal point of this chapter: to what extent do lower national courts make their own, independent examination of CJEU case law?[15]

---

[9] See, e.g., A Komninos, 'Civil Antitrust Remedies Between Community and National Law' in C Barnard and O Odudu (eds), *The Outer Limits of European Union Law* (Oxford, Hart Publishing, 2009), 366.

[10] See Tridimas above n 6 at 403–404.

[11] Ibid. See also Lang above n 1 at 5.

[12] See, e.g., M Bobek, 'The Effects of EU Law in the National Legal Systems', in C Barnard and S Peers (eds), *European Union Law* (Oxford, Oxford University Press, 2014) 142; M Bobek, 'Thou Shalt Have Two Masters; The Application of European Law by Administrative Authorities in the New Member States' (2008) 1 *Review of European Administrative Law* 51.

[13] See, e.g., M Broberg and N Fenger, *Preliminary References to the European Court of Justice* (Oxford, Oxford University Press, 2010); J Komarek, 'In the Court(s) We Trust? On the Need for Hierarchy and Differentiation in the Preliminary Ruling Procedure' (2007) 32 *European Law Review* 467; A Stone Sweet and T L Brunell, 'The European Court and the National Courts: A Statistical Analysis of Preliminary References 1961–1995' (1998) 5 *Journal of European Public Policy* 66.

[14] The importance of the preliminary rulings institute has been clear since some of the CJEU's earliest decisions. See Case 16/65 *Firma G. Schwarze v Einfuhr- und Vorratsstelle für Getreide und Futtermittel*, EU:C:1965:117.

[15] The term 'CJEU case law' refers herein to the jurisprudence of both the Court of Justice and the General Court.

2. THEORY: A THREE-TIERED EU JUDICIARY?

The description of the division of labour within the EU judiciary focuses primarily on the difference in function of EU courts on one hand and national courts on the other.[16] This gives the impression of a two-tiered EU judiciary where, somewhat simplified, the EU courts issue judgments on the interpretation of EU law and the national courts apply that jurisprudence in local disputes.

There are good arguments for rejecting the two-tiered model of the EU judiciary, since it ignores the fact that different national courts have different roles and functions and thereby oversimplifies the situation. An alternative, more complex but also more correct model acknowledges that the EU judiciary has at least three tiers: the EU courts, the highest national courts[17] and the lower national courts.[18]

The fact that EU law does not provide the highest national courts with any special privileges[19] does not mean that they should be lumped together with all the other national courts for the purpose of describing, understanding, and analysing the EU judiciary. The special nature of the highest national courts in relation to the EU courts is widely recognised, not least in the legal literature.[20] It has been argued that higher national courts have 'fought back' against the erosion of their power that emanates from the CJEU.[21]

The interaction between the highest and lower national courts and its consequences for the EU legal order has received less attention. One reason for this may be that the EU courts have staunchly held on to the idea that all national courts are Union courts of general jurisdiction[22] and steadfastly refused to give the highest national courts a role between themselves and

---

[16] See, e.g., Barents above n 2 at 64–65 (describing 'the two pillars of the Community judicial system'); *cf* P Craig, 'The Jurisdiction of the Community Courts Reconsidered' in P de Búrca and J Weiler (eds), *The European Court of Justice* (Oxford, Oxford University Press, 2001) 178 ('It is clear that properly understood we have three types of Community Court, not just two: the ECJ, the CFI, *and* national courts.').

[17] Most obviously supreme, general and administrative courts and specialised constitutional courts.

[18] You could argue for a model with additional tiers, including a distinction between the Court of Justice and the General Court at the EU level and a special category of national courts between the courts of first instance and courts of precedent (appellate courts). However, such further divisions are unnecessary for the purpose of answering the questions posed in this chapter.

[19] Article 267 TFEU distinguishes between national courts 'against whose decisions there is no judicial remedy under national law' and other national courts, but places them in a weaker position vis-à-vis the CJEU than other national courts, not stronger.

[20] See, e.g., AM Slaughter et al (eds), *The European Court and National Courts—Doctrine and Jurisprudence* (Oxford, Hart Publishing, 1998); See Claes above n 5.

[21] See AM Slaughter, 'Judicial Globalization' (1999–2000) 40 *Virginia Journal of International Law* 1103 at 1104–1105.

[22] See Case T-51/89 *Tetra Pak Rausing SA v Commission*, EU:T:1990:41, para 42 ('*the* national courts are acting as Community courts of general jurisdiction'. Emphasis added). See Claes above n 5 at 15.

the lower national courts. This is most explicitly made clear in the CJEU's decision in *Simmenthal II* where the Court held that the Italian *pretore* was obligated by Union law to set aside national law and that the special role preserved for the *Corte costituzionale della Repubblica Italiana* under the Italian constitution was irrelevant when the legal rules applied in the case were of a Union nature. The reason underlying this position is made clear: the full, uniform, immediate, and effective application of Union law in all Member States.[23] Thus, according to the Court of Justice, all national courts are required to apply EU law, including CJEU case law, directly and immediately. This leaves no room for a special relationship between higher and lower national courts and also entails that lower national courts shall consider and apply CJEU case law independently and without considering the opinions of higher national courts.[24]

Under the model expressed in CJEU case law, ordinary national courts functioning as Union courts of general jurisdiction shall apply and enforce Union law, including CJEU case law, independently when adjudicating individual disputes. In so doing, the national courts and the Union courts communicate directly with each other and there is no 'detour' by way of the higher national courts.[25]

Although there are, as is made clear in *Simmenthal II*, good arguments for this model, we do not believe that you can realistically expect lower national courts to completely separate themselves from the higher national courts on matters of Union law. While national judges play a role in the Union judiciary, they are heavily influenced by the national legal culture and have both been trained in and are accustomed to paying close attention to the opinions of the highest national courts. The lower courts' decisions are also much more likely to be reviewed by the higher national courts than by the EU courts and the former, unlike the latter, have the power to overturn them.

Imagine a situation where a Swedish court of first instance is faced with a dispute that involves a question of EU law and where there is relevant CJEU case law governing these questions. If the question is novel, in the sense that it has never formerly been dealt with by Swedish courts of precedent, we would expect the lower court to consider CJEU case law directly and independently. However, if Swedish courts of precedent have addressed the matter, we think it would be naïve to think that the lower court would not at some level be affected. In this manner, and in contrast to the model described above, we imagine and suspect that higher national courts by

---

[23] Case 106/77 *Amministrazione delle Finanze dello Stato v Simmenthal SpA*, EU:C:1978:49, esp. paras 14–20.

[24] From a Swedish perspective, this is similar to the right of every court and public authority to perform judicial review, without waiting for or referring the matter to a higher court. See further, A Eka and D Gustavsson, 'Lagprövning och andra frågor om normkontroll—rapport från en expertgrupp' (2007) *Svensk Juristtidning* 769.

[25] See Model A in Figure 5.1 below.

merit of their position in the national judiciary can impact the application and enforcement of CJEU case law by the lower national courts.[26]

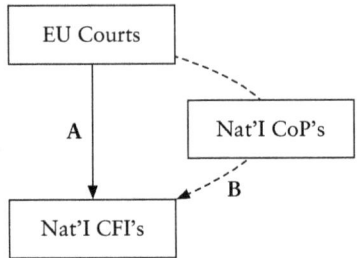

Figure 5.1: Two Models of the EU Judiciary

3. METHOD: MEASURING INFLUENCE

In this contribution, we will explore *to what extent lower national courts are influenced by higher national courts in their application of CJEU case law*. This is achieved by studying the Swedish courts.

As regards the 'lower national courts', we will analyse 402,570 decisions by Swedish courts of first instance (CFI) issued over a two-and-a-half-year period concluding at the end of 2015 (the CFI dataset). These include decisions by both administrative courts (*förvaltningsrätter*) and courts of general jurisdiction (*tingsrätter*) that handle civil as well as criminal cases.[27] If we seek to understand how CJEU case law is actually applied and enforced at the national level, as we do here, the focus ought to be on the national CFI which are responsible for the application and enforcement of Union law in the overwhelming majority of cases.

As regards the 'higher national courts', we examine 12,179 published decisions by the Swedish Supreme Court (*Högsta domstolen*) and the Swedish Supreme Administrative Court (*Högsta förvaltningsdomstolen*)[28] between Sweden's accession to the European Union in January 1995 and August 2014 (the CoP—Courts of Precedent—dataset).

We then study and compare these datasets to determine whether, to what extent, and in what situations the CoP 'influence' the CFI choice of CJEU case law (i.e. decisions by the General Court and the Court of Justice). To do so, we extract and compare references to CJEU case law found in CFI and CoP decisions. We also extract and consider CFI references to CoP decisions.

---

[26] See Model B in Figure 5.1 below.

[27] The total number of CFI decisions during the period studied is about 750,000. Thus, the dataset includes roughly 54% of all CFI decisions during the period in question. However, many of the decisions that are not part of the dataset were decisions in family matters (mainly divorce and custody matters), many of which were undisputed decisions based on joint applications. See Domstolsverket, Domstolsstatistik 2014. Available at: www.domstol.se/Publikationer/Statistik/domstolsstatistik_2014.pdf.

[28] Previously referred to as *Regeringsrätten*.

Thus, we use one court's references to another court's case law as a measurement of the influence that the latter court exerts over the former. These references are studied using three different methods that capture three different ways by which the CoP may influence CFI interpretation and application of CJEU case law. These are described in greater detail below, but briefly stated they are (i) overall CFI/CoP reference to CJEU case law overlap, (ii) CFI reference to CJEU case law cited by CoP, and (iii) CFI co-references to CoP and CJEU case law.

The main findings of this chapter are that, at least in the case of Sweden, higher national courts are capable of and do in practice influence the application of CJEU case law of lower national courts in individual cases, but that in practice this influence is rather limited.

4. 'WE DON'T NEED NO EDUCATION': CFI CITATION INDEPENDENCE

The first approach used here to measure the extent to which Swedish CoP influence the application of CJEU case law by Swedish CFI is what we refer to as CFI citation independence. This assesses whether the CJEU decisions referred to by the CFI are also being cited by the CoP. In other words, we examine how great the overlap is between, on one hand, the CJEU case law cited in individual CFI decisions and, on the other, the CJEU case law cited by Swedish CoP.

The underlying line of reasoning is perhaps best explained using an example. If a Swedish CFI issues a judgment citing two CJEU decisions, the question is whether it found those decisions and decided to cite them because they had previously been cited by *Högsta domstolen* (the Supreme Court) or *Högsta förvaltningsdomstolen* (the Supreme Administrative Court). There are three possible outcomes in such a situation: (i) neither of the two decisions have been cited (0% overlap), (ii) one decision has previously been cited (50% overlap), or (iii) both decisions have previously been cited (100% overlap) by a Swedish CoP.

It is difficult to capture causation but if the CJEU decisions cited by the CFI have never appeared in the CoP jurisprudence, the choice cannot have been a direct result of CoP influence and, conversely, it demonstrates that the CFI is able to identify and apply CJEU case law independently.[29] Is it possible that CoP have influenced the CFI to cite CJEU decisions that they themselves have never mentioned in their decisions? If so, we are talking about a very subtle form of influence that by discussing, for example, EU law more generally and/or citing other CJEU decisions, the CoP have inspired the CFI to explore and cite other elements of EU law.

---

[29] Of course, this would not necessarily mean that the reference was the result of the participating CFI judges' individual research. It is likely that in many cases it is the parties that make the court aware of the existence of relevant EU case law.

If a substantial overlap is discovered you might be tempted to conclude that the CoP have a considerable, positive influence on CFI citation choices, but this is not necessarily true. The fact that a lower court cites a CJEU decision that has appeared in CoP jurisprudence does not necessarily mean that it did so *because* a CoP had previously done so. A plausible, alternative explanation would be that both CFI and CoP cite particular CJEU case law because of a certain quality, such as it being an important precedent on a particular point of law.[30] All we know in such a situation is that it is possible that the lower court was influenced by the choices of the higher court.[31]

In the overwhelming majority of the cases, the CJEU decisions cited by the CFI have never been cited by the Swedish CoP. About two out of three CFI judgments[32] that contain references to CJEU case law have a 0 per cent overlap with the CJEU case law cited by CoP (i.e. they exclusively cite CJEU case law that has never been cited by the Swedish courts of precedent).[33] In only about one in six cases[34] all of the CJEU cases cited by the CFI have appeared in CoP case law.

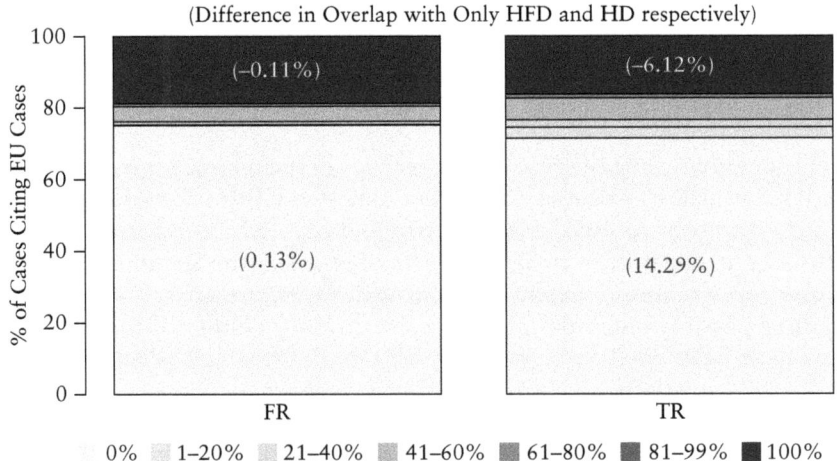

Figure 5.2: **CFI/CoP EU Court Decision Reference Overlap**

---

[30] If we consider CFI decisions further back in time, we might also make the mistake of confusing a correlation that is impossible due to differences in time (e.g. a CFI citing a CJEU decision that was cited by the CoP at a later point in time). This has a minimal impact on this study because the CFI data only consists of more recent cases.

[31] We study influence in these second types of situations in more detail below using different approaches.

[32] 71% for general courts and 75% of administrative courts.

[33] See Figure 5.2 above. As shown, there is 0 per cent overlap between EU case law cited in general CFI and in general CoP decisions in 85 per cent of the cases, but this increases to levels on a par with the administrative CFI when you expand the comparison with all CoP references.

[34] 15% and 19% respectively.

The result is quite strongly divided between no reference overlap (0%) and complete reference overlap (100%), with very little in between. The reason for this clear division is that the overwhelming majority of all CFI decisions citing CJEU case law cite one single decision.[35] The nature of the underlying data thus dictates that most CFI decisions can only be sorted into one of the two categories: 0 per cent or 100 per cent reference overlap.

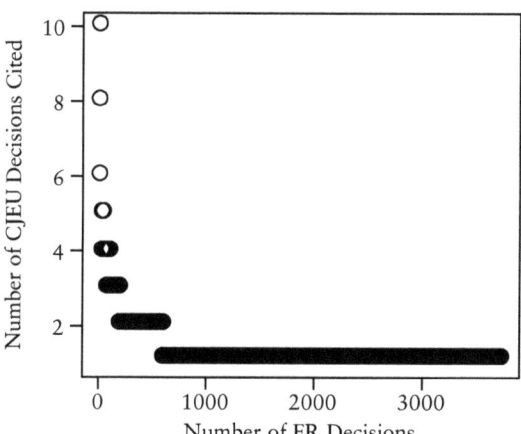

Figure 5.3: Distribution of FR References to CJEU Decisions

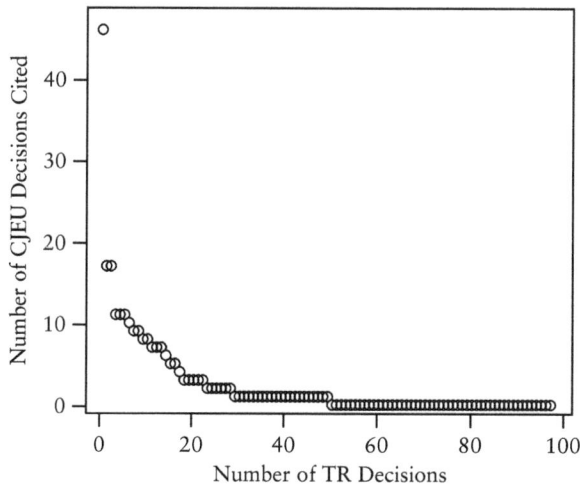

Figure 5.4: Distribution of TR References to CJEU Decisions

[35] See Figures 5.3 and 5.4 above.

This does not affect the observation that Swedish CFI by and large cite CJEU case law that has never been cited by the CoP. As explained above, this finding supports the conclusions that the CFI, to a large extent, consider and apply CJEU case law independently of the higher, national courts. In other words, the CFI do not need the CoP to identify relevant CJEU case law. However, the overlap is so low so as to be somewhat counter-intuitive. Remember, we are not taking into consideration how frequently the higher courts have cited a particular CJEU decision; a single reference in the CoP dataset is sufficient to create an overlap. The fact that the overlap is so low could have a number of explanations. Firstly, it could indicate that the highest courts do not engage with EU law in general and that EU law issues rarely arise before the CoP. However, our previous research indicates that EU law plays an increasingly important role in the highest Swedish courts, demonstrated by the fact that almost 10 per cent of CoP cases had an EU law component in 2014.[36] Secondly, the low overlap could be explained by a tendency of the CoP not to cite CJEU case law, even when engaging with EU law issues. Again, previous research demonstrates that this does not generally hold true. However, higher Swedish courts tend to be rather specific in their use of CJEU case law. More specifically, most CJEU decisions are cited only once and very few decisions accumulate more than a handful of citations.[37] This indicates that the CoP tend to discuss case law that is only relevant in rather specific circumstances. If we assume that the CFI adopt a similar approach, concentrating on CJEU decisions that are specifically relevant to the situation at hand rather than decisions of more general importance, this could contribute to the limited overlap. Finally, and related to the previous discussion, the limited overlap could be an indication of the different legal worlds of the CoP and the CFI. In other words, while both higher and lower courts encounter EU law issues, it might not be the same type of issues.[38]

5. THE MASTER HAS SPOKEN? (POTENTIAL) CoP CITATION INFLUENCE

5.1. What Happens when CoP do Get Involved?

The findings described above show that references to CJEU case law by Swedish courts of first instance cannot, for the most part, be attributed to the very same decisions being cited by Swedish courts of precedent.

---

[36] M Derlén and J Lindholm, 'Festina Lente—Europarättens genomslag i svensk rättspraxis 1995–2015' (2015) *Europarättslig tidskrift* 151, 157.

[37] Ibid, 170–175.

[38] See further section 5.2 below.

However, that does not exclude the possibility that the CoP can and some-times do influence the CFI application of CJEU case law. It is possible—and compatible with the findings above—that the CFI are both willing and tend to 'follow the leader' but that the CoP rarely play along.

Considering that the influence of CoP appears limited to the one in four cases that come before the CFI, it may at first glance seem like this is a question of marginal practical importance. That impression is false for two reasons. First, if the CoP exercise a strong influence on the application of CJEU case law of the CFI in one out of four cases, that significantly impacts the uniform and effective enforcement of EU law. Second, even if they in practice use their influence sparsely, it is both principally and practically problematic if higher national courts are able to exert influence over the application of CJEU case law by lower national courts as it effectively places the EU courts at the mercy of the higher national courts. It is, for example, easy to imagine that higher national courts might be tempted to use this influence if a situation where they strongly disagree with CJEU case law were to arise.

To explore this possibility, we will study judgments by Swedish courts of precedent that contain references to EU case law and examine what impact, if any, these judgments have had on the CFI. By studying the CJEU decisions cited by the CoP, we can also deduce in what situations and on what issues they engage with CJEU case law. This can then be compared to the situations and issues where the CFI do so, giving us some insight into the nature of situations where the CoP exert influence and, conversely, those situations where they do not.

5.2. Cite What I Cite: Very Narrow, but Possibly Deep Influence

There are two possible ways engagement of CoP with CJEU case law may influence the use of CJEU case law in the lower courts. The first way is that CFI might be more likely to apply CJEU case law referred to by the higher courts in EU-related precedents. Such a correlation could be caused by the CoP making the CFI aware of the existence of a CJEU judgment by referring to it or increasing the precedential value of the CJEU judgment in the opin-ion of the lower national courts because the higher national court referred to it, or a combination of these two factors. As discussed below, whether this type of influence is problematic depends on the circumstances.

To study this, we begin by identifying all CJEU decisions ever cited by a Swedish CoP in a published ruling[39] and find that the CoP have all-in-all

---

[39] The CoP only communicates with the CFI through their published opinions; their ability to influence the CFI towards particular EU judgments without explicitly citing them is limited.

cited 209 unique CJEU decisions.[40] We then examine if and how frequently the Swedish CFI have cited these decisions.[41]

We find that most CJEU decisions cited by the Swedish CoP have never or very rarely been cited by the Swedish CFI[42]—59 per cent of all CJEU decisions cited by Swedish CoP have never been cited by the CFI during the period in question.[43] Among the remaining decisions, 58 per cent have only been cited once or twice by the CFI. Thus, of all the unique CJEU decisions ever cited by Swedish CoP, about 83 per cent[44] have never or so rarely been cited by the CFI that any connection between the two is unlikely. Phrased differently, only 17 per cent of the CJEU case law cited by the CoP has

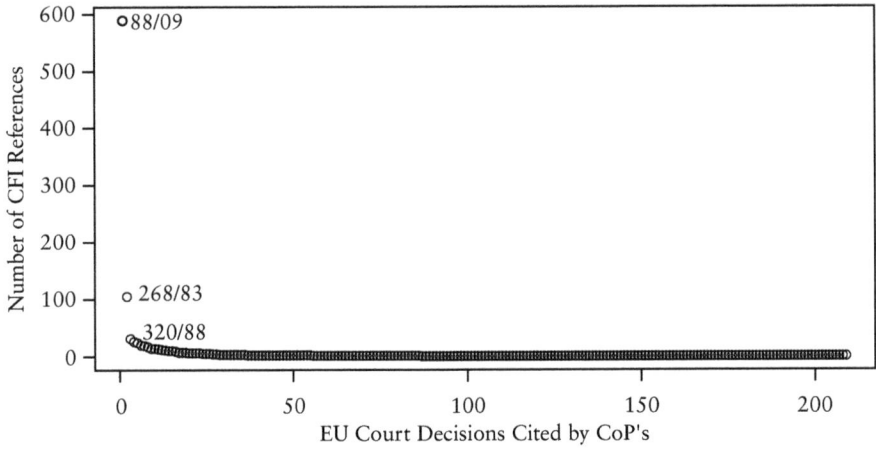

Figure 5.5: CFI References to CoP Cited EU Court Decisions

---

[40] Many of the decisions cited by the CoP have been cited in several CoP decisions and the total number of references to EU case law is therefore substantially higher. Although it is not directly pertinent to the research question examined in this chapter, we feel that it is worth noting that this must be considered a high number of cases, at least significantly higher than we had expected. The diversity in references supports our previous conclusion that Swedish courts have a rather instrumental approach to EU law and CJEU case law. See Derlén and Lindholm (n 36) 173–174.

[41] Some might argue that the fact that the CFI did not refer to an EU court judgment does not necessarily mean that it did not read, follow, and apply it in the case. It is impossible to empirically prove or disprove the claim that the judges were influenced by something that they intentionally left out of the judgment. It does, however, seem unlikely to us that the lower courts would do this on a larger more systematic scale, particularly under these circumstances where the higher courts through their explicit references have clearly signalled that it is both relevant and appropriate to cite the EU decisions in question.

[42] See Figure 5.5 above.

[43] 123 out of 209 EU court decisions.

[44] 173 out of 209 EU court decisions.

appeared more than twice in CFI judgments and where it is possible that the CFI reference is a sign of CoP influence.

Thus, much like the absence of a CoP reference to a CJEU decision does not seriously impact its chances of being cited by CFI, four times out of five a CoP referring to a CJEU decision has no discernible effect on the lower court's tendency to cite the same case. This suggests, quite strongly, that the Swedish CoP cannot easily and effectively steer the Swedish CFI towards CJEU case law simply by citing it.

It is more difficult to explain this pattern. It seems extremely unlikely that the CFI would refrain from citing relevant CJEU case law because it has already been cited by the CoP. One possible explanation is that Swedish CFI in general pay limited attention to CoP decisions. However, it seems unlikely considering that even though precedence is not *de jure* binding in the Swedish legal system, it plays an important role and is *de facto* followed.[45] In our opinion, the most likely explanation for the observations is that Swedish CFI and CoP deal with different types of EU-related disputes and issues and that much of the CJEU case law cited by the CoP is therefore of limited relevance to the lower courts.[46]

Two CJEU judgments deviate quite sharply from the general trend. The first is the CJEU's judgment in *Graphic Procédé* regarding the classification of transactions for VAT purposes. More specifically, the case concerned the classification of printing services for assigning VAT.[47] In the wake of *Graphic Procédé*, Swedish courts, including general and administrative courts at all levels, have received and decided many cases dealing with the VAT-classification of printing services,[48] including many complex cases regarding the legal consequences of classification and reclassification of print-related services.[49] Thus, the CJEU's interpretation of EU law in *Graphic Procédé* gave rise to extensive practical and complex legal consequences in Sweden, most of which were not governed by EU law, and the resolution of which required the involvement of both Swedish CFI and CoP. It seems quite clear that, in this case, the involvement of CoP was necessary to ensure the uniform and effective enforcement of EU law in Sweden, and did not constitute improper or problematic influence of the lower courts.

The second exceptional case, *Rompelman*, also concerns VAT. The case concerned two Dutch nationals' right to repayment of VAT on payments

---

[45] See, e.g., G Bergholtz and A Peczenik, 'Precedent in Sweden' in DN MacCormick et al (eds), *Interpreting Precedents* (Farnham, Ashgate, 1997).

[46] See also section 5.3.

[47] Case C-88/09 *Graphic Procédé v Ministère du Budget, des Comptes publics et de la Fonction publique*, EU:C:2010:76 (regarding the classification of reprographic activities).

[48] *Graphic Procédé* is generally relied upon by Swedish courts for the legal rule that printed products shall be assigned 6% VAT-rate instead of the standard 25%.

[49] See, e.g., HFD 2011 not 66; HFD 2014 not 15; HFD 2014 ref 14; HFD 2015 ref 69; NJA 2015 s 1072; NJA 2016 s 799.

on a not-yet-constructed property that they were eventually going to let.[50] Although there are examples of Swedish courts citing *Rompelman* for the CJEU's conclusion that such pre-payments can entitle a VAT-repayment,[51] it is more commonly cited for the general rule that 'it is for the person applying to deduct VAT to show that the conditions for deduction are met'.[52] This explains why references to *Rompelman* appear in a large number of CFI and CoP decisions: there are numerous VAT-repayment-related disputes each year in Sweden and CJEU case law, regarding the placement of the burden of proof, will be relevant in many of those disputes.

In conclusion, our analysis reveals that Swedish CFI are unlikely to cite specific CJEU decisions because the CoP have cited them—in the overwhelming majority of cases a CoP reference has no measurable impact on the lower courts—and when there is a significant overlap it seems attributable to the fact that the type of dispute or the legal questions concerned is a common one, like VAT.[53]

5.3. Cite the Citation: Influence by Replacement

The findings above support the conclusion that CJEU case law citation overlap between Swedish CFI and CoP is quite limited. The most likely explanation for our findings is that while both CFI and CoP encounter EU law issues and cite CJEU case law, they engage with EU law on quite different matters.

If there is no national precedent on how to resolve an EU-related legal matter, a lower-court judge has no other option than to engage directly with original EU sources, including CJEU case law. However, if the national courts of precedent have delivered an opinion on the matter at hand, we expect that the lower-court judge would be inclined to at least consider the higher court's interpretation and arguments since the judge (i) is both accustomed and expected to follow the higher court's decision on non-EU-law-related matters, (ii) wishes to avoid having his or her decision overturned on appeal, and (iii) can save time (which is in short supply in the lower courts) researching EU law independently and *de novo*.

For example, imagine a Swedish court of first instance faced with a dispute where there is relevant CJEU case law and that this case law has been discussed in the published decisions of one of the Swedish courts of precedent. As concluded above, it is rare that the lower court judge reads the

---

[50] Case 268/83 *Rompelman and Rompelman-Van Deelen v Minister van Financiën*, EU:C:1985:74.

[51] See, e.g., RÅ 2002 note 26.

[52] *Rompelman*, para 24. See, e.g., RÅ 2004 ref 112; RÅ 2010 ref 98; HFD 2013 ref 12. There are also many examples from the lower Swedish courts.

[53] Besides *Graphic Procédé* and *Rompelman*, this is also the case with, e.g., Case C-320/88 *Staatssecretaris van Financiën v Shipping and Forwarding Enterprise Safe BV*, EU:C:1990:61 (third most frequently cited by CFI).

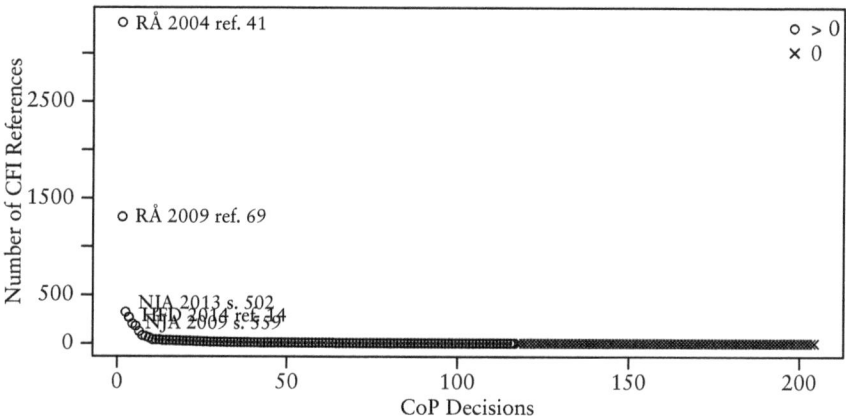

Figure 5.6: CFI References to CoP Decisions Citing EU Court Decisions

higher court's decision and cites the same or similar CJEU court decisions. However, it is possible that the lower court judge regards the higher court's decision as such a strong source of law on the issue and relies on the higher decision, by itself or along with relevant CJEU case law.

While we can understand and sympathise with a lower court judge who chooses the latter approach, it is still problematic. The approach is not entirely dissimilar to a researcher using secondary sources and carries the same potential problems; the secondary sources may have misinterpreted the primary sources and there may be new primary sources that have not been considered in the secondary sources.

We use a multi-step approach to examine whether Swedish CFI have such tendencies. We begin by identifying all Swedish CoP decisions that contain references to CJEU case law.[54] We then identify and isolate CFI decisions that cite those EU-related CoP decisions.[55] This information is interesting in itself as it shows us which EU-related CoP decisions may have had the greatest impact on the interpretation of EU law by the CFI.[56]

Figure 5.6 demonstrates that most EU-related CoP decisions are of very limited use in lower courts: 43 per cent of them have never been cited by the CFI in the period studied,[57] and most others were only cited rarely. However, a handful of CoP decisions have been cited very frequently. The clear leader is RÅ 2004 ref 41, concerning patient mobility and free movement, with 3,339 references in the CFI dataset. The runner-up is RÅ 2009 ref 69, with 1,303 references, concerning public procurement. These two judgments

---

[54] The data considered contains 205 such CoP decisions.
[55] The data considered contains 6,235 such CFI decisions.
[56] See Figure 5.6 above.
[57] 88 decisions.

are in a league of their own, with the third most cited case far behind with 317 references. This is NJA 2013 s 502, where the Swedish Supreme Court reversed its position on *ne bis in idem* and tax surcharges following the *Åkerberg Fransson* case from the CJEU.[58] The list of frequently cited judgments also include HFD 2014 ref 14, concerning tax assessment and value added tax,[59] and NJA 2009 s 559, concerning the expulsion of EU citizens due to criminal activity, with 263 and 198 references respectively.

The fact that EU-related CoP judgments follow a power law distribution in the CFI dataset, where a few judgments are cited extensively and most judgments are practically never used, is not surprising in itself, since practically all citation networks display this tendency.[60] However, it is interesting from the perspective of CoP as gatekeepers. The fact that some CoP judgments are cited extensively indicates that the highest courts indeed have a significant potential as gatekeepers for lower courts in EU-related matters. However, this influence is limited to a handful of cases, whereas most CoP judgments are never or very rarely cited by the CFI. It is reasonable to assume that the leading cases, discussed above, deal with EU issues that frequently arise in lower courts, while many of the other judgments deal with more specific issues. Examples of this include RÅ 2001 ref 69, concerning VAT and breakfast served at hotels, and NJA 2004 s 662, concerning the EEA agreement and state liability.

As a next step, we examine whether CFI judgments citing a particular EU-related CoP decision also include references to CJEU case law. We refer to this as the CoP decision's co-reference rate. If every CFI decision that contains a reference to the CoP decision also contains references to CJEU case law, the co-reference rate is 100 per cent. Conversely, if none of the CFI decisions citing the CoP decision cite any CJEU case law, the co-reference rate is 0 per cent. The examination of the co-reference rate includes all CJEU case law, not just the judgment or judgments cited by the CoP, as it is possible that the CFI might find other CJEU cases relevant.

We would expect most CoP decisions to have quite a high co-reference rate. Since the CFI decisions cite CoP decisions citing CJEU case law, it is reasonable to assume that there is relevant CJEU case law that the CFI could cite in its judgment[61] and as Union courts of ordinary jurisdiction we expect

---

[58] Case C-617/10 *Åklagaren v Hans Åkerberg Fransson*, EU:C:2013:105.

[59] This forms part of the extensive litigation concerning VAT on printing services, in the wake of the above-mentioned *Graphic Procédé* case from the CJEU. For a comment see, e.g., U Hedström, 'HFD:s beslut om att efterbeskatta kunder i de s.k. tryckerimomsmålen—ändring av praxis?' (2014) *Skattenytt* 245.

[60] In fact, this holds true for most complex networks, R Albert and AL Barabási, 'Statistical Mechanics of Complex Networks' (2004) 74 *Review of Modern Physics* 47, 49, and the European Court of Justice, M Derlén and J Lindholm, 'Peek-a-boo, It's a Case-Law System! Comparing the European Court of Justice and the United States Supreme Court from a Network Perspective' (2017) 18 *German Law Journal* 647.

[61] This is not necessarily true in every individual case. The CoP decision may contain statements of law that are entirely unrelated to EU law and it is possible that the CFI is citing that part. It is, therefore, important to manually confirm what is being cited.

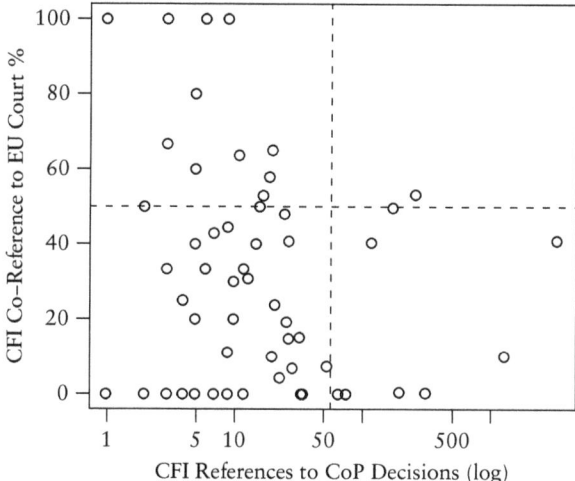

Figure 5.7: CFI References to EU-Related CoP Decisions

the CFI to cite such case law independently and faithfully. However, as illustrated by Figure 5.7, this hypothesis does not hold true.

In fact, nearly half of the relevant CFI judgments[62] only cite the Swedish CoP decisions and no CJEU judgments. This is a surprisingly high number. However, we again see significant differences between individual CoP decisions. For some CoP judgments, the co-reference rate is high, even as high as 100 per cent. To find examples of the latter, we have to go to judgments with relatively few CFI citations. This includes HFD 2011 ref 28, concerning value added tax on sailboats, RÅ 2006 ref 38, concerning investment funds and HFD 2012 ref 29, concerning public service contracts, all with between 6 and 9 references. Among CoP judgments with a higher number of citations from CFI, we find a co-reference rate of about 50 per cent or higher. This includes RÅ 2009 ref 43 (co-reference rate 51 per cent) and RÅ 2008 ref 35 (co-reference rate 43 per cent), both concerning public procurement and the right to withdraw an invitation to tender. When it comes to the top five judgments mentioned above, HFD 2014 ref 14 has a co-reference rate of 53 per cent and RÅ 2004 ref 41 scores very high, with 79 per cent.

However, the vast majority of judgments have a very low co-reference rate. This includes two of the judgments mentioned above, NJA 2013 s 502 and NJA 2009 s 559, where the co-reference rate is close to zero.[63] RÅ 2009 ref 69, the second most cited EU-related CoP decision, also scores low on the co-reference scale, with about 11 per cent.

---

[62] 3,031 of 6,236 CFI decisions.
[63] 1/317 (or 0.3%) and 1/198 (or 0.5%) respectively.

How can the low co-reference rate be explained? We identify three possible explanations for the absence of separate references to CJEU case law by the CFI. First, and most obviously, the CFI could be citing the CoP judgments for reasons entirely unrelated to EU law. This would seem to hold true at least for certain CoP cases. For example, the above-mentioned case NJA 2009 s 559 clearly includes non-EU related issues. As part of its judgment, the Supreme Court discussed both the penalty for pickpocketing and expulsion of EU citizens convicted of crimes. A number of CFI cases cite the judgment on the issue regarding the relevant penalty for pickpocketing, without any EU law dimension.[64] However, NJA 2009 s 559 is also used by lower courts regarding the expulsion of EU citizens and the Citizens' Rights Directive[65] with no references to CJEU case law.[66]

Second, the CFI could be referring to a discussion concerning national law that is fundamentally related to EU law. In such cases an underlying EU law question is resolved by the higher court, based on CJEU case law, and the lower courts see no need to discuss said case law or EU law dimension themselves. For example, in RÅ 2009 ref 69, mentioned above, the Supreme Administrative Court discussed the respective role of the courts and the parties in public procurement proceedings, more specifically whether the court could take into consideration circumstances not discussed by the parties. The court observed that the CJEU had left this issue to be decided by the procedural rules of the Member States,[67] and continued to discuss how the Swedish rules on administrative procedure should be applied regarding public procurement. Based on this discussion, the Supreme Administrative Court concluded that the party claiming that an error had been committed also had the responsibility to clearly explain the circumstances on which he or she based the complaint. This conclusion has been cited, practically verbatim, by lower administrative courts in many public procurement cases. Typically, the lower court will—so to speak—jump straight to the conclusion of the Supreme Administrative Court and not discuss the underlying judgment of the CJEU, thus implicitly accepting the CoP interpretation of

---

[64] See, e.g., Stockholms tingsrätt's judgment in case number B 8550-13, 1 July 2013; Kalmar tingsrätt's judgment in case number B 4271-12, 17 April 2013; Malmö tingsrätt's judgment in case number B 1688-14, 13 March 2014.

[65] Directive 2004/38/EC of the European Parliament and of the Council of 29 April 2004 on the right of citizens of the EU and their family members to move and reside freely within the territory of the Member States amending Regulation (EEC) No 1612/68 and repealing Directives 64/221/EEC, 68/360/EEC, 72/194/EEC, 73/148/EEC, 75/34/EEC, 75/35/EEC, 90/364/EEC, 90/365/EEC and 93/96/EEC, OJ L 158, 30.4.2004, pp 77–123.

[66] See, e.g., Uddevalla tingsrätt's judgment in case number B 865-14, 8 April 2014; Stockholm's tingsrätt's judgment in case number B 2018-15, 2 April 2015; Attunda tingsrätt's judgment in case number B 828-15, 24 March 2015.

[67] Case C-315/01 *Gesellschaft für Abfallentsorgungs-Technik GmbH (GAT) v Österreichische Autobahnen und Schnellstraßen AG (ÖSAG)*, EU:C:2003:360.

that judgment.[68] Cases such as RÅ 2009 ref 69 contain both EU and national law elements, but unlike NJA 2009 s 559, these cannot be separated from each other. The EU law issue is foundational and decides the ambit of the discussion about Swedish administrative procedural law. While it makes sense for lower courts to refer to the conclusion of the Supreme Administrative Court when it comes to the issue of how the Swedish rules on administrative procedure should be applied regarding public procurement, the absence of references to the underlying CJEU judgment could hide the EU law dimension.

Thirdly, and most controversially, the lower court could in fact be citing the citation (i.e. referring only to the CoP judgment even for the EU law issue). An example of this is HFD 2014 ref 14, discussed above, concerning tax assessment and value added tax. Here, the Supreme Administrative Court decided on the consequences of the *Graphic Procédé* judgment of the CJEU, according to which printed products should be assigned a 6 per cent VAT-rate instead of the standard 25 per cent. The Supreme Administrative Court discussed several judgments of the CJEU before concluding that the Swedish Revenue Service had the right to alter previous decisions regarding VAT on printing services, for suppliers and buyers of the services alike. HFD 2014 ref 14 has been cited extensively by lower administrative courts, but they have taken different approaches to the use of CJEU case law. Several of the CFI judgments mention some CJEU case law, at least the foundational decision in *Graphic Procédé*.[69] However, other CFI judgments obscure the EU dimension by only referring to Swedish legislation and the CoP judgment as if no EU dimension existed.[70] This approach is sometimes adopted even if the plaintiff explicitly makes reference to the EU principles of legal

---

[68] See, among many others, Förvaltningsrätten i Stockholm's judgment in case number 9957-15, 26 August 2015; Förvaltningsrätten i Stockholm's judgment in case number 12213-15, 1 July 2015; Förvaltningsrätten i Stockholm's judgment in case number 26716-13, 4 February 2014; Förvaltningsrätten i Stockholm's judgment in case number 1944-15, 10 April 2015; Förvaltningsrätten i Stockholm's judgment in case number 5747-15, 8 May 2015; Förvaltningsrätten i Uppsala's judgment in case number 3249-13E, 15 August 2013; Förvaltningsrätten i Stockholm's judgment in case number 7796-14, 7 July 2014; Förvaltningsrätten i Härnösand's judgment in case number 1337-14E, 1338-14E and 1339-14E, 11 July 2014; Förvaltningsrätten i Uppsala's judgment in case number 5493-13E, 28 March 2014.

[69] As noted above, the co-reference rate for HFD 2014 ref 14 is about 53%. For examples of administrative CFI judgments referring to HFD 2014 ref 14 as well as CJEU case law, see, e.g., Förvaltningsrätten i Malmö's judgment in case number 3403-13, 23 September 2014; Förvaltningsrätten i Malmö's judgment in case number 12786-13, 30 July 2014; Förvaltningsrätten i Malmö's judgment in case number 5243-13, 11 July 2014; Förvaltningsrätten i Linköping's judgment in case number 8211-11, 5 December 2014; Förvaltningsrätten i Linköping's judgment in case number 8617-13, 11 December 2014; Förvaltningsrätten i Karlstad's judgment in case number 1232-14 and 4739-14, 20 May 2015.

[70] See, e.g., Förvaltningsrätten i Luleå's judgment in case number 1885-13, 4 September 2014; Förvaltningsrätten i Falun's judgment in case number 303-15, 18 December 2015; Förvaltningsrätten i Stockholm's judgment in case number 587-13 and 594-13, 11 June 2015.

certainty and legitimate expectations.[71] In these cases the CFI are clearly citing the citation, resolving the issues as if they were solely domestic and obscuring the EU law dimension.

It is not possible to quantify how many of the CFI references concern internal rather than EU dimensions in the underlying CoP judgment (i.e. scenario 1 above). However, it seems unlikely that this could serve as a general explanation for the low co-reference rate. Even if the CoP judgments contain issues unrelated to EU law, we would still expect a significantly higher co-reference rate. It is reasonable to assume that in many situations, the lower court is, in fact, citing the citation—in other words referring only to the CoP judgment even for the EU law dimension (i.e. scenario 3 above). This is inherently problematic, as it obscures the EU law dimension and makes the CFI dependent on the interpretation of CJEU case law performed by the CoP.

6. CONCLUSIONS—IS THERE SOMETHING ROTTEN IN THE STATE OF SWEDEN?

The three tests used in this study suggest that the answer to whether Swedish CoP influence the application of CJEU case law by CFI is complicated, perhaps more so than one might initially imagine.

On the one hand, this study's findings suggest that, generally speaking, Swedish courts of first instance identify and apply relevant CJEU case law independent of whether this has been dealt with by Swedish CoP or not. This 'reference independence' is true regardless of how you measure it: the CFI never or rarely cites most CJEU court decisions cited by the CoP and most CJEU court decisions cited by CFI have never been cited by the CoP. Differently put, when viewed as a whole and when focusing on references to CJEU decisions, the Swedish CoP's influence as gatekeepers or filters appears quite marginal. This would seem to support the idea, championed by the CJEU, that all national courts, regardless of their position in the national legal order, are Union courts. Our findings seem to indicate that the CoP and CFI live in somewhat different worlds: the data shows that both are confronted by EU law-related issues, but differences in citation behaviour could be explained by the fact that they are not confronted by the same issues.

However, our study shows that when Swedish CFI have found and cited a CoP decision concerning an issue relating to EU law, they do not consistently consider relevant CJEU case law. Thus, the influence of the CoP on the CFI enforcement of CJEU law can be and is quite high in situations where they

---

[71] See, e.g., Förvaltningsrätten i Stockholm's judgment in case number 2438-15, 12 March 2015.

make decisions on matters of EU law that the CFI subsequently cite. This is highly surprising, even controversial, as it suggests that Swedish CFI have on some matters effectively replaced the primary source of law—CJEU case law—with an interpretation in a secondary source of law—a national CoP decision.

To put things in perspective, let us imagine that something similar occurred in a federal legal order, such as in the USA. In 1973, the United States Supreme Court famously declared in *Roe v Wade* that the US Constitution included a right to have an abortion.[72] Soon thereafter and explicitly on the basis of the US Supreme Court's decision in *Roe v Wade*, the Supreme Court of Minnesota concluded in *State v Hodgson* that the state of Minnesota was precluded from interfering with abortions.[73] Imagine if inferior Minnesota courts subsequently exclusively referred to *State v Hodgson* as the source for the right to have an abortion, completely disregarding *Roe v Wade*.

A possible, more nuanced, understanding of these findings is to admit that the interplay between national law and EU law is both important and complicated; that the CoP are the ultimate arbiters of matters of national law and interpreters of national law; and that this—perhaps inevitably and legitimately—gives them some influence over how the CFI apply and enforce case law-based EU law.

---

[72] 410 US 959, 93 S Ct 1409 (1973).
[73] 204 NW2d 199 (Minn 1973).

6

The Role of the Court in Limiting National Policy-Making

Requiring Safeguards against the Arbitrary Use of Discretion

ANGELICA ERICSSON

1. INTRODUCTION

IN A LEGAL order like that of the EU, determining how various issues should be regulated is an intrinsically delicate task. Regulation is generally produced both at a central and a decentralised level, according to the federalist principle of subsidiarity. However, it may be that there are no central EU-level rules that specifically regulate a given legal issue, but that this issue still falls within the realm of the (admittedly quite elusive) 'scope of EU law'. One of the main objectives of this chapter is to explore what role the Court of Justice of the European Union[1] plays in this specific type of situation. How does it engage in the determination of how such an issue can be regulated by the national policy-maker?

Since the CJEU has been entrusted with an interpretative monopoly with regard to the meaning of EU law, this court is actually liable to determine the limits of national policy-making both in the context of preliminary ruling procedures and in the context of infringement proceedings brought by the Commission. Thus, the Court is routinely called upon to issue authoritative interpretations in the ambivalent area where the EU policy-maker has not specifically regulated an issue but where EU law still imposes itself—notably, but not exclusively, through the Treaty provisions on free movement.[2] This can be a rather sensitive task where the Court has to determine the effects

---

[1] Hereafter the 'CJEU' or simply the 'Court'.

[2] Also the existence of EU secondary legislation can sometimes bring an issue within the scope of EU law, even if that legislation does not itself regulate it (e.g. when a Member State enacts enforcement measures connected to the said legislation).

of the relevant EU law in the face of strong national interests concerning a given policy area. In fact, due to the broad scope of application of the Treaty rules, there is hardly any area of socio-economic life that can escape the application of these rules.[3]

The exploration carried out in this chapter will, therefore, not focus on a particular policy area but will instead home in on certain standards employed by the Court when performing its task. Special attention will be given to a number of instances where the CJEU has assessed national regulation with reference to what you might call 'safeguards against the arbitrary use of discretion'.

However, before addressing the appearance of these standards in the Court's case law, a brief theoretical discussion on the role of the Court in relation to national policy-making is provided in section 2. The discussion in this section, which touches upon various claims about the degree of activism that can be ascribed to the CJEU, will serve as a basis for assessing the different tools of judicial review that the Court has made use of when devising limits to the Member States' policy-making powers. Moreover, section 3 provides some insights into the functioning of the proportionality assessment and its relationship with the occasional recognition of a national margin of appreciation in different policy areas. Describing what must be the most notorious tool of judicial review in internal market law; this section, however, mainly serves to provide a context to section 4. Section 4, which in truth constitutes the heart of this chapter, contains a concrete examination of how the Court has limited national policy-making by requiring safeguards against the arbitrary use of discretion. These safeguards are split into different categories and examined in relation to the proportionality assessment. Lastly, some conclusions are drawn concerning the role which the Court is effectively playing when it requires such safeguards.

2. IS IT ACTIVIST FOR THE COURT TO LIMIT NATIONAL POLICY-MAKING?

As an international court in a so-called *sui generis* legal order, there are no self-evident answers to the role that the CJEU should play in relation to national policy-making. It is therefore relevant to account for the different views on whether the Court, when it puts limits on national policy-making powers, acts in accordance with its role or oversteps its mandate.

Views on the merits of the very existence of an international court are divided. Arnull notes that such courts have been seen, by some,

---

[3] S de Vries, 'Safeguards and Opportunities for the Protection of Fundamental Rights within the EU Single Market' (2016) 1 *Europarättslig Tidskift* 69, 73.

as undemocratic and as a threat to the achievement of national policy objectives while others have praised them for raising the credibility of international commitments due to the increased probability of violations being detected and accurately labelled as non-compliance, thus maximising the long-term value of a multilateral agreement for all parties.[4]

In this regard, you may argue that it lies in the very nature of the common EU project that its accomplishment might validly impede the achievement of certain national policy objectives. However, the Member States would only allow limits to their policy-making, in the context of a multilateral agreement, if equivalent limits were effectively imposed on the others parties to this agreement. In this sense, the EU legal order, enforced by the CJEU, solves the 'prisoner's dilemma' facing national governments.[5] Hence, the CJEU has a crucial role to play in enforcing the limits on national policy-making which flow from the EU legal order, in the sense of ensuring the enforcement of a multilateral agreement.

Rest assured, however, that not everyone has appreciated the way the Court has gone about ensuring this enforcement. In fact, the CJEU has been said to have a 'pro-EU interpretative bias' and, hence, to favour the interpretative approach and outcome that enhances further integration.[6] Such a one-sided interpretative bias does not square easily with the principle of subsidiarity. In fact, as argued by Bogojević and Groussot, this principle should not only be taken into account as a tool of judicial review of EU positive actions, it 'should also be conceptualised as a tool of legal interpretation'.[7] This so-called 'covert subsidiarity' finds support in Article 1 in the Protocol (No 2) on the application of the principles of subsidiarity and proportionality, which states that each EU institution (including the Court) 'shall ensure constant respect for the principles of subsidiarity and proportionality, as laid down in Article 5 of the Treaty on European Union'.

In this respect, loud critical voices have been raised, accusing the Court of 'going wild' in the sense of being activist.[8] When used to describe a court, it should be noted that the word 'activist' generally constitutes an insult,

---

[4] A Arnull, 'Me and My Shadow: The European Court of Justice and the Disintegration of European Union Law' (2007) 31 *Fordham International Law Journal* 1174, 1175f.

[5] M Höreth 'The Least Dangerous Branch of European Governance? The European Court of Justice Under the Checks and Balances Doctrine' in M Dawson, B De Witte and E Muir, *Judicial Activism at the European Court of Justice* (Cheltenham, Edward Elgar Publishing, 2013) 37.

[6] M Bobek 'The Court of Justice of the European Union' in A Arnull and D Chalmers, *The Oxford Handbook of European Union Law* (Oxford, Oxford University Press, 2015) 151, 173.

[7] X Groussot and S Bogojević, 'Subsidiarity as a Principle of European Constitutional Law' in L Azoulai (ed), *The European Union as a Federal Order of Competences* (Oxford, Oxford University Press, 2014) 234.

[8] With Hjalte Rasmussen setting the tone.

depicting a 'court that has behaved improperly by straying beyond the limits of the judicial function, by misusing its powers'.[9]

In an attempt to evaluate whether the Court really is, as some critics claim, 'activist' in this sense, Arnull has assessed it in the light of certain phenomena which might expose a given court to such an epithet.[10] Among others, he dealt with the phenomenon of so-called 'judicial legislation' and the phenomenon of striking down arguably constitutional actions of other branches of government. As for claims of 'judicial legislation', Arnull concluded that the CJEU has indeed often been accused of seeking to achieve ends which should (according to the critics) have been left to the Union legislator or the Member States to decide, but that such accusations have rarely been based on a developed theory of where the limits of the judicial function are located.[11] On the other hand, he concluded that the Court is not normally criticised as 'activist' in the sense of striking down arguably constitutional actions of other branches of government.[12] However, it must be noted that Arnull, in this regard, only considered the actions of Union branches of government—not Member State branches of government.

When Lenaerts, in his capacity as the President of the Court, made a statement about the allegation that his institution was a 'politically driven catalyst for European integration', he firmly proclaimed that its role was to uphold the law, 'nothing less and nothing more'.[13]

This conception of the role of the Court might seem modest, but does not exclude significant consequences for national policy-making. In fact, it has been claimed that the Court acts as a 'constitutional adjudicator' every time it ensures that in the interpretation and application of the Treaties, the law is observed, in line with its obligation under Article 19(1) TEU.[14] This holds particularly true in relation to the judicial review of arguably constitutional actions of Member State branches of government, as this type of review always presupposes choices regarding the constitutional limits to State or public intervention.[15] Even if the Court is not itself competent to directly engage in a judicial review of national policy measures, its interpretation of EU law—combined with the principle of primacy—imposes, in practical

---

[9] A Arnull, 'Judicial Activism and the European Court of Justice: How should Academics Respond?' in M Dawson, B De Witte and E Muir, *Judicial Activism at the European Court of Justice* (Cheltenham, Edward Elgar Publishing, 2013) 215.

[10] ibid 216ff.

[11] ibid 217.

[12] ibid 216.

[13] In an interview with the *Financial Times*, published 22 November 2016. Available at www.ft.com.

[14] E Sharpston and G De Baere, 'The Court of Justice as a Constitutional Adjudicator' in A Arnull, C Barnard, M Dougan and E Spaventa (eds), *A Constitutional Order of States?* (Oxford, Hart Publishing, 2011) 124.

[15] M P Maduro, *We, the Court* (Oxford, Hart Publishing, 1998) 59.

terms, on the national courts to engage in such a review and draw all practical consequences from a finding of incompatibility with EU law. In particular, when the CJEU provides an interpretation of EU law in relation to a legal issue that is not specifically regulated by EU law, this interpretation translates into standards of judicial review of national measures—effectively limiting national policy-making.

The criticism concerning strong judicial review of arguably constitutional actions of other branches of government has traditionally been based on the so-called counter-majoritarian difficulty and the claim that judges (as opposed to democratically elected politicians) have no special insight into major substantive constitutional dilemmas.[16] Nevertheless, it is doubtful whether this criticism would carry the same force concerning the CJEU's role in the context of a judicial review of national policy measures. In this regard, Maduro has argued the following:

> Contrary to the traditional conception of judicial activism addressed to the protection of minorities against the democratic majority will, European judicial activism can better be described as majoritarian activism: promoting the rights and policies of the larger European community (the majority) against the 'selfish' or autonomous (depending on the point of view) decisions of national polities (the minorities).

Against the backdrop of these diverse proclamations concerning the role of the Court and whether this institution oversteps its boundaries, the following sections will examine more closely the tools that the Court develops in practice when it engages in the judicial review of national measures.

3. PROPORTIONALITY ASSESSMENT AND NATIONAL MARGIN OF APPRECIATION

Arguably the most important tool when it comes to a judicial review of national measures based on EU law is the proportionality assessment, which has been considered the 'crucial legal methodology of the contemporary era' and a 'key feature of post-war constitutional law'.[17] The structure of the proportionality assessment is generally divided into different prongs which are cumulative in nature. Hence, a national measure which restricts EU law can only be deemed proportional if it pursues a legitimate aim, is both appropriate and necessary (i.e. there are no less restrictive means) to achieve this aim, and is proportional in the strict sense. To conduct this assessment,

---

[16] A Arnull, 'Judicial Review in the European Union' in A Arnull and D Chalmers, *The Oxford Handbook of European Union Law* (Oxford, Oxford University Press, 2015) 376, 380.

[17] P-A Van Malleghem, *Proportionality and the Erosion of Formalism* (Doctoral thesis at the Faculty of Law of KU Leuven, 2016) 15 and 23.

you first have to establish precisely what the legitimate aim pursued is and how restrictive the measure to be assessed actually is. Otherwise, it is impossible to evaluate the proportionality and conduct the balancing which is inherent in this assessment.

As a tool of judicial review, the proportionality assessment allows the judiciary to take into account national interests (as external justifications) while ensuring, in a structured manner, that the national policy-maker is not unduly encroaching on relevant EU law. However, according to Azoulai, this is a framework in which national authorities (as opposed to the EU) are continuously forced to justify themselves with regard to the objectives of integration before a judicial body. He has also stated that, by finding 'individual public law rights' to flow from EU law, the Court has, systematically been able to subject all kinds of national public interests to a proportionality assessment.[18] In fact, according to the Court's case law, Member States must always exercise their policy-making power in compliance with EU law, even in policy areas which have not been conferred on the EU, such as those of direct taxation, criminal law, education, social protection or civil status.[19]

As has already been noted in the previous section, the Court has sometimes been charged with overstepping its mandate and going too far in assessing issues which are of a policy nature. A solution that has been proposed would be for it to accord a degree of deference to the national policy-maker, by granting a margin of appreciation.[20]

Petursson has concluded that a deferential approach, with reference to a margin of appreciation, is applied in EU law, but that more weight has been placed on the application of the proportionality principle of the Court, with or without references to deference doctrines.[21] In this regard, he has noted that authors generally place the EU margin of appreciation within the context of the proportionality assessment but that there are calls for the CJEU to use deferential judicial review in a clearer and more structured manner.[22]

With this in mind, it would probably be inappropriate to qualify the Court's case-by-case recognition of a national margin of appreciation as a self-standing tool of judicial review. Nevertheless, this recognition might conceptually be thought of as a 'tool modifier', in its relation to the proportionality assessment. This modifier would normally reduce the intensity of the judicial review, as it—at least in theory—would diminish the possibility

---

[18] L Azoulai, 'The European Court of Justice and the Duty to Respect Sensitive National Interests' in M Dawson, B De Witte and E Muir (eds), *Judicial Activism at the European Court of Justice* (Cheltenham, Edward Elgar Publishing, 2013) 169f.

[19] ibid 171.

[20] G T Petursson, *The Proportionality Principle as a Tool for Disintegration in EU Law* (Doctoral thesis at the Faculty of Law at the University of Lund, 2014) 114.

[21] ibid 191.

[22] ibid 189f.

for the judiciary to discredit the proportional nature of a given restrictive measure and, hence, to declare that the national policies encroach 'unduly' on existing EU law. Two clear examples of when the award of a margin of discretion actually seems to have resulted in a deferential judicial review are the judgments in the *Omega* case[23] and the *Perez and Gomez* case.[24] This type of deferential judicial review largely corresponds to the concept of 'covert subsidiarity', mentioned in section 2, and a broad understanding of judicial subsidiarity.[25]

It is, however, hard to determine the precise effects of this modifier, as the Court has stated that even if 'Member States have a broad discretion when choosing the measures capable of achieving the aims of [a certain legitimate] policy, ... that discretion may not have the effect of undermining the rights granted to individuals by the Treaty provisions in which their fundamental freedoms are enshrined.'[26]

4. SAFEGUARDS AGAINST THE ARBITRARY USE OF DISCRETION

Turning now to an alternative and less well-documented tool of judicial review that could become relevant in non-regulated areas where Member States have a broad discretion; 'safeguards against the arbitrary use of discretion'. The modest aim in this section is to showcase a selection of judgments where it appears that the outcome of the judicial review of national measures depend on the existence (or lack) of these safeguards.

To identify such safeguards against the arbitrary use of discretion, the case law of the CJEU has been scanned for instances where the Court seems to attach normative weight to the presence or absence of a 'systemic potential' for an unfettered disregard of EU law. It should be stressed that for the Court to find that such a potential exists, it does not have to be proven that a Member State has actually disregarded EU law or even that it would effectively be likely to do so. However, if the abovementioned safeguards are absent, a potential disregard of EU law would not be made visible and could, therefore, continue with impunity. It should be possible to identify a judgment where such safeguards are required when the CJEU, in essence, declares that a national regulatory measure under review can only be compatible with EU law if the surrounding structures are designed to preclude the occurrence of deviations from EU law through arbitrary decision-making.

---

[23] Case C-36/02 *Omega* [EU:C:2004:614].
[24] Cases C-570/07 and C-571/07 *Perez and Gomez* [EU:C:2010:300].
[25] X Groussot and S Bogojevic, 'Subsidiarity as a Principle of European Constitutional Law' in L Azoulai (ed), *The European Union as a Federal Order of Competences* (Oxford, Oxford University Press, 2014) 234.
[26] Case C-201/15 *AGET Iraklis* [EU:C:2016:972] para 81.

The following sub-sections will provide different categories of these safeguards against the arbitrary use of discretion and, to enable a better understanding of how and when the Court would require such safeguards; particular attention will be given to the specific context in which the Court has done so. Where in the Court's reasoning can you find such requirements and what is their relationship with the proportionality assessment?

4.1. Access to Judicial Remedy

The judiciary of any given legal order is usually entrusted with the mission to ensure that public power is not abused or exercised arbitrarily. Therefore, one obvious safeguard against an arbitrary exercise of national discretion would be the involvement of national courts in the control of this exercise. When individuals derive rights from EU law, the CJEU does indeed routinely require that there should be access to a national judicial remedy, even when no specific remedy is imposed by EU legislation and the Member States, therefore, enjoy institutional and procedural autonomy.[27] A variant of the following formula is routinely reiterated by the Court in these circumstances:

> ... in the absence of relevant [Union] rules it is for the domestic legal system of each Member State to designate the courts and tribunals having jurisdiction and to lay down the detailed procedural rules governing actions for safeguarding rights which individuals derive from [Union] law, provided, first, that such rules are not less favourable than those governing similar domestic actions (principle of equivalence) and, secondly, that they do not render in practice impossible or excessively difficult the exercise of rights conferred by [Union] law (principle of effectiveness) ...[28]

Moreover, if the national measure at issue constitutes an examination or authorisation procedure established by the national legislature in order to pursue a national protective aim, the Court has developed further requirements for the procedure that would precede the access to judicial remedy. Notably, in the *Dynamic Medien* case, the Court held that the examination procedure at hand must be 'readily accessible, can be completed within a reasonable period, and, if it leads to a refusal, the decision of refusal must be open to challenge before the courts'.[29] It can be noted that, due to these

---

[27] Even if the relevant piece of secondary EU legislation does not require access to a judicial remedy, it could certainly be argued that it is generally required by primary EU law, through Article 19(1) TEU and Article 47 of the Charter of Fundamental Rights of the European Union (the 'Charter'). In this sense, the Court could not reasonably be accused of being 'activist', in the sense of 'judicial legislation', when requiring that EU rights should be legally enforceable within the national legal orders.

[28] eg Case C-55/06 *Arcor* [EU:C:2008:244] para 166.

[29] Case C-244/06 *Dynamic Medien* [EU:C:2008:85] para 50.

additional requirements, both the effective access to a judicial control of the discretion exercised in the examination procedure, as well as the timely manner in with the judge will be able to exercise this control, are ensured.

As for the context of these requirements in the *Dynamic Medien* case, the Court announces them right at the end of its reasoning and it is somewhat unclear if they are to be regarded as self-standing imperatives or as an element of the necessity prong of the proportionality assessment.

4.2. Legal Certainty and Foreseeability of a Regulatory Framework

Much like access to a judicial remedy, the principle of legal certainty is intrinsically linked with the concept of the rule of law (as opposed to an arbitrary rule of man). In EU law, the principle of legal certainty 'requires in particular that rules involving negative consequences for individuals should be clear and precise and their application predictable for those subject to them'.[30] It follows from this definition of the principle of legal certainty that its aim is to ensure that rules are foreseeable for the individual who is subjected to them.

The importance which the CJEU attaches to such foreseeability is apparent in its judgment in the *Laval* case. In this judgment, the CJEU found the national regulatory framework to be 'characterised by a lack of provisions, of any kind, which are sufficiently precise and accessible that they do not render it impossible or excessively difficult in practice for [a foreign service provider] to determine the obligations with which it is required to comply as regards minimum pay' and thereby deemed it to be unjustifiable under EU law.[31]

As for the context of this firm conclusion by the Court, it can be found right at the end of the judgment. Without directly relating to a specific prong of the proportionality assessment, this conclusion might be read, in light of the foregoing point, as if the regulatory framework could not be deemed to be 'appropriate means' by which a Member State may legitimately require foreign undertakings to comply with their rules on minimum pay and, therefore, could not be justified in the light of the public interest objective at hand.

Another particularly interesting judgment with regard to legal certainty and foreseeability, which deserves to be treated in some detail, is the one handed down by the Court's Grand Chamber in the *AGET Iraklis* case.[32] This case concerned a Greek regulation imposing a framework on the

---

[30] Case C-17/03 *VEMW* [EU:C:2005:362] para 80.
[31] Case C-341/05 *Laval* [EU:C:2007:809], para 110.
[32] Case C-201/15 *AGET Iraklis* [EU:C:2016:972].

ability for undertakings to effectuate collective redundancies. According to the contested regulatory provision, a national authority could, by reasoned decision, after taking account of the documents in the file and 'assessing the conditions in the labour market, the situation of the undertaking and the interests of the national economy', decide not to authorise some or all of the projected redundancies.[33]

The Court assessed this provision both in relation to the freedom of establishment, enshrined in Article 49 TFEU, and in relation to the freedom to conduct a business, enshrined in Article 16 of the Charter. In light of the broad discretion that Member States enjoy when choosing the measures capable of achieving the aims of their social policy, the Court concludes that the establishment of a framework governing the circumstances in which collective redundancies may be effectuated is capable of complying with the mentioned provisions of EU primary law.[34]

So far, the Court keeps a rather deferential stance; accepting, in principle, the national policy choices at hand. However, towards the end of its judgment, it declares that 'it must be established whether the particular detailed rules [of the contested national provision]—and especially the three criteria which the competent public authority is called upon to take into account for the purpose of deciding whether it opposes collective redundancies— are such as to ensure that [this provision in fact complies with the relevant requirements of EU law]'.[35] It seems like the Court views these criteria as the surrounding structures that should limit arbitrariness. When assessing them, the Court first declares that the criterion of 'interests of the national economy' cannot be accepted, as it is linked to an economic aim, and then moves on to conclude that the other two criteria, namely the 'situation of the undertaking' and the 'conditions in the labour market', are formulated in terms which are too general and imprecise.[36] In a decisively worded paragraph, the Court draws the following conclusion about the lack of legal certainty in the national legislation:

> Even though the [contested national provision] states that the power not to authorise collective redundancies ... must be exercised by analysing the documents in the file, while taking account of the situation of the undertaking and the conditions in the labour market, and must result in a reasoned decision, it is clear that, *in the absence of details of the particular circumstances in which the power in question may be exercised*, the employers concerned do not know in what specific objective circumstances that power may be applied, as the situations allowing its exercise are potentially numerous, undetermined and indeterminable and leave the authority concerned a broad discretion that is difficult to review. Such criteria which are not precise and are not therefore founded on objective, verifiable conditions go

---

[33] ibid para 10.
[34] Case C-201/15 *AGET Iraklis* [EU:C:2016:972] paras 81, 93 and 94.
[35] ibid, para 95.
[36] ibid, paras 96–99.

beyond what is necessary in order to attain the objectives stated and cannot therefore satisfy the requirements of the principle of proportionality ...[37]

In relation to the requirement of access to a judicial remedy (see above), the Court states the following:

> ... whilst the fact that the exercise of such a power of opposition may be reviewed by the national courts is necessary for the protection of undertakings in the light of the application of the rules on freedom of establishment, it cannot, however, suffice on its own to make good the incompatibility with those rules of the two aforementioned assessment criteria [since] the legislation concerned also fails to provide the national courts with criteria that are sufficiently precise to enable them to review the way in which the administrative authority exercises its discretion ...[38]

As can be deducted from these two paragraphs of the judgment in the *AGET Iraklis* case, national authorisation/opposition schemes, which need to be justified in relation to the EU fundamental freedoms, should be bestowed with a whole cast of safeguards against an arbitrary use of discretion. Even if the national authority, as in this case, is obliged to give reasons to substantiate its decision and this decision is subject to a judicial control, the Court does not seem to be satisfied that this authority's use of its discretion could be effectively monitored. In fact, when the Court states that the factual situations covered by the general and imprecise criteria are 'potentially numerous, undetermined and indeterminable and leave the authority concerned a broad discretion that is difficult to review', it signals both a lack of foreseeability for the person wishing to enforce her EU rights and a fatal problem regarding the possibility of subjecting the national authority's decisions to an effective judicial control.

In this judgment, the Court squarely positions its reasoning about the lack of underlying objective, verifiable conditions within the necessity prong of its proportionality assessment. An interesting point to note when comparing the different parts of this judgment is that the Court insists on the fact that a framework for opposing collective redundancies would have been deemed necessary and proportionate, had it not been for the lack of safeguards against the arbitrary use of national discretion. It can, therefore, safely be concluded that the lack of these safeguards was decisive when the Court reached its judgment in this case.

4.3. Decision-making Structures Free from Vested Interests

Whereas the safeguards presented in the two sub-sections above concerned the quality of regulatory frameworks and the access to administrative or

---

[37] ibid, para 100 (emphasis added).
[38] ibid, para 101.

judicial procedures, safeguards against the arbitrary use of discretion may also concern the actual structuring of the national delegation of decision-making power. In the area of the general prohibition of public distortion of competition, two cases concerning a Member State-induced conflict of interest serve as relevant examples of the requirement that decision-making structures should be kept free from vested interests.

In the *ERT* case, the CJEU concluded that the coupling of exclusive rights, both to transmit and to retransmit television broadcastings, was incompatible with Union law, when it was liable to create an abusive behaviour by the monopoly holder.[39] In other words, the mere probability of induced abuse of a dominant position is enough for the granting of exclusive rights to be condemnable in the light of Union law.[40] In line with the requirements for the other safeguards, the part of the *ERT* judgment which examines the structural propensity for arbitrariness concludes the Court's treatment of the question at hand (the rules on competition).

In the *MOTOE* case, an organisation had been given the administrative power to limit access to a market in which it itself operated, thereby placing this organisation at an obvious advantage over its competitors—in the sense that it might prevent the participation of competitors but never have its own participation prevented.[41] At the very end of the judgment, the CJEU put particular focus on the fact that the administrative power had been transferred without being subject to 'restrictions, obligations and review' which could lead it 'to distort competition by favouring events which it organises or those in whose organisation it participates'.[42]

The requirement for safeguards against the arbitrary use of discretion resulting from these two cases is clearly a self-standing requirement, as there is no mention of a proportionality assessment in this context.

5. CONCLUSION

What can be deducted from the selection of judgments presented above concerning the Court's role in limiting national policy-making in areas which have not been specifically regulated by the EU? Does the fact that the Court, in a variety of different cases, seems to require safeguards against the arbitrary use of discretion have any significance in this regard?

Firstly, it can be concluded that the Court certainly does not shy away from its mission of ensuring the enforcement of the multilateral agreement

---

[39] Case C-260/89 *ERT* [EU:C:1991:254] para 37.
[40] P Slot, 'Rättsutlåtande om betydelsen av EG:statsstödsregler och konkurrensrätt för svensk bostadsmarknad och hyreslagstiftning', *EU, allmännyttan och hyrorna, Bilagor*, SOU 2008:38, 74.
[41] Case C-49/07 *MOTOE* [EU:C:2008:376] para 51.
[42] ibid, paras 52–53.

that has evolved into the EU legal order. You might even question whether its demands for such safeguards may provoke critics to call it out as being an 'activist' court (again). Could these demands qualify as a product of so-called 'judicial legislation'? If you consider that the resulting limits on national policy-making would require an action by the EU legislator, the Court has indeed been activist in developing these demands. It should be noted that none of them (with the obvious exception of the right to an effective judicial remedy) can be found in EU primary or secondary law. However, if you adhere to Maduro's take on the analytical framework of institutional choice and his emphasis on the 'majoritarian approach' of the CJEU, you might claim that the Court acted entirely within the limits of its judicial function. In fact, one of the justifications for this 'majoritarian approach' is the underlying suspicion that the Member State will have a natural tendency to favour the interests of its own citizens (effectively con-stituting its electorate and the legitimating force of its democracy), rather than taking account of the interests of other EU citizens. Subsequently, if you already consider arbitrary decision-making to be undesirable in the individual's own national context (where she is at least part of the elector-ate), it is not hard to understand why it would be even more undesirable in a federal system. If it could, thereby, be established that it is actually highly appropriate for the CJEU to require safeguards against the arbitrary use of national discretion, it could not validly be taunted as 'activist' when in fact it would only be acting within its mandate.[43]

Secondly, with regard to the claims that the Court should, preferably in a structured and clear manner, take the principle of subsidiarity into account as a tool of interpretation to engage in deferential judicial review of national measures, it is possible to see the requirements for safeguards against the arbitrary use of discretion as a move in this direction. Already the Court's occasional recognition of a margin of appreciation for Member States in certain policy areas has the potential to modify the proportionality assess-ment in order to accommodate the so-called 'covert subsidiarity' to a greater extent. Recognising a greater margin of appreciation should, in principle, translate into fewer limits on national policy-making. I would argue that when the Court requires safeguards against the arbitrary use of discretion, it is able to accommodate this 'covert subsidiarity' to an even greater extent. Even if the demands for safeguards might be perceived as an invasive judi-cial review (in the sense that the CJEU would make a strong statement about the unjustifiable nature of the national structure, when such safeguards are lacking), the Court could actually leave the core ambitions of national

---

[43] Such an understanding of the role of the Court and of its demands for safeguards against the arbitrary use of discretion could even be used as an explanatory model to give a more nuances view on certain (by no means all) of the cases where the Court has been criticised for being too activist. See, A Ericsson, 'The Many (Mis)readings of the Laval Case' (2016) 1 *Europarättslig Tidskrift* 113.

policy-making untouched. To make my point clear; the Court is not limiting a Member State from pursuing a progressive health plan when it requires the healthcare authorisation scheme to be based on objectively verifiable criteria (the substance of the criteria is left to the Member State), it merely restricts the ways to structure such a health plan. This tool of judicial review could leave many doors open for the national policy-maker, but would force her to carefully consider which combination of safeguards to put in place to ensure that the measure will not be deemed to harbour any potential for arbitrariness.

Thirdly, the way in which the Court has introduced its demands for safeguards against the arbitrary use of discretion, as showcased above, can hardly be qualified as a 'structured and clear manner'. Granted, a certain coherence can be attributed to the fact that these demands are most often found close towards the end of the Court's legal reasoning and that they seem to carry a decisive normative weight, in the sense that the absence of the such safeguards would most likely lead to the conclusion that the national measure is incompatible with EU law. However, the Court does not seem to have put any greater effort into conceptualising these demands. Indeed, it is not even clear whether they should be seen as a part of the proportionality assessment (and if so, under which prong) or perceived as a completely independent imperative. Hettne has concluded that, since these procedural and structural guarantees have been applied in a case-sensitive manner, they cannot be seen exclusively as an aspect of proportionality.[44] In this regard, Prechal has argued convincingly that, even if guarantees such as those regarding administrative and judicial procedure have often been formulated in the context of the proportionality assessment, these guarantees do not share the balancing rationale of this assessment and could legitimately be treated as a separate tool of judicial review.[45]

Lastly, regardless of whether the demands for safeguards against the arbitrary use of discretion should be viewed as a part of the proportionality assessment or as a separate tool of judicial review, these demands have the potential of becoming a workable tool for EU judicial review—one which could be readily usable by the national judiciaries. A national judge should reasonably, if she finds that a national measure, which falls within the scope of EU law, is not accompanied by appropriate safeguards against arbitrary decision-making, feel confident to set aside such a measure on the basis of a EU law. However, for such a tool of judicial review to be truly workable on a more general level, this new acquaintance needs to become far more familiar.

---

[44] J Hettne, 'Administrative Law as a Key to Market Integration?' in P Cardonnel, A Rosas and N Wahl (eds), *Constitutionalising the EU Judicial System—Essays in Honor of Pernilla Lindh* (Oxford, Hart Publishing, 2012) 164.

[45] S Prechal, 'Free Movement and Procedural Requirements: Proportionality Reconsidered' (2008) 3 *Legal Issues of Economic Integration* 201.

7

Institutional Balance as Constitutional Dialogue

A Republican Paradigm for the EU

DESMOND JOHNSON*

1. INTRODUCTION: A REPUBLICAN PARADIGM OF NON-DOMINATION FOR THE EU

THE EU CONSTITUTIONAL order suffers from a legitimation deficit.[1] This chapter posits that the republican model of institutional balance as constitutional dialogue constructed here can diminish this deficit, by ensuring the exercise of public power in the EU is *balanced*. This constitutional model demands that individuals and collective societal forces—legal, political, economic, and cultural—are 'free and equal' to pursue their vision of the public good to achieve republican ideals. It promotes *ex-ante* and *ex-post* processes of a legal and political nature in different dialogical fora of contestation, negotiation, and reconciliation.

* This work is the outcome of ongoing discussions with many academic colleagues and friends. I am particularly grateful for the invaluable comments and constructive feedback from David Jenkins, Mikkel Jarle Christensen, Marina Lostal, Jeff Dahl, William Worster, Stefania Marassi, Ana Bobic, and Jacob Oberg. I would also like to thank all those who participated in the stimulating conference this volume is based on, particularly the editors of this volume, Mattias Derlén and Johan Lindholm. Furthermore, I express my gratitude to my Research Assistants, Asiyih Barker and Francesca Minetto. Finally, I would like to thank the University of Copenhagen, Faculty of Law and Max Planck Institute for Comparative Public and International Law in Heidelberg, for providing inspiring research environments that helped me further develop many of the ideas in this chapter.

[1] See, Lord and Magnette arguing that contestation and a plurality of views concerning the legitimacy of the EU may actually enhance, and not weaken, the overall legitimacy of the EU constitutional order: C Lord and P Magnette, 'E. Pluribus Unum? Creative Disagreement about Legitimacy in the EU' (2004) 42(1) *Journal of Common Market Studies* 183; P Craig, 'Integration, Democracy, and Legitimacy' in Craig and de Burca (eds) *The Evolution of EU Law* (Oxford, Oxford University Press, 2011) 13.

Questions concerning how to *balance* public power and individual and political self-determination within a constitutional order are universal.[2] Republican thought has been an essential strand of constitutionalism designed to achieve such a balance since antiquity.[3] The central tenets of republicanism include non-domination, non-arbitrariness, self-governance, pluralism, and the pursuit of the public good.[4] These essential elements of republicanism are designed to ensure limited government by preventing the arbitrary interference with individual and political self-determination by those that exercise public power.[5] Such a non-dominating republican paradigm aims to ensure an institutional balance that reconciles competing societal interests, legitimacy claims, and constitutional values while achieving the public good.

This chapter explores the case law of the Court of Justice of the European Union (CJEU) on institutional balance to investigate whether the EU constitutional order adheres to fundamental themes of republicanism and if this is desirable. Currently, the EU and its institutions exercise real 'coercive' and autonomous power through the adoption of binding acts and decisions that shape the balance between the exercising of public power and individual and political self-determination. The exercising of such power in the EU is subject to and limited by an array of different societal forces operating at different levels of governance. Compared with national constitutional orders, however, the Union system of decision-making processes and institutional, legal, and political structures and arrangements are complex and suffer from the perception of a democratic and accountable deficit.[6] Such widespread perceptions lead to deeply contentious debates concerning the legitimation of the EU constitutional order.[7] As shown in section 4, the case law of the CJEU on institutional balance is a paradigmatic example of such contestation.

Questions concerning the nature, role, and scope of the institutional balance are vital for the legitimation of the EU constitutional order. Such issues involve how public power is balanced and exercised within the EU and its Member States.[8] Ultimately, questions involving institutional balance inevitably arise because it fundamentally shapes the future of

---

[2] MJC Vile, *Constitutionalism and the Separation of Powers* (Liberty Fund, 1998); TA Aleinikoff, 'Constitutional Law in the Age of Balancing' (1987) 96(5) *The Yale Law Journal* 943; CR Farina, 'Statutory Interpretation and the Balance of Power in the Administrative State' (1989) 89(3) *Columbia Law Review* 452.

[3] P Pettit, *Republicanism: A Theory of Freedom and Government* (Oxford, Oxford University Press, 1997); CR Sunstein, 'Beyond the Republican Revival' (1988) 97 *Yale Law Journal* 1539.

[4] Civic Virtue is also a fundamental element of many republican theories, but beyond the scope of this chapter. MA Fitts, 'Look Before You Leap: Some Cautionary Notes on Civic Republicanism' (1988) 97(8) *The Yale Law Journal* 1651.

[5] See Pettit, *Republicanism* above n 3.

[6] A Follesdal and S Hix, 'Why There is a Democratic Deficit in the EU: A Response to Majone and Moravcsik' (2006) 44(3) *Journal of Common Market Studies* 533.

[7] G Majone, 'Europe's "Democratic Deficit": The Question of Standards' (1998) 4(1) *European Law Journal* 5.

[8] Y Devuyst, 'The European Union's Institutional Balance after the Treaty of Lisbon: Community Method and Democratic Deficit Reassessed' (2008) 39 *Georgetown Journal of International Law* 247.

the EU.[9] Accordingly, competing perspectives of the institutional balance are axiomatic. Such questions focus on the ubiquitous subject, *who governs* and how *best* to reconcile competing visions of the public good. Essentially, who has the *ultimate authority* to determine what the institutional balance is and explicate its role in the EU constitutional order? Such debates lead to the central question, whether and, if so, how a republican model of institutional balance as constitutional dialogue can add value to our understanding of the CJEU's position in shaping the institutional balance and its role in the EU constitutional order.

The structure proceeds in the following manner. First, the analysis traces the republican origins of the institutional balance, elucidates central tenets of the principle, and puts forth a republican model of institutional balance as constitutional dialogue. Second, it explores who has the ultimate authority to interpret and shape the institutional balance and its role in the EU constitutional order. Third, the analysis shifts to explore how the CJEU has created, applied, and interpreted the institutional balance to achieve the public good from its perspective. Finally, the analysis concludes that institutional balance is a product of multi-actor and interactive processes, not the sole terrain of any societal force within the EU.

2. INSTITUTIONAL BALANCE AS LEGITIMATE GOVERNMENT

Institutional balance rests on the notion that to achieve legitimate government, a constitutional order must have a balanced interaction between different societal forces. Accordingly, a central tenet of institutional balance is the continuous ambition to establish and promote a balanced interaction between societal forces that find solutions to constitutional conflicts. This demands constitutional actors operate on behalf of the public good rather than particular factional self-interests, linking institutional balance with republicanism.[10]

2.1. Core Tenets of Institutional Balance within the EU

The institutional balance is a fundamental characteristic of self-government and an essential constitutional norm in the EU that governs the relations between Union institutions.[11] Different actors have competing views concerning how public power is balanced and exercised in the EU. The discourse has traditionally focused on the relations between the actors in the

[9] L Cram, 'Introduction to Special Issue on the Institutional Balance and the Future of EU Governance: The Future of the Union and the Trap of the "Nirvana Fallacy"' (2002) 15(3) *Governance* 309.

[10] C Mouffe, 'Democratic Citizenship and the Political Community' in C Mouffe (ed) *Dimensions of Radical Democracy: Pluralism, Citizenship, Community* (New York, Verso, 1992) 225.

[11] AM Sbragia, 'Conclusion to Special Issue on the Institutional Balance and the Future of EU Governance: The Treaty of Nice, Institutional Balance, and Uncertainty' (2002) 15(3)

institutional triangle, the European Parliament, the Council, and the Commission, as well as the CJEU case law governing such interactions. Yet, institutional balance should be understood as a multi-level concept shaping relations beyond the seven Union institutions listed under Article 13.2 of the Treaty on the European Union (TEU).[12]

Since the EU is a multi-level system of governance, it is not only an arduous task to limit the scope of the concept to the seven Union institutions, but it is also undesirable. Institutional balance is shaped and influenced by a number of dialogical interactions: the relationship among Union institutions; the relationship between the EU and Member States; the relationship between the Member States and EU institutions; and the relationship between the Member States.[13] Additionally, since the EU is a multi-level polity that exercises 'real' public power, it shapes the balance between the exercise of public power and individual and political self-determination.[14] This means that the concept shapes relations between a broad array of multi-level actors including Union institutions, Member States, the peoples of Europe, and public and private interest groups operating in EU civil society.[15] From this viewpoint, institutional balance captures the multi-level nature of EU governance.

This understanding requires a clarification of the two distinct approaches of the institutional balance, one legal and one political.[16] As Jacqué explains, the legal approach concentrates on the formal Treaty provisions and the case law of the CJEU.[17] The political approach, however, is a broader and more dynamic understanding of the concept that incorporates formal law as well as soft law and governance processes that develop in constitutional practice and can be considered *extra-legal*.[18]

Governance 393; G De Búrca, 'The Institutional Development of the EU: A Constitutional Analysis' in P Craig and G de Búrca (eds), *European Union Law: An Evolutionary Perspective* (Oxford, Oxford University Press, 1999).

[12] See, Art 13.2 TEU which states: 'The Union's institutions shall be the European Parliament; the European Council; the Council; the European Commission, the Court of Justice of the European Union, the European Central Bank, and the Court of Auditors.' Consolidated Version of the Treaty on European Union [2012] OJ L 326/13.

[13] Extensive research concerning the relationship between the Member State Courts and CJEU has occurred. For an analysis focusing on the relationship between national and EU courts within the EU judiciary and the potential for lower national courts to complete their own independent examination of CJEU case law, see, Derlén and Lindholm, Chapter 5 in this volume.

[14] For a competing view, see M Chamon, 'The Institutional Balance, and Ill-Fated Principle of EU Law?' (2015) 21 *European Public Law* 371.

[15] S Smismans, 'The Constitutional Labelling of "The Democratic Life of the EU": Representative and Participatory Democracy' in A Føllesdal and L Dobson (eds), *Political Theory and the European Constitution* (Abingdon, Routledge, 2004), 122.

[16] JP Jacqué, 'Principle of Institutional Balance' (2004) 41 *The Common Market Law Review* 383.

[17] Ibid.

[18] S Smismans, 'Institutional Balance as Interest Representation: Some Reflections on Lenaerts and Verhoeven' in C Joerges and R Dehousse (eds), *Good Governance in Europe's Integrated Market* (Oxford, Oxford University Press, 2002); P Craig, 'Institutions, Powers, and Institutional Balance' in P Craig and G de Búrca, *The Evolution of EU Law* (Oxford, Oxford University Press, 2011), 41–85.

De Búrca famously details the challenges with the legal positivist approach in her 'critique of formal-legal constitutionalism'.[19] Similarly, commentators such as Craig, Smismans, and Curtin each argue that the positivist approach is both 'partial and misleading', reflecting the 'formal constitution' rather than the 'real' constitution.[20] To reflect constitutional reality, this republican model utilises the political dimension of institutional balance. This broader political understanding of institutional balance better captures the dynamism and the complex realities of EU governance.

2.2. Ongoing Contestation of Institutional Balance

Institutional balance is a republican mode of governance used to describe the constitutional and institutional structures, processes, practices, and decision-making apparatus within EU governance.[21] Institutional balance rests on the republican notion that the constitutional rules of the game are shaped and influenced by an array of different societal forces with different sources of legitimacy that compete and cooperate in search of the public good.[22] From this viewpoint, institutional balance demands that each of the different phases of EU governance have multiple actors that exercise public authority. Thus, it is based on a complex web of overlapping authority between different societal forces operating at multiple levels of governance. This captures the mutual interdependency, multi-functionality, pluralistic and overlapping system of shared constitutional authority in the EU that often operates in a heterarchical rather than hierarchical nature. Importantly, the institutional balance is continuously shaped and reshaped; it is not in a fixed state of affairs, but a dynamic concept. The institutional balance in the EU varies depending on the policy area, the decision-making procedure, and legal basis provided for in the Treaty. Accordingly, a single permanent institutional balance across all phases of EU governance does not exist.

---

[19] G de Búrca, 'The Institutional Development of the European Union: A Constitutional Analysis' in P Craig and G de Búrca (eds), *European Union Law: An Evolutionary Perspective* (Oxford, Oxford University Press, 1999) 61. For other accounts explaining that legal positivism is not capable of reflecting the complexities of EU constitutional reality, see, D Curtin, 'EU Constitution as Architecture: Separation of Powers in the Twenty-first Century' in De Regels en Het Spel: *Opstellen Over Recht, Filosofie, Literatuur en Geschiedenis Aangeboden aan Tom Eijsbouts* (The Hague, TMC Asser Press, 2011), 123–33.

[20] Ibid.

[21] G Majone, 'Delegation of Regulatory Powers in a Mixed Polity' (2002) 8(3) *European Law Journal* 319.

[22] As Burtt explains, perhaps *the* distinguishing feature of republicanism is the fundamental role it accords to political virtue, exemplified by the public good. S Burtt, 'The Good Citizen's Psyche: On the Psychology of Civic Virtue' (1990) 23(1) *Polity* 23.

3. THE REPUBLICAN MODEL OF INSTITUTIONAL BALANCE
AS CONSTITUTIONAL DIALOGUE

This republican model ties two strands of constitutional thought—institutional balance and constitutional dialogue—together in pursuit of the republican ideals linked with good governance.[23] The model concentrates on an essential element of constitutionalism—balance—that explores the relationship between the exercise of public power and self-determination. The republican understanding of balance recognises that in certain contexts, different societal forces must exercise public power and make decisions that may limit self-determination. Yet, a vital element from the republican perspective is that such actors must prevent the arbitrary interference with individual and political self-determination. This model understands that the arbitrary interference with individual and political self-determination is less likely to occur when multiple actors with different constitutional perspectives participate in each of the different phases of public power—law-making, executing, interpreting, and regulating. For these reasons, normative aims linked with republican ideals are particularly appealing for the multi-level system of EU governance. The question remains, however, whether the EU realises these republican aims.

A survey of the literature illustrates the *ubiquitous* nature of this issue—how to reconcile public action with self-determination—within constitutional discourse.[24] The problem concerns how to ensure a balanced interaction between the exercise of public power, and individual and political self-determination when a society consists of a multitude of societal forces with competing viewpoints concerning what the public good is and how best to govern to achieve it. The following section briefly elucidates central tenets of republicanism, non-domination, and a two-pronged reading of self-determination—individual and political—which is shaped by a long strand of republican thought.[25]

---

[23] Q Skinner, *The Foundations of Modern Political Thought, Volume 1: The Renaissance* (Cambridge, Cambridge University Press, 1978); J Pocock, *The Machiavellian Moment: Florentine Political Thought and the Atlantic Republic Tradition* (Princeton University Press, 1975).

[24] For a seminal assessment of this relationship at the national level concerning the evolution of the separation of powers, see, A Hamilton, J Jay, and J Madison, *The Federalist Papers* (The Floating Press 2011); see Vile above n 2; EM Magill, 'The Real Separation in Separation of Powers Law' (2000) 86(6) *Virginia Law Review* 1127.

[25] The work of Dawson and de Witte is particularly influential concerning this two-prong understanding of self-determination. See M Dawson and F de Witte, 'Constitutional Balance in the EU after the Euro-Crisis' (2013) 76(5) *The Modern Law Review*, 817.

3.1. The Essential Element of Non-domination in Republicanism

Non-domination is a focal point in republican thought.[26] This republican ideal is designed to promote the *freedom* and *equality* of each societal actor.[27] As Hickey states, 'to be free, on a republican analysis is to enjoy resilient protection from domination, where domination is understood as unchecked powers of interference enjoyed by another agent'.[28] From this republican perspective, legitimate governance is based on the notion that no societal force can *unilaterally* control the distinct processes of governance.

Skinner argues that republican thought has traditionally understood freedom as non-interference—freedom from restraint.[29] Yet, it is important to note that non-interference with individual liberty does not guarantee non-domination because Skinner's version of non-interference focuses on the negative conception of individual liberty.[30] On the other hand, Pettit argues that domination 'is subjection to an arbitrary power of interference of another', regardless of whether those in a dominant position exercises that power.[31] Thus, Pettit argues that non-domination focuses on both the negative aspect of individaul liberty—the freedom from interference and the positive aspect of individual liberty—the freedom to engage in the political process within a constitutional order. For this reason, contemporary republican discourse offers non-domination, rather than non-interference, as the central tenet of contemporary republicanism.[32] Pettit, a vociferous proponent of non-domination as an essential element of republicanism, exemplifies this evolution.

Pettit contends that the ideal of non-domination is 'the one and only yardstick by which to judge the social and political constitution of a community.'[33] From this view, republican thought contends that individuals, or groups, who are 'dominated by others are not free but slaves.'[34] In Pettit's usage of the concept, slavery is a condition where individuals or

---

[26] F Schuppert, 'Non-Domination, Non-Alienation and Social Equality: Towards a Republican Understanding of Equality' (2015) 18(4) *Critical Review of International Social and Political Philosophy* 440.

[27] Schuppert emphasising the importance of the concept of equality in republican thought. ibid.

[28] T Hickey, 'The Republican Virtues of the "New Commonwealth Model of Constitutionalism" (2016) 14(4) *International Journal of Constitutional Law* 794 at 795.

[29] See, Skinner above n 23; Similar to Skinner, many contemporary strands of republicanism argue that freedom from restraint, (non-interference) is an essential element of republicanism. JM Balkin, 'Republicanism and the Constitution of Opportunity' (2015) 94 *Texas Law Review* 1427.

[30] P Pettit, 'Keeping Republican Freedom Simple: On a Difference with Quentin Skinner' (2002) 30(3) *Political Theory* 339.

[31] Ibid, 340.

[32] Ibid, 339.

[33] See Pettit above n 3 at 80.

[34] See Pettit above n 3.

groups lack freedom and self-rule.[35] Slavery is the antithesis of republicanism, from this view as it prevents individuals from being 'free and equal', since slaves were subject to domination and the arbitrary will of another societal force.[36] In this context, slavery is arbitrary government, since people can not make laws or govern for themselves.[37] Consequently, since slavery promotes the domination of particular societal forces, it prevents societal actors from exercising individual and political self-determination within a constitutional order.

3.2. Individual Self-Determination as Non-domination

Individual self-determination reflects the demand for individuals to be free from domination.[38] This republican understanding stresses that each individual may have different—even diametrically opposed—understandings of what the public good is and how best to govern to realise it. For this reason, to achieve republican aims, each individual must be 'free and equal'.[39] Each must be able to identify and articulate its unique view on how best to govern.[40]

Inevitably, different constitutional visions develop and continuously conflict with one another, as each societal element is designed to represent different and competing legitimacy claims, societal interests, and constitutional norms. This reflects the perpetual state of societal conflict in which constitutional questions must be resolved.[41] Since the different constitutional visions on how best to govern in a matter that achieves the public good compete with one another, distinct fora must be established which would allow for contestation and deliberation over competing constitutional issues.[42] This provides the framework to establish ongoing negotiation and reconciliation of the divergent viewpoints in a multi-actor and interactive

---

[35] Ibid.

[36] Different forms of slavery exist, seen, for instance, in the Roman incarnation and the racialised American form. This chapter is not addressing the atrocities that were caused by systematic and institutionalised slavery in the United States of America. For a critique of the use of the concept in republican thought in the context of American history, see, DJ Watkins, 'Slavery and Freedom in Theory and Practice' (2016) 44(6) *Political Theory* 846–70; See also JM Balkin and S Levinson, 'The Dangerous Thirteenth Amendment' (2012) 112 *Columbia Law Review* 1459 at 1497 (noting 'the founding generation's view of slavery as anti-republicanism and unjustified domination').

[37] Ibid, 1484.

[38] See Pettit above n 3.

[39] See de Búrca above n 19; Dawson and de Witte above n 25; T Hickey, 'The Republican Virtues of the New Commonwealth Model of Constitutionalism' (2016) 14(4) *International Constitutional Law Journal* 794.

[40] See Dawson and de Witte, above n 25.

[41] E Carolan, *The New Separation of Powers: A Theory for the Modern State* (Oxford, Oxford University Press, 2009).

[42] See Smismans above n 18; Craig above n 18 at 41.

deliberative process.[43] In the EU, the process of national referenda and the European Citizens' Initiative are examples of societal forces attempting to realise individual self-determination.[44]

3.3. Political Self-determination as Non-domination

The second element of self-determination, political self-determination, recognises the need to have constitutional processes that can reconcile these competing viewpoints when they inevitably clash. Accordingly, this model recognises that non-domination, non-arbitrariness, pluralism, and dialogical deliberation are essential elements of this two-pronged understanding of self-determination. From the viewpoint of this model, this demands non-dominating dialogical fora that can achieve republican aims and reconcile competing claims of constitutional authority. Such fora must incorporate *ex-ante* and *ex-post* procedural and substantive norms (process norms) of a legal and political nature.

This dialogical reading of institutional balance requires a complex matrix of constitutional rules designed to promote fora for contestation and reconciliation of constitutional conflicts concerning how to achieve the public good. Consequently, societal forces are subject to a mixture of different control and coordination mechanisms: enshrined in constitutional texts (Treaties); codified in formal mechanisms; or soft law and governance processes that may develop in practice, including clearly articulated legislative objectives; judicial review; budgetary controls; the active participation of public and private interest groups; public and private monitoring bodies; the input of specialised bodies with technical expertise, such as agencies and other regulatory bodies.[45] As de Búrca notes, such dialogical mechanisms are spelled out in the Treaty by the Court in its interpretation and application of the Treaty, by an array of societal forces through a range of legal and extra-legal mechanisms.[46] Such actions establish and reinforce political and legal checks and balances that promote process norms linked with a dialogical understanding of institutional balance. This includes the promotion of the rule of law in relation to the interpretation and the application of the Treaty, and protecting institutional prerogatives.[47]

Process norms can include the duty to give reasons, rules on transparency and access to information, rules concerning the participation of different

---

[43] Ibid.
[44] A Karatzia, 'The European Citizens' Initiative and the EU Institutional Balance: On Realism and the Possibilities of Affecting EU Lawmaking' (2017) 54(1) *Common Market Law Review* 177.
[45] See Majone above n 7 at 27.
[46] See de Búrca above n 19 at 56.
[47] Ibid; see Majone above n 7.

actors including interest groups, and the duty to meet standards of good administration.[48] Since each of the dialogical participants must give reasons and justify their decisions, this allows each actor the opportunity to exchange ideas and reflect on different viewpoints. This will enhance the legitimation of the decisions, as outcomes are based on a rational debate.

This provides the frame for each societal force to be checked and held politically and legally accountable, while also providing each an opportunity to participate in a non-dominating dialogical deliberation concerning contested constitutional issues. Essentially, procedural and substantive processes that ensure that each societal force is 'free and equal' to articulate and promote its vision of the public good in an open and fair deliberative process.[49] For these reasons, this model is designed to explain interactions between competing societal interests: majoritarian and non-majoritarian; judicial and non-judicial; public and private; and formal and informal elements, within EU governance. In the process, the model shows that the participation of different actors in the exercise of each of the various processes of governance, can help legitimate EU decision-making.

3.4. A Dialogical Understanding of Institutional Balance

This model of institutional balance as constitutional dialogue is designed to achieve constitutional values linked with republicanism. This model demands that an ongoing non-dominating dialogue occur between different societal forces concerning how best to resolve constitutional conflicts and achieve the public good. Such a model provides the framework to ensure a balanced interaction exists between societal forces representing competing societal interests, legitimacy claims, and constitutional norms.[50] This interaction promotes a deliberative democratic process that aims to ensure an institutionalised and constructive dialogue, between different societal forces that interact in pursuit of the public good.[51] In this republican paradigm, no single actor has the ability to *unilaterally* say what the institutional balance is and explicate its role in the EU constitutional order. A multitude of different actors are involved in an ongoing multi-actor and deliberative process involving how to resolve questions concerning the institutional balance.

This non-dominating dialogue is *constitutional* since it aims to contribute and shape the basic norms that govern the actions of societal forces who

---

[48] M Shapiro, 'The Giving Reasons Requirement' (1992) 1 *University of Chicago Legal Forum* 179.

[49] See Pettit above n 31.

[50] In the context of the EU, see Dawson and de Witte above n. 25; D Yuratich, 'Article 13(2) TEU: Institutional Balance, Sincere Co-Operation, and Non-Domination during Lawmaking?' (2017) 18(1) *German Law Journal* 1.

[51] G Graziano, 'Institutional Balance in the EU. The Prodi Administration as a Reforming Commission' (2008) *European Working Paper*, 9.

exercise public power within a constitutional order.[52] Each actor, representing distinct societal elements, brings their unique perspective to a constitutional conflict.[53] Accordingly, each actor must be 'free and equal' to reflect, articulate, and then voice their constitutional vision concerning how best to govern in a manner that achieves the public good and realises individual and political self-determination.[54]

The pluralistic inclusion of multiple actors in the exercise of every power is an essential element in the constitutional disposition of power within the EU constitutional order. This is consistent with a central tenet of republicanism, non-domination. Non-domination requires the inclusion of different societal elements in each phase of EU governance to prevent any single societal force from controlling the distinct decision-making processes in the EU. This demands that each of the different exercises of power in the EU involve multi-actor processes. In the EU, such multi-actor processes are evident in the law-making process (Commission, European Council, and European Parliament), the application of those laws (Commission, European Council, and Comitology Committees) in the interpretation of the laws, (CJEU, national courts, and Commission), the regulatory process (Commission, EU agencies, and national representatives), and in agenda setting (European Council, Commission, and Council). For this reason, societal actors, whether judicial; extra-judicial; majoritarian; non-majoritarian; and technocratic, exert varying degrees of power, while operating at different levels of governance, such as subnational; national; supranational; and international. Such actors are embedded in the divergent processes of decision-making in the EU constitutional order.

This leads to the mutual interdependence of the creation of norms—a multi-actor and interactive process of shaping and reshaping constitutional norms, including the institutional balance.[55] This requirement of multi-actor and interactive processes promotes the republican notion of non-domination, as it is designed to prevent any single actor from dominating any process of EU governance. Under the republican model, any societal element is able to contribute to the gradual emergence of these mutually interdependent shared constitutional norms. Each is able to participate in an ongoing process that continuously shapes and then reshapes the meaning of these norms over time. In this way, each societal element can engage in a multi-actor and interactive dialogical process that allows each to participate in the making, application, and interpretation of constitutional norms. The institutional balance exemplifies this mutually interdependent and shared

---

[52] A Meuwese and M Snel, 'Constitutional Dialogue: An Overview' (2013) 9(2) *Utrecht Law Review* 123.
[53] Ibid.
[54] See Pettit above n 31.
[55] See Hickey above n 28.

creation of constitutional norms. This dialogical interaction is deliberative and has legitimating force, as it can potentially resolve, or at least diminish, societal tensions concerning the institutional balance. Importantly, this also brings to the fore the concept of constitutional dialogue.

Constitutional dialogue is a concept that is meant to reconcile competing sources of authority.[56] The concept was originally introduced as a way to reconcile competing legitimacy claims between the legislature and the judiciary. From a republican perspective, understanding interactions between the two actors as a dialogue enhanced the legitimation of constitutional decision-making as it prevents either the legislature or judiciary from reigning supreme. The concept, however, has also been used in a broad sense to incorporate the range of societal forces beyond the legislature or judiciary that exercise public power in contemporary systems of constitutional governance.[57] It is this broad understanding of constitutional dialogue, which is most apt to reflect the complexities of EU governance and applied in this model.

This overlapping system of mutually interdependent, competitive, and coordinated exercises of public authority is best captured in the republican model of institutional balance as constitutional dialogue. This model demands that constitutional authority is dispersed across an array of societal forces and that a number of different actors are involved in each of the distinct processes of constitutional decision-making. Now that the meaning of the institutional balance has been explicated and the republican model of institutional balance as constitutional dialogue constructed, the Chapter shifts focus to the question: who has the *ultimate authority* to say what the institutional balance is?

4. WHO HAS THE ULTIMATE AUTHORITY ON THE INSTITUTIONAL BALANCE? THE ROLE OF THE CJEU IN SHAPING THE INSTITUTIONAL BALANCE

The CJEU, in two seminal decisions, *Van Gend en Loos* and *Costa*, created 'a new legal order', distinct from those operating at the national or international level and established constitutional norms in direct effect and supremacy that declared its decisions were supreme over the Member

---

[56] The concept of constitutional dialogue in the US can be linked to Bickel's famous counter majoritarian difficulty. L Fisher, *Constitutional Dialogues: Interpretation as Political Process* (Princeton University Press 2014); B Friedman, 'The History of the Countermajoritarian Difficulty, Part One: The Road to Judicial Supremacy' (1998) 73 *New York University Law Review* 333; In the Canadian context, see, PW Hogg and AA Bushell, 'The Charter Dialogue between Courts and Legislatures (Or Perhaps the Charter of Rights Isn't Such a Bad Thing after All)' (1997) 35(1) *Osgoode Hall Law Journal* 75.

[57] J Bohman, 'Expanding Dialogue: The Internet, the Public Sphere, and Prospects for Transnational Democracy' (2004) 52(1) *The Sociological Review* 131.

States.[58] Significantly, the CJEU has also demonstrated that the EU is of a 'constitutional' nature.[59] It frequently proclaims that the EU is based on the rule of law and that the European Treaty is a Union constitution that provides the CJEU a fundamental role in settling constitutional disputes between institutions.[60] *Les Verts* is a paradigmatic example of the CJEU's institutional perspective concerning the constitutional nature of the EU. It declares that the EU is based on the rule of law, and that decisions taken by Union actors and the Member States must comply with the 'constitutional charter', the Treaties.[61] Further, the Court has utilised the preliminary reference procedure and the legal basis requirement to maximise its scope and shape the EU constitutional order from its perspective.[62]

4.1. The CJEU's Role in the EU Constitutionalisation Process

The seminal judgments of *Van Gend* and *Costa* by the CJEU in the early stages of the European integration process in the 1960s show that the CJEU fundamentally influences the nature of EU governance and the balance between constituent elements.[63] The Court famously declared in *Van Gend en Loos* that 'the EEC created a new legal order of international law compromising both Member States and their nationals, where in limited fields the Member States limited their sovereign rights for their benefits'.[64] The CJEU declares that the then Community is a unique entity, distinct from either nation states or international organisations. Importantly, in doing so, the CJEU sets the frame for a constitutional disposition of powers distinct

---

[58] Case 26/62, *Van Gend en Loos* EU:C:1963:1, [1963] ECR 003; Case 6/64, *Costa v ENEL* EU:C:1964:66, [1964] ECR 585.

[59] AS Sweet and TL Brunell, 'Constructing a Supranational Constitution: Dispute Resolution and Governance in the European Community' (1998) 92(1) *The American Political Science Review* 63.

[60] Article 2 TEU now declares that the EU is based on the rule of law. Where the Court clearly lays out that it is the European judiciary, and not that of the Member State that determines the validity of measures enacted by the institutions See, Case 11/70, *Internationale Handelsgellschaft* EU:C:1970:114, [1970] ECR 1197; L Bauer, 'The European Court of Justice as a Constitutional Court' (2009) 3(4) *International Constitutional Law Journal* 268.

[61] In *Les Verts*, the CJEU states that 'the Community is based on the rule of law, inasmuch as neither its Member States nor its Institutions can avoid a review of the question whether the measures adopted by them are in conformity with the basic constitutional charter, the Treaty established a complete system of legal remedies and procedures designed to permit the Court of Justice to review the legality of measures adapted by the institutions'. Case 294/83 *Les Verts v Parliament* EU:C:1986:166, [1986] ECR 1339, para 23.

[62] For a detailed analysis of judicial politics in the EU, from various viewpoints. See, A Vauchez, 'The Transnational Politics of Judicialization. *Van Gend en Loos* and the Making of EU Polity' (2010) 16(1) *European Law Journal* 1; H de Waele and A van der Vleuten, 'Judicial Activism in the European Court of Justice—The Case of LGBT Rights' (2010) 19 *Michigan State International Law Review* 639.

[63] See *Van Gend en Loos* above n 58: *Costa v ENEL* above n 58.

[64] See *Van Gend en Loos* above n 58.

from constitutional arrangements at the national level or at the international level. Accordingly, the Court's articulation of the EEC as a 'new legal order' is a transformative event shaping the institutional balance and how public power is balanced within the EU.

Meanwhile, in *Costa*, the Court stated that the Treaty is an innovative, autonomous, and distinct source of law that cannot be overturned by domestic legal provisions without the very nature of the Union legal order itself being questioned.[65] *Costa* demonstrates, from the CJEU's institutional perspective, that Union law has supremacy or primacy and therefore prevails over the laws of the Member States of the Union.[66]

The CJEU could have limited its reasoning in both judgments to conform to the conventional understanding of international law. Under this reading, states are 'masters of the Treaties'.[67] From this view, the Member States and their constitutional order would remain supreme over the law of the European Union.[68] Instead, the CJEU greatly expanded the scope of Union law. The transformative decisions laid down in the 1960s by the CJEU explicitly challenged the applicability of this conventional understanding of the international law to the EU legal order. In the process, it significantly altered the path of European integration.

These two ground-breaking decisions illustrate the CJEU's vital role in interpreting the Treaties and resolving constitutional conflicts. The discourse concerning the relationship between the CJEU and the highest national courts has been particularly significant to debates concerning EU governance. These decisions created an ongoing dialogue relating to the relationship between the EU and national legal orders.[69] Despite general acceptance of the CJEU's role in the integration process, at no time has there been unanimity among different societal forces concerning how to resolve constitutional conflicts that arise between the two legal orders.[70]

The notion of supremacy has caused profound controversy among certain national courts and legal commentators.[71] The national courts pushed back when they felt the CJEU was taking a stance that interfered with their

---

[65] *Costa v ENEL* above n 58.

[66] Ibid.

[67] KJ Alter, 'Who Are the "Masters of The Treaty"?: European Governments and The European Court of Justice' (1998) 52(1) *International Organization* 121.

[68] Bobíc offers a comprehensive pluralistic account of the European constitutional space, illustrating how Member States courts have attempted to limit the impact of CJEU decisions. See, A Bobíc, Chapter 3 in this volume.

[69] M Claes and M de Visser, 'Are You Networked Yet? On Dialogues in European Judicial Networks' (2012) 8(2) *Utrecht Law Review* 100.

[70] Bobíc uses the concept of constitutional pluralism to highlight the ongoing contestation concerning how public authority is balanced by courts operating at the national and EU level. See above n 68.

[71] This has been intensely debated by certain national courts within the Member States. The Lisbon Judgment by the German national court is a pragmatic example of debates concerning the supremacy of EU law, BVerfG, Judgment of the Second Senate of 30 June 2009—2 BvE 2/08.

constitutional authority under national constitutions.[72] Thus demonstrating that national courts also have a fundamental role to play in shaping the institutional balance. Increasingly, concerns over 'judicial activism' are espoused as the CJEU's case law arguably significantly contradicts the objectives and ideals of Member States when the original European Treaties were created in the 1950s. As Alter argues, the CJEU has transformed the European legal order so fundamentally, that its decisions now routinely challenge the fundamental objectives of the European project, including interference with national sovereignty and the interests of individual and the collective Member States.[73]

The Court also claims that it has the ultimate authority both to say what the institutional balance is and to explicate its role in the EU constitutional order.[74] The CJEU uses this authority and the wide discretion it has interpreted for itself to settle constitutional conflicts. The Court utilises its role under Article 19 TEU to significantly impact the institutional balance and ensure the rule of law under the Treaty.[75] The CJEU has used the uncertainty in Treaty provisions that are often vague and unclear as a frame to promote its constitutional vision of the public good within the EU. As a result, the Treaty has been labelled 'an incomplete contract' by Herieter and Farrell.[76] This has provided the CJEU with the power to frequently interpret the Treaty in a meta-teleological manner.[77] As Bradley argues,

it is the very open-ended character of the relevant Treaty provisions which has enabled the Court of Justice to develop a coherent theoretical structure of inter-institutional relations in the Community decision-making process, based on the

---

[72] Decisions by national courts in Germany, Denmark, and the Czech Republic are illustrative of this. In the EU, the debate over whether the CJEU has the ultimate authority to decide the balance of power between Member States and EU institutions is much more vigorous than debates concerning the relationship between EU institutions. The numerous constitutional courts of the Member States that have weighed in on the topic demonstrate the serious questions that arise over these issues. see M Herdegen, 'Maastricht and the German Constitutional Court; Constitutional Restrains for an "Ever Closer Union' (1994) 31 *Common Market Law Review* 235; see also, Transcript of the Record of Judgments for the Danish Supreme Court. The Danish Supreme Court's Judgment of 12 August 1996, UfR 1996 1300 H.

[73] See Alter, above n 67; For analysis demonstrating how courts and judges in Scandinavian Member States may attempt to resist CJEU decisions, as 'a true democracy should elevate parliament over the other branches.' See, M Wind, Chapter 11 in this volume.

[74] The Treaty explicitly provides the CJEU with general jurisdiction to hear disputes involving EU law and settle constitutional conflicts. See Articles 263 and 264 TEU. A notable exception is the area of Common Foreign Security Policy (CFSP); See Case C-70/88 *European Parliament v Council* EU:C:1989:604 [1989], Opinion of Advocate General Van Gerven.

[75] See, Consolidated Version of the Treaty on European Union [2012] OJ L 326/13, art 19(1).

[76] H Farrell and A Héritier, 'Codecision and Institutional Change' (2007) 30(2) *West European Politics* 285.

[77] Öberg J, 'The Rise of the Procedural Paradigm: Judicial Review of EU Legislation in Vertical Competence Disputes' (2017) 13 *European Constitutional Law Review* 248.

notion of the institutional balance intended by the Treaty, which is underpinned by a set of substantive and procedural legal rights and obligations.[78]

However, the CJEU has been labelled 'an activist court', as serious questions are raised in relation to its case law on institutional balance. *Chernobyl* and *ESMA* illustrate how the CJEU promotes an institutional balance that is, arguably, not reflected in the Treaty. Nevertheless, it is now generally accepted that the CJEU plays a fundamental role in settling constitutional disputes over the balance of powers within the EU.[79]

4.2. The CJEU Creates, Applies and Interprets the Institutional Balance

The Court's essential role in establishing and maintaining the institutional balance is evident in its landmark decision in *Meroni,* a case involving the delegation of powers and the first reference to institution balance in the EU.[80] According to *Meroni*, the principle of institutional balance derives from the distribution of powers established in the Treaties.[81] However, it is in its *Chernobyl* decision where the CJEU most precisely elucidates its institutional perspective on what the institutional balance is and how the concept shapes the EU constitutional order.[82]

The central issue in *Chernobyl* involved the ability of the European Parliament (EP) to bring an action for annulment.[83] The EP was consulted by the Council, but argued that the Commission used the wrong legal basis to reduce its role in the lawmaking process.[84] The Council vehemently rejected

---

[78] The coherence, or lack thereof, of the institutional structure, is intensely disputed and a central aspect of discussions involving the institutional balance. Nevertheless, Bradley is correct when he argues that the unclear Treaty provisions have provided the Court with the opportunity to shape the institutional balance. See, KSC Bradley, 'Maintaining the Balance: The Role of the Court of Justice in Defining the Institutional Position European Parliament' (1987) 24 *Common Market Law Review* 41.

[79] L Azoulai, and D Dehousse, 'The European Court of Justice and the Legal Dynamics of Integration' in A Menon and S Weatherill (eds), *The Oxford Handbook of the European Union* (Oxford, Oxford University Press, 2012).

[80] In *Meroni*, the Court did not use the term institutional balance, but instead referenced the balance of powers between institutions is guaranteed in the Treaty. Nonetheless, this is considered the first reference of the institutional balance: 'From that provision there can be seen in the balance of powers which is characteristic of the institutional structure of the Community a fundamental guarantee granted by the Treaty in particular to the undertaking and association of undertaking to which it applies.' See Case 9/56 *Meroni* EU:C:1958:7, [1958] ECR 00133.

[81] *Chernobyl* is an essential case governing the constitutional disposition of powers. Case C-70/88 *European Parliament v Council (Chernobyl)* EU:C:1990:217 [1990] ECR I-2041; Consolidated Version of the Treaty on European Union [2012] OJ L 326/13, art 13(2).

[82] Ibid, paras 1–6.

[83] In this case, the EP was seeking an annulment of a Council Regulation involving the maximum permitted levels of radioactive contamination of food items in the market in the aftermath of the nuclear accident in Chernobyl. See *Chernobyl* above n 81, paras 1–6.

[84] Instead of Article 31 of the Euratom Treaty, the EP argues that Article 100a of the EEC Treaty is the proper legal basis. Importantly, the latter provision, allows for a greater role for the EP in the decision-making process under the co-decision procedure, now the ordinary legislative procedure after the Lisbon Treaty. See *Chernobyl* above n 81, paras 1–6.

the action claiming that, pursuant to the Treaties and CJEU's *Comitology* decision, the EP does not have the right to bring an action for annulment.[85]

From the CJEU's perspective, it is the Treaties that have created an institutional balance within the EU constitutional order that distributes powers and assigns a particular role for each institution in order to achieve the public good—Union objectives established in the Treaties.[86] From the CJEU's perspective, since each institution has its constitutional tasks, the institutional balance shall not be altered in a manner not envisaged by the Treaty itself. From the legal dimension of institutional balance, such changes run contrary to the rule of law and interfere with the ability to achieve Union objectives.[87] *Chernobyl* also declares that a legal remedy should be available when an actor takes actions that circumvent the institutional balance.[88]

The Court places itself at the center of disputes between Union institutions. It declares that

> the Court, which under the Treaties has the task of ensuring that in the interpretation and application of the Treaties the law is observed, must therefore be able to maintain the institutional balance, and consequently, review the observance of the Parliament's prerogatives when called upon to do so by the Parliament, by means of a legal remedy which is suited to the purpose which the Parliament seeks to achieve.[89]

Accordingly, *Chernobyl* also lays down a general principle that a Union institution has the ability to protect its prerogatives and, thus, its institutional position.[90]

The *Chernobyl* decision exemplifies the increasing perception that the CJEU is an activist court. The criticism of the CJEU for this decision was particularly striking since the Treaty, under Article 173 EEC, explicitly provided an exhaustive list of potential litigants who could request the CJEU

---

[85] In *Chernobyl*, the Council argues that the then recently decided *Comitology* case, where the Court rejected a similar claim by the EP, should be used as precedent to deny the EP claim in *Chernobyl*. See, Case 302/87, *European Parliament v Council (Comitology)* EU:C:1988:461 [1988] ECR 05615.

[86] In the CJEU's formulation of the institutional balance, the Court states, 'the treaties set up a system for distributing powers among the different Community institutions, assigning to each institution its own role in the institutional structure of the Community and the accomplishment of the tasks entrusted to the Community." The Court adds that "observance of the institutional balance means that each of the institutions must exercise its powers with due regard for the powers of other institutions'. See *Chernobyl* above n 81, paras 21–23.

[87] This has essentially been codified in the Lisbon Treaty. 'Each institution shall act within the limits of the powers conferred on it in the Treaties, shall in conformity with the procedures, conditions, and objectives set out in them.' Consolidated Version of the Treaty on European Union [2012] OJ L 326/13, art 13(2).

[88] See *Chernobyl* above n 81, paras 21–23.

[89] Ibid.

[90] As the Court states, 'it is the Court's duty to ensure that the provisions of the Treaties concerning the institutional balance are fully applied and to see to it that the Parliament's prerogatives, like those of the other institutions, cannot be breached without it having available a legal remedy, among those laid down in the Treaties, which may be exercised in a certain and effective manner'. See *Chernobyl* above n 81, paras 21–23.

review EU legislation.[91] Therefore, the CJEU unilaterally expanded the list of litigants in a manner contrary to the explicit text of the Treaty. Some argue that in certain cases, such as *Chernobyl*, the Court has gone beyond the strict letter of the law and provided the EP with powers that were not attributed to the assembly in the Treaty.[92] However, the CJEU reasoned that it was respecting the general principle of representative democracy to justify its *Chernobyl* decision.

Chernobyl highlights that the CJEU creates constitutional norms that augment the powers of the EP in the name of democratic deliberation. This, from the Court's reasoning, was necessary to secure the public good, and to ensure that the EP—the democratically elected assembly at the EU level—has the ability to have its voice heard in the law-making process. Since the relevant Treaty provisions were not amended to recognise the EP's increasing powers in constitutional reality, the CJEU unilaterally incorporated such changes in decisions it rendered.[93] Further, the *Chernobyl* decision has been justified, since the Treaties were later amended by the Member States to reflect the decision.[94] From this perspective, the ability for *extra-judicial* actors to exercise constitutional review of the CJEU's constitutional interpretation of Union law can and should take place on a systematic basis.[95]

The CJEU has continuously played a role in promoting the ability of the EP to contribute to an ongoing dialogue over contested issues during the EU law-making process. This is particularly noticeably in situations where the EP is in a comparatively weak position to the Council; this is evident in cases such as *Isocluse* and *Roquette*. *Chernobyl* is illustrative of how the Court promotes a dialogue between divergent actors within the law-making process. The Court has also promoted dialogic deliberation in a number of other cases, specifically in the area of consultation and re-consultation.[96] In this regard, the CJEU has promoted the principle of sincere cooperation, in order to ensure both the EP and the Council are engaging in non-dominating dialogue when exercising law-making authority.[97]

The CJEU's creation, application, and interpretation of institutional balance, epitomises its role in settling constitutional conflicts concerning how

---

[91] See de Waele and van der Vleuten above n 62.

[92] P Neill, 'The European Court of Justice—A Case Study in Judicial Activism' *European Policy Forum* (1995); TC Hartley, *Constitutional Problems of the European Union* (Oxford, Hart Publishing, 1999), Chapters 2 and 3.

[93] S Prechal, 'Institutional Balance: A Fragile Principle with Uncertain Contents', in T Heukels, Blokker N and M Brus (eds), *The European Union After Amsterdam: A Legal Analysis* (Amsterdam, Kluwer Law International, 1998).

[94] JWR Reed, 'Political Review of the European Court of Justice and Its Jurisprudence' (1995) *Harvard Jean Monnet Working Paper* 13/1995.

[95] Ibid.

[96] Case 139/79 *Maizena v Council* EU:C:1980:250, [1980] ECR 3393; Case C-65/93 *Parliament v Council* EU:C:1995:91 [1995] ECR-643.

[97] See Yuratich above n 50.

public power is or ought to be balanced in the EU. The Court—when deciding cases involving institutional balance—creates a rule by developing the concept of institutional balance in *Meroni*, applies and develops the concept further in *Chernobyl*, and continues to reinterpret the concept in later decisions.

Importantly, the CJEU is often called upon to act as a problem solver, to reconcile competing societal forces representing distinct legitimacy claims, constitutional values, and societal interests across Europe—Union institutions and other bodies, national courts, national governments, national parliaments, public and private interests groups, and the peoples of Europe.[98] In this way, the CJEU engages with judicial and extra-judicial societal forces to provide its view on how best to resolve constitutional conflicts concerning the institutional balance. This allows it to act as a dialogical forum that provides a fair process for contestation, negotiation, and reconciliation between different societal forces.

From a republican perspective, this illustrates that the CJEU creates constitutional rules, then applies and interprets them to promote and maintain the institutional balance. The CJEU exercises judicial review and utilises meta-teleological interpretation to further promote European integration and achieve the ultimate objectives of the Treaty. In other words, the CJEU utilises such teleological interpretation to achieve its vision of what the public good *is* and *ought* to be within the Union.

The CJEU has played a vital role in the constitutional development of the EU.[99] From a republican perspective, the CJEU aims to ensure public power is exercised in a non-dominating fashion. Through its case law, the CJEU has shaped how constitutional conflicts concerning institutional balance are settled. For this reason, cases such as *Meroni* and *Chernobyl* are of vital importance to a proper understanding of the institutional balance, as they highlight how the CJEU engages in a dialogical process to shape and reshape the institutional balance. Despite its important role shaping how the institutional balance impacts EU governance, the CJEU does not have a monopoly on the meaning of the institutional balance; nor can it unilaterally determine what the public good is, or ought to be, in the EU. Instead, a range of actors operating at different levels of governance are involved in the shared creation of constitutional norms, including the institutional balance. It is important to note that the CJEU has continuously been involved in an ongoing dialogue with other societal forces over how best to resolve constitutional conflicts within the pluralistic and multilevel system of EU governance.[100]

---

[98] M Dawson, 'Constitutional Dialogue Between Courts and Legislatures in the European Union: Prospects and Limits' (2013) 19(2) *European Public Law* 369.

[99] See Arnull, Chapter 1 in this volume.

[100] A Rosas, 'The European Court of Justice in Context: Forms and Patterns of Judicial Dialogue' (2007) 1(2) *European Journal of Legal Studies* 121.

5. EXTRA-JUDICIAL ACTORS AND THE MUTUAL INTERDEPENDENCY OF THE INSTITUTIONAL BALANCE

Extra-judicial societal forces use a variety of formal and informal processes to shift the institutional balance in a manner that fundamentally shapes the EU constitutional order.[101] The actors in the institutional triangle—the Commission, European Parliament, and Council—and beyond continuously contest and re-interpret the institutional balance laid down by the Court.[102] For example, one of the most transformative shifts of institutional balance in the EU constitutional order has been the increasing power of the EP.[103] This is particularly evident when the EP's increasing powers are compared to those of the Council and the Commission. The powers of the latter two institutions have remained relatively the same throughout European integration and they have often fiercely resisted the rise of the EP.[104]

5.1. The EP Shaping the Institutional Balance

The EP has transformed from an advisory body—an elected assembly—with little coercive power into a 'real' player in EU governance. As Hix describes, the EP is now a constitutional agenda-setter able to fill gaps left by the 'incomplete contracts' established in the Treaties through its constitutional interpretation.[105] This also allows the EP to shape the institutional balance through legal and extra-legal processes—CJEU case law, inter-institutional agreements, and budgetary negotiations.[106] By using such processes as strategic tools, the EP has enhanced its institutional position in the EU's constitutional order, with the objective of obtaining an 'equal' status to the Council in the law-making process. It now exercises significant legislative,

---

[101] See Smismans, above n 18.

[102] The 2010 Framework Agreement between the European Parliament and Commission is a classic example of how two actors, in this case the EP and the Commission arguably go beyond the Treaties to shape the institutional balance, Framework Agreement on Relations between the European Parliament and the European Commission, OJ 2010 No L304/47.

[103] G Tsebelis, 'The Power of the European Parliament as a Conditional Agenda Setter' (1994) 88(1) *American Political Science Review* 128; S Hix, 'Constitutional Agenda-Setting Through Discretion in Rule Interpretation: Why the European Parliament Won at Amsterdam' (2002) 32(2) *British Journal of Political Science* 259.

[104] H Farrell and A Héritier, 'Formal and Informal Institutions under Codecision: Continuous Constitution-Building in Europe' (2003) 16(4) *Governance: An International Journal of Policy, Administration, and Institutions* 577.

[105] See Hix above n 103.

[106] A pertinent example of this is inter-institutional agreements in a number of areas. See the 2010 Framework Agreement on relations between the European Parliament and the Commission. Official Journal L 304, 20/11/2010 P. 0047—0062.; see also budgetary inter-institutional agreements.

budgetary, and oversight authority.[107] Thus, the EP has utilised various processes with the objective of achieving the republican aim of non-domination in the EU law-making process.

The EP has often sought assistance from the CJEU to strengthen its role in EU decision making. Perhaps the most striking of these examples is *Chernobyl*, as analysed above. Yet, in other cases, such as *Roquette*, the CJEU has stressed the fundamental importance of having the democratic assembly participate in EU decision-making processes.[108] In *Roquette,* the central issue was whether the European Parliament had the right to intervene to protect its right to be consulted during the consultation procedure under Article 230 Treaty of the European Community (now Article 263 TFEU).[109] The Court held that the EP has a general right to intervene to protect its prerogatives, therefore annulling the Council measure because the latter institution failed to consult the EP before passing its instrument.[110] In such cases, the Court utilised the parliamentary interpretation of the institutional balance to enhance the EP's role and ensure its voice is heard in the governing process.[111] In this context, the CJEU is emphasising the need for a multi-actor dialogical deliberation in the law-making process. Such a dialogical process also promotes the idea of non-domination, preventing the Council from unilaterally controlling the EU law-making process.

5.2. European Agencies Shaping the Institutional Balance

European agencies provide another illustrative example of extra-judicial actors that have the potential to shift the institutional balance and transform its role in the EU constitutional order.[112] The question of the precise role of agencies in the EU constitutional order, and how they impact (or ought to impact) institutional balance, has caused fundamental inter-institutional debates between the EP, the Council, and the Commission.[113] The debates often lead to justifiable legitimacy concerns over the nature, powers, resources, and functions of EU agencies.[114]

---

[107] The EP has largely obtained this objective, Consolidated Version of the Treaty on European Union [2012] OJ L 326/13, arts 289–94.

[108] See Case 138/79, *Roquette v Council* EU:C:1980:249, [1980] ECR 3333.

[109] Ibid; see also, Case 139/79 *Maizena v Council* EU:C:1980:250, [1980] ECR 3393.

[110] E Vos, 'European Agencies and the Composite EU Executive', in M Everson, C Monda and E Vos (eds), *European Agencies Inbetween Institutions and Member States* (Kluwer Law International, 2014).

[111] See Smismans above n 18.

[112] See Vos above n 110.

[113] DR Kelemen, 'European Union Agencies', in A Menon and S Weatherill (eds), *The Oxford Handbook of the European Union* (Oxford, Oxford University Press, 2012) 383.

[114] RH Van Ooik, 'The Growing Importance of Agencies in the EU: Shifting Governance and the Institutional Balance' in D Curtin, RA Wessel (eds), *Good Governance and the European Union: Reflections on Concepts, Institutions and Substance* (Antwerp, Intersentia, 2005).

Contestation between different societal forces in the EU is increasingly evident in recent case law, where the CJEU has suffered intense criticism for decisions following the unprecedented euro-crisis, such as *Pringle* and *ESMA*.[115] The euro-crisis led to the creation of new financial supervisory authorities in the EU.[116] These were granted significant powers, with the objective of addressing ongoing threats to European and national financial markets.

The most pertinent aspects of the debate were not whether such actors were needed to combat threats to the European financial market. It is generally recognised that such bodies are often justified as a functional necessity, since they have unique technocratic expertise and the ability to address complex technical questions.[117] Instead, the precise placement of such bodies, their powers, and what *ex-ante* and *ex-post* control mechanisms would exist to hold such actors accountable caused the most controversy. Serious concerns were raised as such actors operate largely outside the constitutional framework established in the Treaty. Another major criticism was the role of the EP. It was left largely outside the new supervisory framework. Instead of having a significant role in the establishment of these agencies, similar to the EU ordinary legislative procedure, the EP had mere consultation rights. This meant that the elected assembly at the EU level was unable to exercise 'real' power in one of the most fundamental crises in the history of EU integration.

Nevertheless, the Court validated the use of such financial supervisory frameworks, raising justifiable concerns over the legitimation of CJEU decisions and its ability to act as a neutral observer rather than a rubber stamp for national governments.[118] Despite legitimate concerns involving the accountability, transparency and control mechanisms available to hold ESMA to account, the CJEU concluded that the legal basis and the powers ESMA can exercise were legal. This was a similar result to the CJEU's *Koster* decision, which confirmed the legality of comitology committees under the Treaty.[119] The financial crisis—which has wreaked havoc over much of the EU for almost a decade—is not the only profound turbulence and

---

[115] Case 370/12 *Pringle v Government of Ireland and Others* EU:C:2012:675, [2012]; Case 270/12 *UK v European Parliament and Council of the European Union(ESMA)* EU:C:2014:18, [2014].

[116] Council, *Conclusions*, 29 June 2012, EUCO 76/12, p.1.

[117] Case C-270/12 *United Kingdom Great Britain and Northern Ireland v European Parliament and Council of the European Union(ESMA)* EU:C:2014:18, [2014].

[118] Case 270/12 *UK v European Parliament and Council of the European Union* EU:C:2014:18, [2014].

[119] C di Noia and M Gargantini, 'Unleashing the European Securities and Markets Authority: Governance and Accountability after the ECJ Decision on the Short Selling Regulation (Case C-270/12)' (2014) 15(1) *European Business Organization Law Review* 1.

uncertainty currently facing the EU.[120] National referenda are increasingly a forum for the peoples of the EU to shape the institutional balance.

5.3. The Peoples of Europe Shaping the Institutional Balance

The peoples of the EU have often played a significant role in the European integration process through referenda at the national level.[121] Throughout the years, there have been a number of national referenda concerning vital issues of European integration: enlargement, the euro, opt-outs, bailouts, migrant quotas, and the European Constitution.[122] Among the most influential were the close referenda, causing great debate, concerning the ratification of the Maastricht Treaty in 1992[123] and the European Constitution in 2005.[124]

In 2016, the United Kingdom European Union Referendum (Brexit) caused political shockwaves across Europe and around the globe. In a historic 'non-binding' referendum, the question was posed whether the United Kingdom should leave, or remain in, the EU. Nearly 52% of the people voted to leave the Union. This vote has led to a number of dialogical deliberations, negotiations, and meetings concerning the precise processes and mechanisms by which a Member State can leave the EU.[125]

Since the Brexit vote, an ongoing dialogue at different levels of governance over how to reconcile competing visions of the future of UK–EU relations have occurred. This involved the peoples of Britain, the British Parliament, the British Government, the British Supreme Court, the European Council, the European Commission and the European Parliament. This includes significant decisions by the British Supreme Court[126] and British Government. Brexit has the potential to fundamentally transform the institutional balance and its role in the EU constitutional order. Accordingly, understanding national referenda as a form of constitutional dialogue

---

[120] European Commission, *The Future of Europe: Reflections and Scenarios for the EU27 by 2025* (White Paper COM, 2017).
[121] A Szcerbiak and P Taggart *EU Enlargement and Referendums,* (Abingdon, Routledge, 2013).
[122] Directorate-General for Internal Policies. Policy Department Citizen's Rights and Constitutional Affairs, 'Referendums on EU Matters' (2017) PE 571.402.
[123] MN Franklin, C van der Eijk, '*Referendum Outcomes and Trust in Government: Public Support for Europe in the Wake of Maastricht*' (1995) 18 *West European Politics* 101.
[124] See Dutch European Constitution referendum, 1 June 2005; French European Constitution referendum, 29 May 2005. Available at: www.cfr.org/backgrounder/european-union-french-dutch-referendums.
[125] European Council, 'European Council (Art. 50) Guidelines for Brexit Negotiations', Press Release 29/04/2017.
[126] *R v Secretary of State for Exiting the European Union* [2017] UKSC 5.

exemplifies that through national referenda, the peoples of Europe can fundamentally transform the institutional balance.[127]

6. CONCLUSION

This chapter proposes a republican model of institutional balance as constitutional dialogue to explore the institutional balance and its role in the EU constitutional order. The central objective of this chapter was to put forth a republican model of institutional balance as constitutional dialogue that provides insights into the ongoing, multi-actor and interactive processes of EU governance. This analysis highlights constitutional conflicts concerning who has the ultimate authority to say what the institutional balance is and determine its role in the EU constitutional order. Through the lens of republicanism, this model provides unique insights concerning the dynamism of the institutional balance that better reflect the complex realities of EU governance than traditional positivist readings. Consequently this chapter shows how constitutional dialogue adds value to the existing discourse concerning debates on the institutional balance in the EU.

The preceding analysis vividly illustrates how the CJEU has played an essential role in constitutional conflicts concerning the institutional balance. According to the Court's institutional perspective, when exercising judicial review, it has the ultimate authority to unilaterally ensure the manner in which societal forces operate in accordance with the rule of law and institutional balance established in the Treaty. Since establishing the concept of institutional balance in *Meroni* and continuously shaping and reinterpreting it, the CJEU has been instrumental in *balancing* the interactions between societal forces in the EU.

The CJEU has the means, motive, and opportunity to act autonomously of other societal forces in an attempt to promote their institutional perspective and protect institutional prerogatives concerning how to achieve the public good.[128] Extra-judicial societal forces, however, also fundamentally shape the CJEU's decisions. Legal positivists often fail to capture the complex realities of a constitutional order and fail to reflect the role of extra-judicial constitutional interpretation. Consequently, this chapter eschews the notion that can be found in most traditional positivist readings, that the institutional balance is unilaterally shaped and formulated (or dominated) by the CJEU.[129]

---

[127] Directorate-General for Internal Policies. Policy Department Citizen's Rights and Constitutional Affairs, 'Referendums on EU Matters' (2017) PE 571.402.

[128] CJ Carruba, M Gabel and C Hankla, 'Judicial Behavior under Political Constraints: Evidence from the European Court of Justice' (2008) 102(4) *American Political Science Review* 435.

[129] The conventional view concentrated on CJEU case law and is linked with legal positivists. See Smismans above n 18.

The CJEU does not have a monopoly on constitutional interpretation in the EU. It is important to emphasise that a range of actors—legal, extra-legal, majoritarian, non-majoritarian, and technocratic—shape, and are shaped by the institutional balance. For this reason, the model put forth in this chapter demands a systematic reinterpretation of institutional balance from a dialogical perspective that emphasises republican values.

This dynamic dialogical understanding of institutional balance based on deliberative interaction between competing societal forces shows that EU governance is heterarchical rather than hierarchical in nature. An array of societal forces utilise a number of distinct formal and soft law and governance processes to interact in an ongoing dialogical process with the aim of governing societal relations, resolving societal conflicts, and reconciling competing legitimacy claims and constitutional perspectives.

Institutional balance is based on shared constitutional authority, mutual interdependence and the multifunctionality of societal forces. Demanding that multiple societal forces participate in the exercise of each power. The ongoing, multi-actor, and interactive processes of EU governance, require different societal forces engage in negotiation, contestation, and ultimately reconciliation concerning the competing visions of the institutional balance, and how best to govern to achieve the public good in the EU. Such processes require dialogical fora where the different societal forces can be counterbalanced against one another.

The CJEU offers just one type of dialogical forum to resolve constitutional conflicts concerning the institutional balance and the public good in the EU. Extra-judicial fora are also vital avenues for contestation and reconciliation. This depiction better reflects the intricacies of contemporary governance and the evolution of the institutional balance in the EU constitutional order. This republican model enhances the legitimacy of the EU constitutional order, as each societal force is free and equal to engage in a constitutional dialogue over the meaning of the institutional balance and shows how to achieve the public good in a manner that secures republican governance in the EU.

8

House of Cards in Luxemburg?

A Brief Defence of the Strategic Model of Judicial Politics in the Context of the European Union

OLOF LARSSON AND DANIEL NAURIN

1. INTRODUCTION

T HIS CHAPTER WILL make a claim that may appear absurd to many European legal and political science scholars, namely that we have something to learn from the Americans when it comes to courts and politics in Europe. We outline a brief defence of the Separation of Powers model (SOP) of judicial politics, and its application to the Court of Justice of the European Union (CJEU) on theoretical and empirical grounds. The SOP model is a positive theoretical model, which was developed to understand the interaction between the executive, legislative and judicial branches of power in the United States.[1] Versions of it have subsequently been exported by political scientists and international relations scholars to other contexts.[2]

---

[1] BA Marks, 'A Model of Judicial Influence on Congressional Policymaking: Groove City College v. Bell', (1988) *The Hoover Institution Working Papers in Political Science*; JA Ferejohn and B R Weingast, 'A Positive Theory of Statutory Interpretation' (1992) 12 *International Review of Law and Economics* 263; L Epstein and J Knight, *The Choices Justices Make* (CQ Press, Washington, DC, 1998); JA Segal, 'Separation-of-Powers Games in the Positive Theory of Congress and Courts' (1997) 91 *The American Political Science Review* 28.

[2] G Garrett, 'International Cooperation and Institutional Choice: The European Community's Internal Market' (1992) 46 *International Organization* 533; G Garrett, 'The Politics of Legal Integration in the European Union' (1995) 49 *International Organization* 171; G Garrett and BR Weingast, 'Ideas, Interests, and Institutions: Constructing the European Community's Internal Market' in J Goldstein and RO Keohane (eds), *Ideas and Foreign Policy* (Cornell University Press, Ithaca, New York, 1993); G Vanberg, 'Legislative-Judicial Relations: A Game-Theoretic Approach to Constitutional Review' (2001) 45 *American Journal of Political Science* 346; G Grendstad, WR Shaffer and EN Waltenburg, 'Revealed Preferences of Norwegian Supreme Court Justices' (2010) 123(1) *Tidsskrift for Rettvitenskap* 73–101.

These applications have often been strongly contested.[3] Critics have raised concerns about theoretical imperialism on behalf of American political scientists, who tend to see cold-hearted strategies wherever they look. European judges are different from their American colleagues, it is argued. They base their decisions on law-based syllogistic reasoning, not on politics or partisan ideology.[4] Rationalist-strategic theories like the SOP model seem to have more in common with the TV series House of Cards than European legal realities. They do not take into account the legal culture and the inherent meaning and functioning of law as it works on this side of the Atlantic.[5]

Our defence of the SOP model is a moderate one. We do not claim that this theoretical approach fully captures the decision making of the CJEU or any other court in liberal democracies. It is a parsimonious theory, which aims to capture *some* aspects of judicial behaviour, and contributes to explaining *parts* of the development of legal integration in Europe. Other theories are needed to complete the picture. We do claim, however, that it captures *significant* parts of the interaction between law and politics. In our view, emphasising the political-strategic features of the CJEU is important as a realistic counterweight to, on the one hand, the tendency in the history of European legal integration to tell a normative story of the CJEU as the impartial saviour of European integration that fits with the preferred narrative of Euro-lawyers and judges,[6] and, on the other, the naïve idea that judges only speak the law.[7] We argue that legal integration is driven by law and politics, and that judicial behaviour takes both factors into account. The SOP model provides a convincing—albeit incomplete—theoretical account of how that interaction works, which corresponds well with the empirical facts on the ground.

The rest of the chapter contains, firstly, a brief summary of the core assumptions and propositions of the SOP model, and secondly, an equally brief summary of our empirical research on the position-taking of the CJEU and the Member State governments.

---

[3] G Davies, 'Legislative Control of the European Court of Justice' (2014) 51 *Common Market Law Review* 1579; G Davies, 'The European Union Legislature as an Agent of the European Court of Justice' (2016) 54 *Journal of Common Market Studies* 846–61; A Stone Sweet and T Brunell, 'The European Court of Justice, State Noncompliance, and the Politics of Override' (2012) 106 *American Political Science Review* 204; A Grimmel, 'Judicial Interpretation or Judicial Activism? The Legacy of Rationalism in the Studies of the European Court of Justice' (2012) 18 *European Law Journal* 518; A Føllesdal, 'Much Ado about Nothing? Claims about Political Appointment to the Norwegian Supreme Court—and What to Do—and Not to Do—about It' (2013) 126(3) *Tidsskrift for Rettvitenskap* 364–71.

[4] J Ferejohn, 'Judicializing Politics, Politicizing Law' (2002) 65 *Law and Contemporary Problems* 41.

[5] See Grimmel above n 3 at 518.

[6] See A Vauchez, 'The Transnational Politics of Judicialization. *Van Gend En Loos* and the Making of EU Polity' (2010) 16 *European Law Journal* 1.

[7] See M Shapiro, 'Judges As Liars' (1994) *Harvard Journal of Law & Public Policy* 155.

2. THE SEPARATION OF POWERS MODEL

The SOP model is based on four basic assumptions.[8]

First, it assumes that judges have *policy preferences*, broadly understood. It means that they have values and ideas about government and society, and that they consider the effects of their decisions on government and society. In the US, scholars usually assume that these preferences can be captured by the same dimension that dominates American politics, the liberal–conservative dimension.[9] Similarly, in domestic European settings, the left-right dimension is considered the most important. For the CJEU, the most salient policy dimension is usually assumed to concern European integration versus national sovereignty. Pollack notes 'there is virtual consensus, among otherwise diverse disciplines and otherwise hostile schools of thought, that the Court should be studied as a unitary actor with a consistent, decades-long preference for European integration'.[10] The sources of this 'More Europe' bias have been identified as the institutional interest of the court in strengthening EU law over national law,[11] and as the ongoing socialisation of judges into a European judicial *esprit de corps*.[12]

Second, the SOP model assumes that judges are *rational actors* in the Weberian sense of choosing means to reach goals. It means that they will normally act in a manner that promotes their policy preferences, within the constraints set by law, procedure, professional and social norms. Assuming rationality does not necessarily mean assuming that the judges are perfectly informed about the effects of their decisions. Rationality may be bounded (i.e. exercised in a context of uncertainty).

Third, the SOP model assumes that the law is *not deterministic*. Often different interpretations and conclusions may be reasonably defended from a legal point of view. The CJEU is bound by the EU Treaties; its decisions follow from primary and secondary law. But EU law is often vague and opens up for different interpretations with different implications for legal integration. It is in these cases that the policy preferences of the judges may play a role.

---

[8] See Marks above n 1; Ferejohn and Weingast above n 4 at 263; Segal above n 1 at 28.

[9] JA Segal and HJ Spaeth, 'The Authors Respond' (1994) 4 *Law and Courts* 10.

[10] MA Pollack, *The New EU Legal History: What's New, What's Missing?* (Social Science Research Network, Rochester, NY, 28 February 2013) 6. Available at: http://papers.ssrn.com/abstract=2207170 (last accessed 29 May 2013).

[11] G Garrett, RD Kelemen and H Schulz, 'The European Court of Justice, National Governments, and Legal Integration in the European Union' (1998) 52 *International Organization* 149; G Tsebelis and G Garrett, 'The Institutional Foundations of Intergovernmentalism and Supranationalism in the European Union' (2001) 55 *International Organization* 357.

[12] A Vauchez, 'Keeping the Dream Alive: The European Court of Justice and the Transnational Fabric of Integrationist Jurisprudence' (2012) 4 *European Political Science Review* 51. However, see Malecki for a critical review: M Malecki, *The Politics of Constitutional Review: Evidence from the European Court of Justice*, 2010. Available at: http://openscholarship.wustl.edu/etd/414.

Fourth, courts are *dependent on others* for the effective implementation of their decisions.[13] In Hamilton's famous words, courts lack both the power of 'the sword' held by the executive, and 'the purse' controlled by the legislature.[14] Thus, a court that makes decisions that upset actors possessing such power risks finds itself ineffective, ignored or overruled. In liberal democracies, where the rule of law is one of the strongest norms in society, outright defiance of court decisions is rare. But compliance may be contained in more subtle ways,[15] and legislative override may reverse the judges preferred policy trajectory.[16]

We argue that these four assumptions are realistic with respect to the CJEU. Over the years, judges of the CJEU have not been shy to display 'a certain idea of Europe'.[17] EU law is often open-ended; there is little reason to assume that judges will not make boundedly rational predictions about the likely effects of their decisions. Furthermore, as an international court with relatively uncertain levels of diffuse social legitimacy,[18] the CJEU is more dependent on state authorities for its effectiveness than most domestic courts.

The four assumptions translate, by means of deductive reasoning, into the following central claims:

(1) Judges decide cases not only based on strict legal analysis and in accordance with professional norms, but also with the purpose of promoting policy preferences (such as European integration).
(2) Judges anticipate reactions from outside audiences and strategically adjust their behaviour.

In the words of Epstein and Knight, judges are *sophisticated policy seekers.*[19] They are sophisticated in the sense that they take measures to avoid provoking a backlash against their preferred policy goals. Such measures may include deferring in the case at hand to the preferences of those who may execute such a backlash. It may also mean engaging in legitimation strategies aimed at sheltering or defending potentially controversial decisions.

---

[13] GN Rosenberg, *The Hollow Hope: Can Courts Bring About Social Change?* 2nd edn (University Of Chicago Press, Chicago, 2008).

[14] *Federalist*, 1788 78.

[15] L Conant, *Justice Contained: Law and Politics in the European Union* (Cornell University Press, Ithaca, NY, 2002).

[16] O Larsson and D Naurin, 'Judicial Independence and Political Uncertainty. How the Risk of Override Impacts on the Court of Justice of the EU' (2016) 70(2) *International Organization* 377–408.

[17] P Pescatore, 'The Doctrine of "Direct Effect": An Infant Disease of Community Law' (1983) 8 *European Law Review* 155.

[18] JL Gibson and GA Caldeira, 'The Legitimacy of Transnational Legal Institutions: Compliance, Support, and the European Court of Justice' (1995) *American Journal of Political Science* 459.

[19] See Epstein and Knight above n 1 at Chapter 3.

It is important to note the words "also" and "not only" in the two claims that are deduced from the four assumptions. A common straw man argument of the SOP model (and rational choice theory generally) is that it claims that policy preferences, strategy and power are the only factors that count. This is not our claim (or indeed the claim of other sensible applications of the SOP model). It would be absurd to argue that legal and professional constraints were not key determinants in the decisions of the CJEU. Moreover, the claim we make is not that decision making in the CJEU is mainly about policy preferences, strategy and power. We claim that *in addition* to legal and professional constraints, decision making in the CJEU is also, and to a significant degree, about policy preferences, strategy and power.

The four assumptions and the two claims constitute the core of the theoretical model. It is simple and transparent. The assumptions may be discussed and criticised, the implications may be tested empirically in many different ways. In the next section, we discuss different ways in which we have put the SOP model to test in the context of the CJEU.

3. EMPIRICAL APPLICATION OF THE SOP MODEL TO THE CJEU

Our research is based on a data collection that includes most of the cases in the preliminary reference procedure during a 12-year period, 1997–2008.[20] The project has generated a number of empirical findings that have been presented and published elsewhere.[21] In this section, we will briefly review some of these findings and demonstrate how they speak to the validity of the SOP model as outlined above. Overall, the findings make us more confident that the model is important to understanding judicial politics in the European Union.

We have gathered data on 84 per cent of the preliminary rulings that were filed on the Court's desk during the years 1997 to 2008/between 1997 and 2008 (and decided by the Court up to 2011) amounting to 1,599 cases including 3,845 questions raised by national courts. Not included are those where no oral hearing was held at the Court. An oral hearing will always

---

[20] The project has been pursued in close collaboration with law professors Per Cramér and Andreas Moberg at the University of Gothenburg (although the claims made in this chapter are the responsibility of the authors only). The original data collection was financed by the Swedish Foundation for the Humanities and Social Sciences (Riksbankens Jubileumsfond).

[21] See Larsson and Naurin above n 16; O Larsson and D Naurin, 'Split Vision. Multi-Dimensionality in the International Legal Policy Space'. Paper Presented at the American Political Science Association Annual Meeting, September 1–4, 2016 Philadelphia, PA.; O Larsson M Derlén and J Lindholm 'Speaking Law to Power. The Strategic Use of Precedent of the Court of Justice of the European Union' 50(7) *Comparative Political Studies* 879–907; P Cramér *et al*, 'See You in Luxembourg? EU Governments´ Observations under the Preliminary Reference Procedure' *SIEPS Report No 5* (2016).

be held if one Member State so requests, which means that the missing data is unlikely to include politically salient cases. Our source for the observations of Member State governments is Reports for the Hearing. These are documents made by the Reporting Judge as part of the Court's preparations in the case, including the relevant background to the case and the main arguments made by different parties. The reports contain the original questions posed by the national court as well as summaries of the main arguments of the parties, the Commission and any Member State government that submitted an observation in the case. In our data, 92 per cent of the cases contain at least one government observation, 65 per cent at least two observations and 41 per cent three or more observations.

However, the Court does not publish the actual observations. Reports for the Hearing have not been published since 1993, which means that, since then, it has been very difficult to collect systematic data on the Member States' observations based on public records. Fortunately, we were able to gain access to the reports in the archives of the Swedish Foreign Ministry, on the condition that they would be used only for research purposes.

The coding of the positions proceeded in the following way. First, we identified the key legal issues involved in the questions posed by the national court. These are often formulated/worded as a question that can be answered with a Yes or a No. The next/following step was to define the positions of the actors involved in the process. These positions were subsequently coded according to their implication on legal integration. If a position implied that EU law would restrict the autonomy of Member States, it was coded as 'More Europe'. If no clear implication in terms of legal integration could be drawn from the position, the code was 'Ambivalent'. If the position implied that EU law should not be interpreted as constraining the Member States in the case at hand, the code would be 'Preserved National Sovereignty'.

The data has been analysed using statistical methods. For a more detailed motivation and description of the methods used, we will have to refer to the original publications.[22] There are two main advantages with using large-N studies in this context. First, most scholars tend to draw general conclusions from their work. When making general claims about what a court does, or how judges decide cases, basing the conclusions on five to ten selected cases is *ceteris paribus* less credible then if the conclusions are based on every case before the court. Second, applying statistical tests on the data means making use of the laws of mathematics to reduce the risk of overestimating the findings. Significance tests means putting on a straightjacket that serves to ensure that the inherent tendency towards selective perception does not fool the researcher into seeing patterns that exist only in his or her mind. Put simply, you cannot talk yourself out of a non-significant statistical correlation.

[22] Ibid.

3.1. Findings

Does the CJEU have a tendency to prefer more European legal integration? Our research contains two pieces of evidence that speak to the question of whether CJEU judges have 'a certain idea of Europe', compared to the Member State governments of the EU. First, we can simply compare the positions taken that were coded on the 'More Europe—Preserved National Sovereignty' scale as described above. The left-hand panel of Figure 1 shows that the Member States indeed tend to make interpretations of EU law that are more lenient towards national sovereignty concerns than the CJEU, the General Advocate (AG) and the European Commission. While all Member States have a negative balance, indicating that they defend national sovereignty more often than they promote more legal integration, the CJEU, the Commission and the AG have a positive balance.[23]

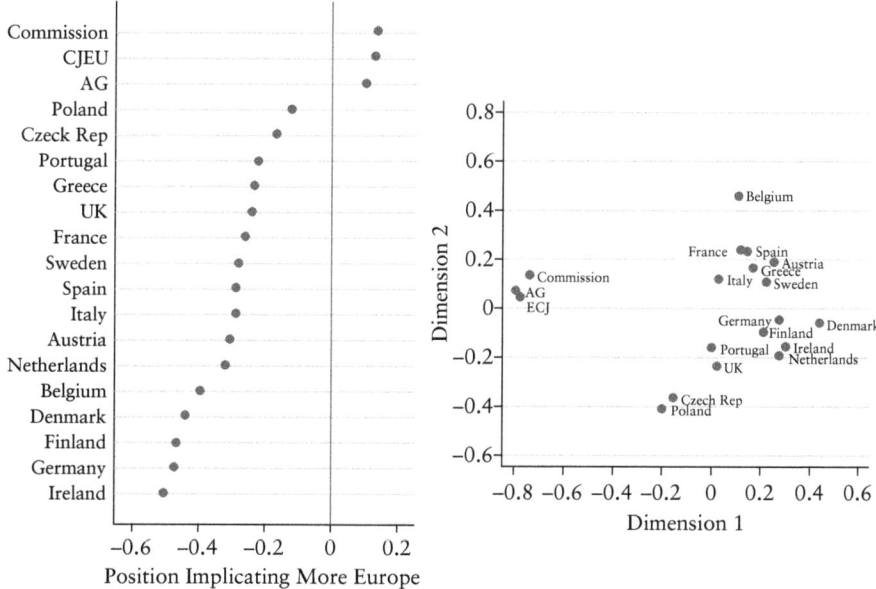

Figure 8.1: Preferences and conflict dimensions in the EU legal policy space

Note: The x-axis of the left-hand figure indicates the balance between positions favouring More Europe vs Preserved National Sovereignty. The right-hand figure shows multidimensional scaling of pairwise similarities. Eigenvalues: 2.51 (dim 1) and 0.91 (dim 2).

Source: Cramer et al 'See You in Luxembourg?'

[23] This is not only a question of Member States defending their own national laws and regulations. The pattern is also similar when we only include observations that were filed in cases originating in other Member States.

The right-hand panel of Figure 1 shows the results of a more inductive approach to the same data.[24] The picture can be read like a distance map, where two actors being closer to each other means that they more often take similar positions in the cases at hand. We find again a clear difference between the supranational actors, including the CJEU, and the Member States. The first dimension is highly and significantly correlated with the hand-coded More Europe—Preserved National Sovereignty scale. The most reasonable interpretation of this pattern is that this is, again, the European integration dimension that shows up in the analysis.

We have also analysed the position of the Member States and the CJEU on the second dimension. In our view, the most credible interpretation is that the second dimension is related to what political economists call 'the varieties of capitalism', and the categories of liberal and social market economies.[25] In brief, liberal market economies are characterised by low levels of taxes and social expenditure, and decentralised labour market relations, while social market economies score high on these scales. We have conducted several statistical analyses that indicate that there is a significant correlation between the position of the Member States on the second dimension and their respective values on these political-economic variables.[26] The pattern is thus a symptom of the major political conflict dimension in Europe, the left-right dimension.

Importantly, we find no evidence that the CJEU takes a distinct position on the second dimension. It does not seem to favour either side in conflicts that relate to highly salient welfare state or labour market issues. What we do find, however, is that when there is a conflict between the Member States on this dimension, the CJEU is more likely to take a decision in favour of More Europe. This makes sense from a strategic Separation of Powers perspective: When Member States are in conflict with each other on the second dimension, the Court has more discretion to promote European integration on the first dimension. The risk that it would face a unified Member State backlash in the form of override, non-compliance or any other hostile reaction is lower when the Member States disagree with each other.[27]

We report on a similar finding in a different study, which uses regression analysis on the same data (the 3,845 legal issues) to identify the correlation

---

[24] This analysis is based on Multidimensional Scaling. We obtain very similar results using other types of dimensional analyses, such as Principal Component Analysis and Optimal Classification.

[25] M Höpner and A Schäfer, *Integration Among Unequals: How the Heterogeneity of European Varieties of Capitalism Shapes the Social and Democratic Potential of the EU* (Max-Planck-Institut für Gesellschaftsforschung, 2012) 429–55; PA Hall and D Soskice, *Varieties of Capitalism : The Institutional Foundations of Comparative Advantage: The Institutional Foundations of Comparative Advantage* (Oxford, Oxford University Press, 2001).

[26] See Larsson and Naurin above n 21.

[27] Ibid.

between the position of Member States and the Court's decisions.[28] This study demonstrates, first, a strong correlation between the positions taken by Member States in their written observations in the proceedings, and the Court's subsequent decisions. Importantly, this is not simply a bivariate correlation stemming from the fact that all actors interpret the same legal texts. By also including the positions of the General Advocate and the Commission in the regression models, we show that there is a significant effect of the observations of Member States independently of the positions of the supranational-legal actors. The effect is also quite important: The chances that the Court decides in favour of More Europe more than doubles—an increase in probability from 0.14 to 0.37—if one major and one smaller Member State argue in favour of More Europe rather than in favour of Preserved National Sovereignty.

Thus, there is a clear correlation between what the Member States say and what the Court does, which goes beyond the legal texts. Furthermore, the same study also finds that the CJEU is more likely to promote European legal integration when the Member States have a harder time agreeing to a unified response in the Council. This is the case when the voting rule in the Council is unanimity rather than qualified majority, such as when the Court interprets the treaties. This is, of course, very much in line with the SOP model. The Court's discretion to promote its policy preferences increases when the political constraints are weaker.

Finally, we have also analysed the effect of the written observations of the Member States on the legal rhetoric of the Court.[29] For this purpose, we have collaborated with Derlén and Lindholm, who have calculated network measures of the CJEU's citations to its own case law.[30] The key finding in our study is that the Court is using more precedent—and more authoritative precedent—when it takes a decision that contradicts the observations submitted by Member States. Thus, the more controversial the Court's decision in the eyes of the Member States, the more the Court increases its efforts to make a persuasive legal argument.

In the regression models, we control for a number of other factors that may also influence the number of citations, such as the salience and complexity of the case and whether the Court's decision is in conflict with the General Advocate's and the Commission's opinions. We use a number of different network measures in the analysis, some of which are more sophisticated than others. The most easily interpretable measure is *outdegree*,

---

[28] See Larsson and Naurin above n 16.

[29] See Larsson, Derlén and Lindholm above n 21 at 897–907.

[30] M Derlén and J Lindholm, 'Goodbye van Gend En Loos, Hello Bosman? Using Network Analysis to Measure the Importance of Individual CJEU Judgments' (2014) 20 *European Law Journal* 667; M Derlén and J Lindholm, 'Characteristics of Precedent: The Case Law of the European Court of Justice in Three Dimensions' (2015) 16 *German Law Journal* 1073.

which is a simple count of how many other cases are cited in a decision. Using this measure, we find that the CJEU cites on average 6.3 previous cases when it takes a decision that goes in the same direction as the (net) position of the member states. However, it cites on average 7.7 cases, when it takes a decision that is in conflict with the Member States' view (i.e. a difference of 1.5 citations).

These analyses of the legal rhetoric of the CJEU also make sense from the perspective of a SOP model. If the CJEU has a preference in favour of more legal integration in the EU, and takes a decision that goes in that direction but which is in conflict with the preferred position of the Member States, then it is rational for the judges to increase their rhetorical efforts. To avoid a negative reaction from those who control the sword and the purse, the Court employs its key weapon—legal authority. Thus, we interpret these finding as evidence that the Court attempts to persuade a potentially critical audience that controversial decisions are strongly embedded in law.

4. CONCLUSIONS

Judges will always deny that their decisions contain elements of policy preferences, strategy and power. Presumably, Shapiro argues, judges could tell the losing party that: 'You have lost because we, the judges, have chosen that you should lose. We have so chosen because we think society would be better off if you lost.' But that would destroy the legitimate authority of the court as an impartial arbitrator, and undermine the norm of rule of law, on which civilised societies are based. Therefore, Shapiro continues

> in all modern societies, and in all cases, judges tell the loser: 'You did not lose because we the judges chose that you should lose. You lost because the law required that you should lose.' That is the answer arrived at to satisfy the losers through hundreds of years of experiments in numerous societies. This paradox means that although every court makes law in a few of its cases, judges must always deny that they make law. I neither criticize nor defend courts as an institution; I simply assert their existential position in the world. They live that paradox; they have lived it in the past and will continue to live it in the future. There is nothing we can do about it, and there is nothing they can do about it. That makes courts part of a distinctive subset of political institutions: one that must always deny that they are wielding political authority when they in fact do wield political authority. Such is the nature of courts. They must always deny their authority to make law, even when they are making law. One may call this justificatory history, but I call it lying. Courts and judges always lie. Lying is the nature of the judicial activity. One must get over the moral *angst* about that and quarrel instead about what law judges make, when, and how fast.[31]

---

[31] See Shapiro above n 7 at 156.

The Separation of Powers model is a positive, not a normative, theory, and thus contains/includes no moral *angst* about judges being sophisticated policy seekers. The purpose of the model is to provide a reasonable account of one aspect of judicial decision making, namely the strategic behaviour of courts in relation to the executive and legislative branches of power, in cases where the law is not deterministic and judges have their own personal ideas about what a just society looks like. The theory's assumptions are not unrealistically demanding in liberal constitutional democracies, and also not for the Court of Justice of the European Union. As our research has demonstrated, its predictions are also consistent with systematic empirical analyses of a large number of cases.

Our conclusion, therefore, is that the specific trajectory of European legal integration is more than just the logical consequence of the inherent meaning of the EU treaties as 'discovered' by the CJEU. It is also not, as the neofunctionalist story has it, the purposeful invention of an unconstrained runaway agent of which the Masters of the Treaties lost control.[32] European legal integration is driven by a court with a certain idea of Europe, and with a sensitive radar to where the political boundaries of its discretion go.

[32] AM Burley and W Mattli, 'Europe before the Court: A Political Theory of Legal Integration' (1993) 47 *International Organization* 41; See Stone Sweet and Brunell above n 3 at 204.

9

Referring Court Influence in the Preliminary Ruling Procedure

The Swedish Example

ANNA WALLERMAN

1. INTRODUCTION

IT HAS BEEN repeatedly held in scholarly literature that national referring courts, by virtue of their role in the preliminary ruling procedure,
enjoy an influential position when it comes to partaking in and influencing the development of EU law.[1] The preliminary ruling procedure, laid
down in Article 267 in the Treaty of the Functioning of the European Union
(TFEU), opens up a direct channel of communication between national
courts and the Court of Justice (CJEU).[2] The national court formulates the
question(s), and the CJEU provides the answer(s). The decision of if, when
and how to seize the CJEU is made at the discretion of the national court
itself. In its order for reference (OfR), the referring court provides not only
the question, but also its factual and legal background, thus essentially providing the Court's first impression of the issue at stake. Furthermore, in
the OfR, the national court has the opportunity to criticise previous CJEU
judgments, defend points of domestic law or national identity, or invite the
Court to take a new stand.

Little research has, however, been undertaken to establish whether
national courts make use of this opportunity to influence the Court of

---

[1] M Bobek, 'Of Feasibility and Silent Elephants: The Legitimacy of the Court of Justice
Through the Eyes of National Courts' in M Adams *et al* (eds), *Judging Europe's Judges: The
Legitimacy of the Case Law of the European Court of Justice* (Oxford, Hart, 2013) 197,
223; T Tridimas, 'Bifurcated Justice: The Dual Character of Judicial Protection in EU Law'
in A Rosas *et al* (eds), *The Court of Justice and the Construction of Europe: Analyses and
Perspectives on Sixty Years of Case-Law* (Amsterdam, TMC Asser Press, 2013) 367, 378f;
A Maitrepierre, 'Le droit de l'Union européenne et le juge français: circonstances et incidences
d'une rencontre' (2007–2008) *Revue des Affaires Européennes* 539 at 545.

[2] On the importance of such dialogue, see the contribution of A Arnull, Chapter 1 in this
volume.

Justice, and virtually none has examined whether such attempts have been successful. This chapter, which constitutes a first, preliminary study in a research project with the working title *As You Sow, So Shall You Reap?*, seeks to fill these gaps as regards the supreme courts of Sweden. The purpose of the chapter is to find out if, how and to what extent these courts make use of the references for preliminary rulings to further particular legal positions, and to what extent they by doing so are successful in influencing the judgment of the CJEU.

The objective is realised through an empirical analysis of the OfRs sent to the CJEU by the Swedish Supreme Court (SC) and Supreme Administrative Court (SAC), and the judgments they have resulted in. The analysis shows that the Swedish supreme courts are generally reluctant to offer an opinion or even argumentation on the questions they refer for preliminary rulings. In consequence, the findings neither confirm nor refute the claims that referring courts play an influential part in the development of CJEU case law.

The argument proceeds as follows. The following section gives an account of previous research of relevance. Section 3 describes the materials used and methods employed by the study. The results of the empirical analysis are presented in section 4. Lastly, section 5 discusses the results and presents some cautious conclusions.

2. PREVIOUS RESEARCH

Several studies have discussed the willingness of national judiciaries to turn to the CJEU with requests for preliminary rulings.[3] These studies have, however, focused on the number of references, rather than their content.

The national courts' use of OfRs to promote a particular legal position has been subject to research particularly from a political science perspective. Drawing on a dataset of free movement and gender equality cases from mainly German, Dutch and British courts, Nyikos has argued that national courts do make strategic use of the possibility to refer cases.[4] She finds that the referring courts have submitted a view on the answer to the referred

---

[3] From the Nordic perspective, see U Bernitz, *Förhandsavgöranden av EU-domstolen: Svenska domstolars hållning och praxis*, SIEPS report 2010:2; U Bernitz, *Förhandsavgöranden av EU-domstolen: Utvecklingen av svenska domstolars hållning och praxis 2010–2015*, SIEPS report 2016:9; M Wind *et al*, 'The Uneven Legal Push for Europe: Questioning Variation when National Courts go to Europe' (2009) 10 *European Union Politics* 63; M Wind, 'The Nordics, the EU and the Reluctance Towards Supranational Judicial Review' (2010) 48 *Journal of Common Market Studies* 1039; M Broberg and N Fenger, 'Variations in Member States' Preliminary References to the Court of Justice—Are Structural Factors (Part of) the Explanation?' (2013) 19 *European Law Journal* 488.

[4] S Nyikos, 'Strategic Interaction among Courts within the Preliminary Reference Process—Stage 1: National Court Preemptive Opinions' (2006) 45 *European Journal of Political Research* 527.

questions in 41 per cent of the cases. In a Swedish context, Leijon and Karlsson have studied the references sent from Swedish courts at all levels of the judiciary between 1995 and 2009. They conclude, *inter alia*, that the cases referred from Swedish courts are fairly equally distributed on the scale from non-political to highly politically sensitive cases and that the referring court offers an opinion in 52 per cent of the cases.[5] Neither study examines to what extent the Court of Justice appears to have been influenced by the views offered by the national courts.

3. METHOD AND MATERIALS

3.1. Materials

Both previous studies rely solely on the materials produced by the CJEU: judgments and in the study by Leijon and Karlsson, Opinions of Advocates General (AG). In contrast, the present study relies both on the OfRs composed by the referring courts and on the judgments of the Court of Justice. It includes all cases that have been decided by the CJEU at the request of the Swedish Supreme Court or Supreme Administrative Court up until 1 July 2016, which renders a total dataset of 40 cases, of which 15 are references from the SC and 25 from the SAC. The OfRs are analysed both individually, in order to determine the degree to which they can be said to betray an interest in the direction of the development of Union law on the part of the referring court, and in comparison with the eventual judgment. The CJEU judgments are analysed only as part of a comparison with the OfR.

3.2. The Analysis of the OfRs

An OfR in the preliminary ruling procedure must include a summary of the dispute before the national court, references to the applicable national and Union legal provisions, and an explanation of the reasons that caused the national court to request a preliminary ruling.[6] Furthermore, the national court is invited to offer its own view on the question(s) referred.[7] All in all, the document should be about ten pages in length.[8]

The analysis of the OfRs has focused on the occurrence of statements aiming or liable to exert an influence over the reasoning of the CJEU. Evidencing the referring court's active interest in Union law, such statements

---

[5] K Leijon and C Karlsson, 'Nationella domstolar som politiska aktörer—främjare av rättslig integration eller försvarare av nationella intressen?' (2013) 115 *Statsvetenskaplig tidskrift* 5.

[6] Art 94 of the Rules of Procedure of the Court of Justice (OJ L 173, 26.6.2013).

[7] Paragraph 17 of the Recommendations to national courts and tribunals in relation to the initiation of preliminary ruling proceedings (OJ 2016/C 439/01).

[8] Ibid, para 14.

will also be referred to as *interest indicators*. Both explicit and implicit elements of persuasion have been taken into account. In particular, the analysis has focused on four parts of the references: (1) the section providing an account of the relevant national law, (2) the reasons for requesting the preliminary ruling, where they go beyond a mere explanation as to why the Article 267 TFEU requirements are fulfilled, (3) the choice and phrasing of the question(s), and of course (4) the proposed answer (if any).

A reproduction or summary of the relevant national rules (1) is required in an OfR. However, such summaries can be 'pure' in the sense that they only recite the text of the relevant statute, or they can include comments added by the referring court such as explanations as to the reasons for a certain legislative choice, or notes on how the rule has been interpreted in case law or scholarly writing. Such comments are liable to either increase the CJEU's understanding of national law, and in the prolongation the chances of it being upheld, or conversely raise doubts as to the EU law compatibility of the rule in question.

As for the reasons for the referral provided by the national court (2), three main factors have been subject to examination. First, whether the national court has made references to any EU legal sources (apart from the provision whose interpretation is being sought); most significantly to previous CJEU case law, where particularly discussions as to how a previous ruling is relevant to the circumstances of the case before the referring court have been considered significant. Secondly, whether the OfR contains argumentation based on distinguishing facts or circumstances in the case at hand, which the national court considers relevant for the interpretation of Union law or the applicability of CJEU precedent. Thirdly, whether there is a discussion as to the result of applying various methods of interpretation, where the national court provides arguments for various outcomes without taking a position of its own. This last factor has been considered particularly significant where it appears to betray an implicit preference for one of the solutions.

Such implied preferences are to be distinguished, however, from factor (4), the preferred outcome, which includes only explicitly stated views on the answer to be given. Lastly, the analysis of the phrasing of the question (3) has mainly consisted in determining whether a question is leading in any direction, either by itself or in conjunction with the other questions asked in the same OfR.

Following this analysis and drawing on the taxonomy developed by Coutron,[9] the OfRs have been organised into three categories based on whether they are mainly descriptive, analytical or argumentative. The categories thus represent three different approaches on the part of the national court.

---

[9] L Coutron, 'La motivation des questions préjudicielles' in E Neframi (ed), *Renvoi préjudiciel et marge d'appreciation du juge national* (Éditions Larcier 2015) 101.

Category A includes cases where the national court simply forwards a question to the CJEU without added analysis and with little or no motivation as to why the question is relevant or its answer unclear. OfRs in this category are signified by neutral descriptions of national law, often consisting of uncommented reproductions of the relevant rules directly from the statute book. Comments on EU law are limited to an explanation as to why the referring courts consider the Article 267 TFEU prerequisites for requesting a preliminary ruling to be fulfilled.

A textbook example of a category A OfR is provided by case C-68/07 *Sundelind Lopez*.[10] The case concerned jurisdiction in matrimonial matters under Regulation No 2201/2003. One Swedish provision, Section 3:2 of the Act (1904:26) on certain international matters relating to marriage and guardianship, is reproduced in the exact wording of the statute and left without further comment. Under the heading 'The need for a preliminary ruling', the referring court notes firstly, that the reasoning of the lower instance courts has been based on Swedish literature (the significance of this fact remains unclear; possibly the SC is suggesting that their research into the legal sources has been unsatisfactory), secondly, that the interpretation of Article 7 of the Regulation is directly decisive for the outcome of the matter, and lastly, that there is no applicable case law from the CJEU.

Category B consists of cases where the national court shows an active interest and provides some insight into Union law, for instance by discussing various possible interpretations, but without expressing an opinion of its own. A typical B case is characterised by a demonstration by the referring court of a considerable level of understanding of EU law and a wish to further the development of EU law or participate in the interpretation thereof. In the typical category B OfR the referring court does so, however, without taking a position on the solution of the case.

Case C-203/12 *Billerud*[11] concerned the calculation of a fine for not surrendering carbon dioxide emission allowances on time pursuant to Directive 2003/87/EC. The questions referred were essentially whether the Directive permitted leniency when the failure to comply with the Directive was merely technical or administrative. The referring court mentioned three different interpretive methods, of which the first would preclude leniency, the third would provide for it and the second allowed for either conclusion. The referring court did not, however, express a preference for either of the interpretations, but simply concluded that the existence of different alternatives meant that there was scope for doubt as to the correct interpretation of the Directive.

Seeing that most of the OfRs included in this study fall into categories A and B, and that the latter category includes orders of a very heterogeneous character, category B has been further divided into three subcategories,

---

[10] ECLI:EU:C:2007:740; NJA 2008 s 71.
[11] ECLI:EU:C:2013:664; NJA 2014 s 79.

designated Ba, Bb and Bc. The typical B case discussed above has been categorised as Bb, whereas the label Ba signifies cases which borders on the
mainly descriptive approach that characterises category A, and Bc desig-
nates cases which contain argumentative elements or where the national
court implicitly hints at a preferred outcome.[12]

Category C, lastly, has been reserved for cases where the national court
displays a clear interest in advancing a certain legal-political position, and
where a preferred answer is explicitly suggested.

Finally, it should be noted that a national court in principle remains
free to choose either of the schematic strategies set out above regardless of
the complexity of the case. There is for instance no necessary correlation
between a complicated legal issue and a more analytical or argumentative
OfR. The length of the OfRs, which typically can be expected to increase
with the complexity of the case, has not been taken into account in the
analysis or classification.

3.3. Measuring Impact: The Comparison between Judgments and OfRs

The analysis of the influence of the national courts' references on the eventual judgments of the CJEU has been carried out by means of a comparison between the two documents in question. In this comparison the study
relies on an adaptation of the method developed by Šadl and Sankari for
evaluating the impact of the AG's Opinion on the judgment of the Court.[13]
As in the analysis of the OfRs, and following the approach taken by Šadl and
Sankari, both explicit and implicit influence has been taken into account.
Considering, however, that the Court of Justice is significantly more reluctant to cite the OfR than the AG's Opinion in its reasoning, the implicit
influence becomes comparatively more important in the present context.

In many cases, national courts, unlike the Advocates General, offer
neither a coherent legal argument nor an answer to the questions. Instead it
becomes necessary to focus on separate elements or parts of the reasoning,
in order to identify instances of correspondence between OfR and judgment. Particular importance has been assigned to (1) the choice of legal
sources relied on by the CJEU, compared to those discussed in the OfR,
(2) the positioning of the question within a legal context (including references to national law or particular characteristics of the case before the
national court), (3) the reasoning of the Court as regards arguments and

---

[12] For an example see case C-540/09 *Skandinaviska Enskilda Banken*, discussed at n 16
below.
[13] U Šadl and S Sankari, 'The Elusive Influence of the Advocate General on the Court
of Justice: The Case of European Citizenship' (2017) *Yearbook of European Law* yex001.
doi: 10.1093/yel/yex001.

interpretive methods brought up by the referring court, and of course (4) the outcome, where the referring court has expressly or implicitly indicated a preferred outcome. Additionally, (5) explicit references to the position or suggestions of the national court by the CJEU have been taken into account.

A correspondence between the OfR and the judgment as to the legal sources cited (1) has been considered significant even in cases where the referring court and the CJEU have arrived at different conclusions, as the correspondence in itself indicates a similar understanding of the problem. As for factors (2) and (3), they are highly context-dependent. The understanding or positioning of the issue (2) is generally most interesting in fields of shared competence and cases which concern the compatibility of national law and EU law, and mainly where the national and Union measures seek to fulfil different purposes. However, also references to particular facts or circumstances regarding the dispute at hand are included here, if the CJEU seizes on a fact or circumstance previously brought forward by the referring court. The reasoning of the CJEU (3) in this context refers not to the whole body of reasons found in the judgment, but to the recurrence of arguments brought forward by the national court. In this analysis it has also been taken into consideration whether a certain argument is part of the *ratio decidendi*, or rather functions as a support for a conclusion already reached, or even constitutes *obiter dictum*. When it comes to arguments addressed by the Court only in order to refute them, they have been considered significant in varying degrees depending on the way in which the referring court has put the argument forward.

As for corresponding outcomes (4), it should be noted that the comparison here includes all cases where an outcome preference can be inferred from the OfR, even though the national court has not explicitly stated it. This category of cases is thus wider than the outcome preferences considered relevant when categorising the OfRs (but builds on factors that have been assigned weight under other headings in that categorisation). Lastly, direct references (5) by the CJEU to the referring court or the OfR have been assigned varying significance depending on the kind of question the reference concerns, with references on matters of fact scoring lower than references on matters of law.

Following this analysis, an overall degree of correspondence—which functions as a proxy for the degree of influence of the referring court—has been established through a holistic assessment of all the factors. The degree of correspondence is expressed utilising a scale from 0 to 5, where 0 indicates no correspondence at all, 1 indicates insignificant levels of correspondence (i.e. not going beyond what can reasonably be expected from two courts deliberating on the same topic (for example, a small overlap on case law cited)), 3 indicates moderate correspondence, such as high levels of correspondence in limited parts of the judgment or an isolated positive reference to the referring court in a matter of law, and 5 indicates a very strong correspondence in reasoning, sources and outcome.

4. FINDINGS

4.1. Findings Related to the OfRs

The Swedish supreme courts generally offer little or no reasoning on the questions referred to the CJEU. Only one of the 40 cases examined (3 per cent) could be referred to the C category. Meanwhile, an overall third of the cases were found to belong to category A, which indicates a lack of any significant indicators of the referring court attempting to influence the CJEU's interpretation of EU law. The distribution is illustrated in Table 9.1.

Table 9.1: Number of OfRs by court and category

	SC	SAC	Total
A	8 (53%)	6 (24%)	14 (35%)
B	7 (47%)	18 (72%)	25 (62%)
C	0 (0%)	1 (4%)	1 (3%)
Total	15	25	40

The B category is the largest one, representing 58 per cent of all OfRs in the dataset and two thirds of the OfRs from the SAC. This category has therefore been broken up into three subcategories, which allows cases that are bordering one of the other categories to be singled out. The results of this subcategorisation are illustrated in Table 9.2.

Table 9.2: Subcategorisation of category B OfRs by court

	SC	SAC	Total
Ba	1 (14%)	5 (28%)	6 (24%)
Bb	4 (57%)	9 (50%)	13 (52%)
Bc	2 (29%)	4 (22%)	6 (24%)
Total	7	18	25

This subcategorisation also permits a more nuanced understanding of the level and direction of activity of the courts. Categories A and Ba include half of the cases in the dataset (52.5 per cent), while categories C and Bc together represent less than a fifth (17.5 per cent). This reaffirms the previous finding, that the Swedish supreme courts tend towards less reasoned OfRs.

In this subcategorisation, it has been particularly relevant to take into account more subtle nuances expressed by the national court. Taken together, a number of more or less inconspicuous statements may contribute to an overall impression of a view implicitly advocated by the referring court. A case from the Bc category provides an illustration:

> The referring court in case C-540/09 *Skandinaviska Enskilda Banken*[14] did not explicitly offer an opinion on the question at issue, which was one of exemptions from VAT. However, under the heading 'The need for a preliminary ruling and the question', where it developed its own reasoning, it did relate two arguments put forward by the applicant in the main proceedings. Furthermore, it appears that the referring court improved these arguments by adding legal sources that were not mentioned in the summary of the party's submission, which is found under a previous heading in the OfR. The referring court also related its own previous case law, which did not support the applicant's position, but noted that the soundness of this jurisprudence had been called into question. Lastly, it noted that the CJEU had not previously had reason to decide whether the relevant exemption rules 'could be construed to include' services such as those at issue in the main proceeding. As a whole, the OfR gives the impression that the referring court favoured the position taken by the applicant in the main proceedings.

As for differences between the courts, it is clear from Table 9.1 that the SAC generally takes a more active position than the SC, particularly in that it has a significantly higher proportion of category B OfRs, and correspondingly a lower proportion of OfRs falling into category A. In the SAC there are also some indications of a development. All category A OfRs from the SAC were referred to the CJEU before 2005, that is to say during the first ten years of Sweden's membership of the Union. In the subsequent ten years and six months covered by the study, the SAC has produced two OfRs pertaining to category Ba, and none to category A. This may indicate that the SAC has developed a greater interest in or understanding of Union law.[15] In the references from the SC, no equivalent or similar development can be discerned; although the number of references increased from only four in the first ten years to eleven in the following ten (not counting references still pending before the CJEU at the study's cut-off date), the proportion of category A OfRs remains largely constant (50 per cent in 1995–2004 compared to 55 per cent from 2005 onwards).

The occurrence of particular interest indicators in the OfRs is indicated in Table 9.3. It should be noted from the outset, however, that the table records any occurrence of the factors in question, but does not include a qualitative assessment of the factor. Therefore, the following discussion cannot take into account whether the OfR refers to one previous CJEU judgment or five, whether a possible interpretation is mentioned in passing

---

[14] ECLI:EU:C:2011:137; HFD 2011 ref 38.
[15] See U Bernitz *Förhandsavgöranden av EU-domstolen* (2016) 102f, who, based on an examination of all preliminary rulings requested by Swedish courts but without breaking down the investigation at the individual court level, finds that the Swedish courts' attitude towards the preliminary ruling institute has matured.

or discussed at length, and so forth. Qualitative aspects have instead been taken into account in the holistic assessment of whether an OfR should be categorised as A, B, or C. The relatively high occurrence of some types of interest indicators even in the A category, where OfRs by definition can be expected to display few such indicators, thus means that those indicators are qualitatively weak, either in the individual case (eg a passing reference to a CJEU precedent) or because some types of interest indicators are by their nature more significant than others; for instance, offering an argument indicates stronger interest than merely suggesting a relevant legal source.

Table 9.3: Occurrence of interest indicators per category

	Comments on Swedish law	EU law sources	Relevant facts	Reasoning	View on outcome	Leading questions
A	50% (7)	29% (4)	14% (2)	0% (0)	0% (0)	14% (2)
B	64% (16)	72% (18)	64% (16)	40% (10)	0% (0)	44% (11)
Ba	67% (4)	33% (2)	67% (4)	17% (1)	0% (0)	33% (2)
Bb	62% (8)	85% (11)	78% (10)	42% (5)	0% (0)	50% (6)
Bc	67% (4)	83% (5)	40% (2)	67% (4)	0% (0)	50% (3)
C	0% (0)	100% (1)	100% (1)	100% (1)	100% (1)	100% (1)
Total	57% (23)	57% (23)	47% (19)	28% (11)	3% (1)	35% (14)

Percentages indicate the prevalence of the factor in relation to the size of each category. Numbers in parenthesis indicate the number of OfRs containing a certain indicator.

As the table shows, the most common display of the referring court taking an interest in EU law or in the outcome of the case is by citing one or more sources of EU law or by adding comments to its account of national law. Both factors were found in 57 per cent of the OfRs. There are, however, notable differences in the distribution of these factors between the categories. References to legal sources were found in 29 per cent of the category A OfRs, whereas in the B category, sources of EU law are cited into three out of four cases. In contrast, variations between the categories when it comes to the treatment of national law are comparatively small, and the occurrence of comments even in category A OfRs is remarkably high: 50 per cent, compared to 64 per cent in category B. This indicates that the presence of comments on national law—and it may be recalled that these are comments that go beyond what is required by the Rules of Procedure[16]—is a poor predictor of the level of interest or activism of the national court, and perhaps also that national courts are not being strategic in their description of national law.

---

[16] See text to n 6 above.

Another interest indicator that is relatively common is the identification by the national court of a particular fact or circumstance in the case pending before it, which distinguishes the case from previous case law or in any other way is likely, in the referring court's opinion, to affect the outcome. In the entire dataset such distinguishing facts are pointed to by the referring courts in 47 per cent of the OfRs. Similar to the citation of EU legal sources, the occurrence of this indicator increases from only 14 per cent in category A to 64 per cent in category B. Here we can only speculate whether this is a strategic choice in the A cases—by not disclosing its analysis on matters of fact the national court retains more choices as to the outcome of the case once the CJEU judgment has been delivered—or if on the contrary it indicates that where a national court takes an interest in EU law, it endeavours to cooperate with the Court.

In case C-441/99 *Gharevheran*,[17] the question concerned the applicant's possibility to rely on the direct effect of Directive 80/897/EEC. The referring court noted that the CJEU in previous judgments had ruled that the directive could not take direct effect, as its provisions left too much discretion to the Member States. However, the national court pointed out in its reasoning that the circumstances of the case at hand were different in that the Swedish legislature had already exercised the discretion in question. In the subsequent judgment this was accepted as a relevant distinguishing factor.

In case C-91/12 *PFC Clinic*,[18] the referring court asked four questions, where the last three mainly served to point out circumstances that the court considered potentially relevant for the answer. The first question was essentially whether plastic surgery and other cosmetic treatments should be exempt from VAT. Further, the SAC asked (emphasis added): (2) Does it affect that assessment if the surgery or treatments are carried out with the *purpose* of preventing or treating illnesses, physical impairments or injuries? (3) If due account is to be taken of the purpose, can the *patient's understanding of the purpose* of the intervention be taken into consideration? and (4) Is it of any importance to the assessment whether the intervention is carried out *by licensed medical professionals*, or that such professionals decide on its purpose? The CJEU, tellingly, decided in its judgment to discuss all four questions together.

Furthermore, the study found that the national court presented one or more arguments or possible answers to the question in just below one third of the cases (28 per cent), and that leading questions occurred slightly in excess of that proportion (35 per cent). Arguments on the question do not occur in category A OfRs, as the presence of arguments by definition places

---

[17] ECLI:EU:C:2001:551; NJA 2002 s 75.
[18] ECLI:EU:C:2013:198; HFD 2013 ref 67.

an OfR in category B or C. In category B arguments were put forward in 40 per cent of the cases. Leading questions occurred in all categories, although only in a relatively modest proportion—14 per cent—of the A cases compared with 44 per cent of the B cases. Two main types of leading questions have been found: questions where the national court asks for permission to favour a particular interpretation, and questions which, by themselves or taken together with other questions asked simultaneously, otherwise contain an element of persuasion.

> An example of the former type of question is provided in case C-170/04 *Rosengren*,[19] where the SC asked if it 'could be held that' a certain national rule fell outside the scope of (then) Article 28 TEC and thus was to be examined only in the light of (the then) Article 31 TEC. The CJEU promptly reworded the question to the more positivist 'whether [the rule in question] must be assessed in the light of Article 31 EC [...] or in the light of Article 28 EC'.
>
> The second type may be illustrated by the questions in the abovementioned case, C-203/12 *Billerud*. In this case, the SC first asked whether certain provisions in the Directive entailed that a penalty must be paid in circumstances such as those in the case before it. In the second question, in the event that the CJEU answered the first question in the affirmative, the SC asked whether the penalty 'will or may be waived or reduced'. The effect of asking these questions in this way is that the CJEU is effectively provided with five different options which provide for various degrees of leniency.

Lastly, as is clear already from the categorisation, only in one case did the national court express an opinion of its own on the answer to be given to a referred question.

> Case C-84/09 *X*[20] concerned a question of whether a sailing boat, which was to be acquired in the UK by a Swedish purchaser and only arrive in Sweden after having been used for recreational purposes in other Member States for 3–5 months, should be subject to VAT in Sweden. In relation to the first three questions, the referring court cited case law and discussed a few different arguments, but did not explicitly state its own view of the problem. On the fourth question, however, the referring court noted that Union law 'did not appear to permit' more than one interpretation. The view of the referring court was thus expressed not as a normative argument, but as a hypothesis or even conviction that a certain answer was the correct one. The referral of the fourth question was motivated not by the referring court's need to know the answer, but by the need for uniform application of law within the Union, as it had been alleged that other (incorrect) interpretations had prevailed in other Member States.

---

[19] ECLI:EU:C:2007:313; NJA 2007 s 941.
[20] ECLI:EU:C:2010:693; HFD 2011 ref 28.

4.2. Findings Related to the OfR–Judgment Comparison

The study has revealed few cases of significant correspondence between the judgments and the OfRs. More than two-thirds of the cases show no or insignificant levels of correspondence. There is no noteworthy difference between the referring courts. The distribution of cases displaying various degrees of correspondence is illustrated in Table 9.4.

Table 9.4: Number of cases by degree of correspondence

	SC	SAC	Total
0	7 (47%)	6 (24%)	13 (33%)
1	4 (27%)	10 (40%)	14 (35%)
2	3 (20%)	3 (12%)	6 (15%)
3	1 (7%)	5 (20%)	6 (15%)
4	0 (0%)	1 (4%)	1 (3%)
5	0 (0%)	0 (0%)	0 (0%)
Total	15	25	40

Case C-137/04 *Rockler*[21] concerned a migrant worker's right to social benefits. The referring court provided some reasoning on the matter in its OfR, where it also discussed previous case law from the CJEU. Judging by this reasoning, the matter considered problematic by the referring court was whether non-discriminatory national measures could even be considered to constitute barriers for the free movement of workers. The CJEU took a more consequence-oriented approach, focusing on the deterring effect of the rule in question and its potential justifiability. The national rule's non-discriminatory character was disposed of in only one sentence (para 18). The reasoning of the CJEU thus followed a path quite different from that (cautiously) pointed at by the referring court. In the overall assessment, the level of correspondence between judgment and OfR was considered insignificant (1), on account of an overlap in the case law cited by the referring court and the CJEU.

A higher level of correspondence can be seen in the first question (of four) in case C-29/08 *SKF*.[22] The question was whether the sale of a subsidiary by a parent company constituted an economic transaction subject to VAT. In its OfR, the referring court cited a number of cases previously decided by the CJEU and attempted to identify decisive aspects of those cases as well as their consequences for the case at hand. Out of the six cases discussed by the referring court, four were relied upon by the CJEU. Furthermore, the CJEU in several paragraphs echoed statements found in the OfR (which in turn drew on

---

[21] ECLI:EU:C:2006:106; RÅ 2006 ref 32.
[22] ECLI:EU:C:2009:665; RÅ 2010 ref 56.

previous case law).[23] The CJEU also referred explicitly to the OfR, albeit on a matter of fact. Based on this question, the overall level of correspondence between the judgment and the OfR has been considered moderate (3), whereas the level of correspondence on the first question, seen in isolation, would be higher.

There are some indications that a greater display of active interest from the referring court may have an influence on the CJEU. Category A OfRs display lower levels of correspondence with the subsequent judgment than category B and C OfRs. This is to be expected; where the national court offers little or no input, there is equally little for the CJEU judgment to correspond with, or indeed to be influenced by. However, even sparsely reasoned OfRs may have an impact.

> The OfR in case 111/05 *Aktiebolaget NN*[24] has been categorised as A. However, in its answer to the first question referred, the CJEU explicitly refers to the OfR three times (paras 29, 36 and 39). Although the references are mainly on matters of fact, it is clear that the description provided in the OfR has influenced the CJEU's analysis, even though the referring court itself refrained from highlighting any facts as particularly important.

Table 9.5 shows that a category A OfR on average displays a 0.64 level of correspondence with the judgment of the CJEU in the same case, whereas a category B reference scores 1.4. Also within the B category, a clear difference can be seen between, on the one hand, the Ba OfRs, which tend to score even lower than the category A ones (but represent a significantly smaller sample), and, on the other, the Bb and Bc OfRs, which on average score around 1.6 on the level of correspondence scale. The differences are again largely consistent between the two referring courts.

Table 9.5: Average degree of correspondence by type of reference

	SC	SAC	Total
A	0.62 (8)	0.67 (6)	0.64 (14)
Ba	*0.00 (1)*	*0.60 (5)*	*0.50 (6)*
Bb	*1.50 (4)*	*1.77 (9)*	*1.69 (13)*
Bc	*1.00 (2)*	*2.00 (4)*	*1.67 (6)*
Total B	1.14 (7)	1.50 (18)	1.40 (25)
C	—	4.00 (1)	4.00 (1)
Total	0.86 (15)	1.40 (25)	1.20 (40)

The numbers in this table indicate the average degree of correspondence for every category of OfRs. Numbers in parenthesis indicate the total number of cases in each category (cf Tables 9.1 and 9.2).

---

[23] See OfR paras 23 and 26 compared to paras 28, 31, and 36 of the judgment.
[24] ECLI:EU:C:2007:195; SAC case no 4224-03.

5. DISCUSSION AND CONCLUSIONS

The findings suggest that the Swedish supreme courts neither attempt to nor succeed in influencing the judicial development of EU law through their use of the preliminary ruling system. This conclusion seems consistent with some previous studies on Swedish courts, while cautiously calling others into question.

Taken together, categories A and Ba include half of the OfRs in the dataset. This may indicate an unwillingness on the part of the Swedish highest instances to enter into dialogue with the CJEU within the preliminary ruling procedure. Thus interpreted, the findings are well in line with previous studies about the Nordic and Swedish courts as 'reluctant Europeans'.[25] The study thereby offers a complement to previous research by noting that the Swedish supreme courts are not only restrictive in entering into dialogue with the CJEU, but that even when a positive decision to refer has been made, restrictiveness continues to characterise the OfRs. It should, however, be pointed out that concise OfRs may have other explanations than disinterest, such as fear of being perceived as biased,[26] or even strategic considerations.[27]

However, the findings also differ from those of previous research about the level of activism in referring courts. One study found that Swedish courts offer their view on the outcome—a factor that would place the OfR in the C category in this study—in as many as 52 per cent of the cases.[28] The current study found only one category C OfR, equalling only 3 per cent of the total dataset. Even if category Bc cases, where the national court more implicitly hints at a particular solution are included, the number found in this study rises only to six cases or 16 per cent in total. The difference may in part be explained by the inclusion in the previous study of both higher and lower court OfRs, as it has been argued that lower courts tend to be more active in offering their opinions than those at the higher levels of the judiciary.[29] However, it is doubtful if this explanation is sufficient, considering the large discrepancy between the findings of this and previous studies. Another possible explanation pertains to the materials relied on; as explained in section 3, this study has analysed the actual OfRs, whereas the

---

[25] See the contribution of M Wind, Chapter 11 in this volume, and further M Wind, 'The Nordics, the EU and the Reluctance Towards Supranational Judicial Review' (2010) 48 *Journal of Common Market Studies* 1039–1063.

[26] See case C-614/14, *Ognyanov*, ECLI:EU:C:2016:514.

[27] See the so-called 'don't ask and the ECJ can't tell' policy, K Alter, *The European Court's Political Power: Selected Essays* (Oxford, Oxford University Press, 2009) 100.

[28] See Leijon and Karlsson above n 5.

[29] See Nyikos above n 4 at 542; Alter, above n 27 at 99ff.

previous study only deduced the position of the national courts from the judgments and AG Opinions.[30]

In this context it should furthermore be noted that the distinction between category B and C OfRs is not necessarily one of the *level* of active interest displayed by the referring court, but rather one of the *form* of this interest. Category B OfRs display an interest in cooperating with the CJEU in the development of Union law by identifying and discussing possible arguments and solutions. In category C OfRs, the referring court instead expresses a preference as to the answer to the question, and explains or attempts to persuade the CJEU that this solution is the most attractive one. Both approaches indicate that the referring court is keen to see and contribute to the successful development of Union law, even though it only in the last-mentioned case claims to know what direction that would be.

As for the comparison between the OfRs and the judgments, this study set out to test claims or hypotheses put forward in scholarly writing as to the allegedly influential position of a national court referring a question to the CJEU. It has found little support for such statements. In this regard, however, several problems connected to the dataset must be emphasised. First, the study has included only 40 cases, which even in the most beneficial of circumstances is rather too small a sample to base general conclusions on. Secondly, the two courts from whose case law the materials have been drawn, practise a tradition of restraint in their relationship with the CJEU, which, as has been shown above, extends to the design of their OfRs. Thus, the materials relied on in this study have been particularly unlikely to exert any discernable influence on the CJEU.

Consequently, the present study cannot confirm the hypotheses regarding the influence of the referring courts. Nor does it amount to a refutation. If anything, the study offers weak indications that there is indeed a positive correlation between a more reasoned OfR and a judgment corresponding at least in parts with the arguments forwarded by the referring court. This finding offers encouragement for further studies.

---

[30] It is clear that this explanation has at least contributed to the different findings. For example, based on the phrase 'It is clear from the order for reference that the national court finds that it is having to apply rules which are probably contrary to provisions of Community law [...]' (AG Opinion in case C-200/98 *X and Y*, ECLI:EU:C:1999:280, para 15), Leijon and Karlsson conclude that the referring court has expressed a view on the relevant national rule's compatibility with Union law in the OfR ('Nationella domstolar som politiska aktörer', at 26). A study of the OfR itself, however, reveals this to be an erroneous assumption. The statement instead appears to express a conclusion reached by the AG himself, on the basis of information provided in the OfR.

APPENDIX: TABLE OF CASES INCLUDED IN THE STUDY, BY REFERRING
COURT AND IN CHRONOLOGICAL ORDER

	Cases included in the study	OfR category	Degree of correspondence
	Supreme Court		
1	C-441/99 *Gharehveran* (NJA 2002 s 75)	Bb	3
2	C-338/02 *Fixtures Marketing* (NJA 2002 s 398, NJA 2005 s 924)	A	0
3	C-267/03 *Lindberg* (NJA 2006 s 246)	A	0
4	C-170/04 *Rosengren* (NJA 2007 s 941)	Ba	0
5	C-316/05 *Nokia* (NJA 2007 s 431)	Bc	0
6	C-432/05 *Unibet* (NJA 2007 s 718)	Bb	1
7	C-98/06 *Freeport* (NJA 2007 s 1000)	Bb	1
8	C-68/07 *Sundelind Lopez* (NJA 2008 s 71)	A	0
9	C-251/07 *Gävle kraftvärme* (NJA 2009 s 194)	A	0
10	C-111/08 *SCT Industri* (Ö 3357/05)	A	1
11	C-263/08 *Djurgården-Lilla Värtan* (NJA 2010 s 419)	Bc	2
12	C-461/10 *Bonnier Audio* (NJA 2012 s 975)	A	2
13	C-203/12 *Billerud* (NJA 2014 s 79)	Bb	1
14	C-279/13 *C More Entertainment* (NJA 2015 s 1097)	A	0
15	C-472/14 *Canadian Oil Company Sweden* (B 2708-13)	A	2
	Supreme Administrative Court		
16	C-241/97 *Försäkringsaktiebolaget Skandia* (RÅ 2000 n 41)	A	0
17	C- 292/97 *Karlsson m fl* (RÅ 2000 n 177–199)	Bc	1
18	C-200/98 *X och Y* (RÅ 2000 ref 17)	Ba	1
19	C-240/99 *Skandia* (3998-1997)	Bb	3
20	C-215/00 *Rydergård* (RÅ 2002 ref 72)	Ba	0
21	C-436/00 *X och Y* (7009-1999)	Bc	2
22	C-15/01 *Paranova Läkemedel* (RÅ 2003 ref 71)	A	0
23	C-422/01 *Skandia och Ramstedt* (RÅ 2004 ref 45)	A	1
24	C-320/02 *Stenholmen* (RÅ 2004 ref 45)	Ba	1

(continued)

(Continued)

	Cases included in the study	OfR category	Degree of correspondence
25	C-169/03 *Wallentin* (RÅ 2004 ref 111)	Bb	1
26	C-412/03 *Scandic Gåsabäck* (RÅ 2005 n 51)	A	0
27	C-137/04 *Rockler* (RÅ 2006 ref 32)	Bb	1
28	C-101/05 *A* (RÅ 2008 ref 44)	A	0
29	C-111/05 *Aktiebolaget NN* (4224-03)	A	3
30	C-458/06 *Gourmet Classic* (RÅ 2009 n 103)	Bb	1
31	C-291/07 *Kollektivavtalsstiftelsen TRR Trygghetsrådet* (RÅ 2009 ref 54)	Ba	1
32	C-29/08 *SKF* (RÅ 2010 ref 56)	Bb	3
33	C-84/09 *X* (HFD 2011 ref 28)	C	4
34	C-540/09 *Skandinaviska enskilda banken* (HFD 2011 ref 38)	Bc	2
35	C-257/10 *Bergström* (HFD 2012 ref 44)	Bb	1
36	C-91/12 *PFC Clinic* (HFD 2013 ref 67)	Ba	0
37	C-632/13 *Hirvonen* (HFD 2016 ref 36)	Bb	3
38	C-686/13 *X* (HFD 2016 ref 14)	Bb	2
39	C-252/14 *Pensioenfonds Metaal en Technie* (2686/12)	Bb	1
40	C-264/14 *Hedqvist* (HFD 2016 ref 6)	Bc	3

10

Citizen Control through Judicial Review

ANNA WETTER RYDE

1. INTRODUCTION

CONSTITUTIONAL PLURALISM IS an inherent part of the EU legal order. It is reflected in the variety of constitutional solutions that are offered at Member State level to, for example, ensure that governments do not abuse their powers. In the present chapter, I will discuss whether the different constitutional solutions for checks and balances in the Member States have an impact on their interaction with the European Court of Justice (ECJ), and if so, whether this could challenge the autonomous EU system for ensuring checks and balances.[1]

The insertion of checks and balances into the constitutional architecture of states is meant to support the political system in its efforts to guarantee legitimacy, accountability and democracy. It is undisputed in all democracies that even though governments are democratically voted into power they must be subjected to rules and regulations and somehow be answerable for their actions and policies. This implies that the majority needs to be scrutinised and examined to rule out the possibility that it would discard duties and abuse its position of power. This scrutiny usually takes place through the creation of checks and balances.

A common system for political checks and balances is the separation of powers, which divides the power between the executive (the government), the legislature (the parliament) and the judiciary (the courts). The executive is accountable to the parliament and may further be held accountable through judicial review by an independent judiciary. The idea of the separation of power is, however, not dominant in all Member States. The Swedish Instrument of Government is an example of a solution, which is not based on the separation of powers of the executive, legislature and judiciary, but rather underlines that the citizen is at the centre of power. The citizens elect the Parliament (the Riksdag), the Riksdag—indirectly—elects

---

[1] I would like to express my gratitude to Jakob Lewander (researcher at the Swedish Institute for European Policy Studies) for his help in preparing the questions discussed in this chapter.

the government, the government governs the country with the help of the administrative authorities, and the courts administer justice in accordance with the directives laid down by the Riksdag in fundamental and other laws. This implies that the judiciary in Sweden has a weaker role in controlling the executive compared to the majority of Member States.

Despite the variety of solutions for checks and balances in the Member States' constitutional orders, the states have agreed on an autonomous EU system for ensuring that legitimacy, accountability and democracy are upheld in the EU. This system has developed over time as European integration has intensified. The EU's gradual enhancement of checks and balances has been particularly intense since the beginning of the Maastricht Treaty negotiations and onwards. Since then, the EU has given more legislative power to the European Parliament, invited national parliaments to carry out subsidiarity checks *ex ante*, provided for a citizens' initiative, introduced the European ombudsman, provided for stronger transparency regimes and better regulation, and enabled citizens to petition the European Parliament. All of these initiatives stimulate the checks and balances in the EU, which in turn supports the overall goal to safeguard legitimacy, accountability and democracy.

Even though the formal prerequisites for citizen control have been continuously strengthened at the EU level, there are indications that political developments imply fewer real opportunities for citizen control. Since the 2004 enlargement, there are indications that the so-called trilogue is used more frequently to resolve political disputes between the Commission, the European Parliament and the Council, Member States tend to vote through consensus in the Council, more policy decisions are made at the European Council level (especially during the so-called 'EU crisis') and the EU's regulation on access to documents seems to be losing its strength.[2] These indications point at the fact that the initiatives created to boost citizen control of the EU Polity seem to be losing ground, mainly because the political tensions at the EU level are running so high that they demand less transparency and more effective instruments in the decision-making process. Some scholars argue that this development started after the 2004 enlargement, which made compromise agreements more difficult to achieve in the formalised rounds, resulting in more pre-negotiation talks and moving the agenda to the informal setting of luncheon tables and Council corridors.[3] In my opinion, the decrease of *ex ante* control needs to be compensated by *ex post* scrutiny or citizens will lose their ability to carry out the necessary controls.

---

[2] Discussions on the reform of Regulation No 1049/2001 have been pending since 2008. Curtin and Leino-Sandberg note that '(..)While one would think that the tendency was—in line with the recent Treaty reforms—to strengthen the rights of citizens further, in fact the opposite seems to be the case, with discussions on reform mainly circulating around new ways to limit citizen access, many of them in rather fundamental ways seem to be at odds with the letter of the Treaties.', D Curtin and P Leino-Sandberg (2016) '*Openness, Transparency and the Right of Access to Documents in the EU. In-Depth Analysis*', (European Parliament Think Tank).

[3] S Hagemann and J De Clerck-Sachsse (2007) 'Decision-Making in the Enlarged Council of Ministers: Evaluating the Facts' (CEPS Policy Brief, No 119).

This chapter departs from the proposition that a higher centralisation of power, which is the result of the gradual integration process, requires effective mechanisms for checks and balances at the EU level. This is especially required in relation to the EU Polity, since its mandate to represent the citizens is strictly limited to the powers conferred on it. Against this background, it is interesting to study when and how the Member States decide to interact with the Court of Justice, being invested with Treaty-based powers to resolve conflicts regarding the limits of EU power.[4] Due to political constraints, however, Member States seem to resort to the court in a very small number of cases; some seem to have completely ruled out the possibility of turning to the ECJ for a legality review.

While the EU system for accountability fills some sort of supplementary function, which can be visualised 'on top of' the national structures serving to control the national Polity, it needs to be taken into consideration that the centralisation of power at the EU level has the effect of aggravating the task of the national actors who are responsible for controlling the Polity. In this new constitutional architecture, composed of both one national and one EU Polity, it is therefore essential to keep an eye on both Polity levels. This is even more important at a time when external threats to the EU imply further EU centralisation, evoking, for example, a closer relationship between national parliaments and national governments and between the EU institutions. Furthermore, at the EU level, the Member States struggle to find political compromises that may effectively resolve the problems they have commonly identified, often under the shadow of European Council meetings.

In this political climate, there is an added risk that the EU acts beyond the limits of its conferred powers. While new political climates may demand difficult compromises, the argument made in this chapter is that such compromises should not be made in the shadow of the citizens but rather in the direct spotlight of a transparent process, clearly mapping out the constitutional values at stake.[5] This is a crucial part of accountability since without it, it will be impossible for the voters to subject the government to citizen control. Acknowledging the difficulties facing the EU Polity in the balance

---

[4] It should be noted that the principle of subsidiarity is traditionally seen as forming part of the *ultra vires* examination, but due to the special character of the principle and the ECJ's approach to it, it is reasonable to leave the examination of the principle to the national parliaments. For an analysis of the possible use of the principle of subsidiarity as a limit to the exercise of EU competence, see further J Öberg, (2016) 'Subsidiarity as a Limit to the Exercise of EU Competences', *Yearbook of European Law* 1–30.

[5] The *Turco* judgment (joined cases C-39/05 P and C-52/05 P, EU:C:2008:374) concerned access to an opinion issued by the Council legal service on a proposal for a legislative act. In its judgment, the ECJ argued that 'the fear expressed by the Council that disclosure of an opinion of its legal service relating to a legislative proposal could lead to doubts as to the lawfulness of the legislative act concerned, it is precisely openess in this regard that contributes to conferring greater legitimacy on the institutions in the eyes of the European citizens and increasing their confidence in them by allowing divergencies between various points of view to be openly debated'(para 59).

between effective EU policy-making and respecting the need for a transparent decision-making process, the present chapter looks at the possibility of further stimulating the *ex post* control of the EU Polity.

2. PURPOSE AND METHOD

The purpose of this chapter is to identify structural asymmetries in the choices made by EU governments to request a legality review by the ECJ, within the framework of an action for annulment in accordance with Article 263 of the Treaty on the Functioning of the European Union (FEUF), and to discuss whether the Member States' reluctance to use the *ex post* alternative has a negative impact on the EU internal order, created partly to hold the EU Polity accountable for its actions. Actions for annulment are given a symbolic meaning, in relation to the other types of judicial actions, since the political decision for a review to be performed by the judiciary is made at the behest of the governments, which have been part of the disputed decision themselves.[6] Furthermore, this examination by the court is arguably something very different from the role of the judiciary in settling conflicts between parties, since actions for annulment examines the actual validity of legal norms.

This chapter seeks to establish what the incentives are for EU governments to turn to or not to turn to the ECJ to request an *ultra vires* examination of the legislation. In relation to enhancing accountability, it is argued that a judicial review should exclusively focus on the *ultra vires* review, since it offers a constitutional method for ensuring compliance with the principle of conferred powers. In this context, it should be recalled that when the EU acts *ultra vires*, it has failed to adhere to the limits of its competences, which are embodied in the founding Treaties. In effect, *ultra vires* is the reverse of the competence coin, which makes it unacceptable in a democratic government.[7]

This chapter presents data on the actions for annulment referred to the ECJ by the 15 Member States that have been EU Members since 1995. The data is used to provide a background for the further discussions on whether the right for Member States to refer an action for annulment meets the need to secure robust EU structures for checks and balances in the EU constitutional order.

The survey on the actions for annulment referred to the ECJ by the Member States uses a typology to measure the 'strength' of objections

---

[6] It should be noted that the data collected for this chapter does not rule out the possibility that a Member State can be involved in a case, indirectly, through the preliminary reference procedure. The mechanism enables national courts to request an opinion on the legality of an act.

[7] P Craig, 'The ECJ and *ultra vires* Action: A Conceptual Analysis' (2011) 48 *Common Market Law Review* 395–437.

by the Member States. It is argued that the strongest type involves cases where Member States object to the mere legality of an EU legal act (directive or regulation), adopted by the EU legislator directly or by an institution with delegated powers. These are referred to as 'strong cases'. In contrast, the weakest type (i.e. 'weak cases', arguably involves cases where Member States react to what they find to be an unfavourable decision often involving them, by questioning the legality of the decision). In this particular case, Member States often complain about a specific measure with direct financial consequences for the country. Such cases include state aid decisions. Although legislative acts may also have financial effects, they are labelled strong cases as they refer to the decision of the legislator, while the weak cases instead address the Commission and the Council in their administrative capacity.

The study has been limited to the period between 1995 and 2016. As a methodological point of departure, it is acknowledged that the ECJ offers a political arena for the Member States, where they may invest juridical and political capital for determining the pace and direction of European legal integration. In that sense, the decision of Member States to intervene and refer cases to the ECJ is primarily a political matter. In addition, the decision to refer a case to the ECJ may also be explained by the constitutional cultures of the Member States. In this chapter, I focus on actions for annulment, examining whether they are particularly indicative of the diversity of the constitutional traditions of the Member States. If so, this could be explained by the fact that actions for annulments invite the judiciary to examine the legality of a political decision, a scenario that is alien to many majoritarian democracies.

3. WHEN AND WHY DO MEMBER STATES RESORT TO THE CHOICE OF LEGALITY REVIEW?

In this chapter it is assumed that all Member States have an equal interest in defending their policy preferences in the ECJ, especially since they all have an equal footing in the court. This makes the ECJ a unique political arena for the Member States, as no other European institution offers them an equal voice. In effect, we should expect all Member States to use the court in a similar manner for the purpose of defending their national interests. However, as will be shown, this is not really the case.

It is possible to divide the parties that may bring actions (all types of actions) to the ECJ into two basic groups; (i) the national courts that under certain conditions are *obliged* to refer cases to the ECJ and (ii) the Member States, the European Parliament, the Council and the Commission and private individuals and entities who *have a right* to refer cases to the court under certain circumstances.[8] These two groups of referees have tradition-ally different incentives for interacting with the ECJ. While the national courts may be obliged by EU law to request a preliminary ruling to settle a national case, the referral by governments would more often be subjected to strategic domestic concerns. Such concerns may include political EU bar-gaining capital, fear of having to pay damage compensation and concerns relating to their relationship with national constitutional courts. It should, however, be noted that the national courts may also subject their decision to request a preliminary reference to strategic choices.[9] This implies that the difference between national courts and governments may not be so great after all, even though the governments are clearly under no EU obligation to initiate a proceeding in the ECJ, whilst the national courts are.[10]

The relatively narrow referral grounds available to the EU citizens are to a certain extent legitimised and remedied through judicial review within the judicial systems of the Member States in collaboration with the ECJ. The preliminary reference procedure thus plays an essential role in safeguard-ing the correct interpretation of Union law but it arguably plays a minor role in securing that the EU law is valid.[11] Furthermore, political scientists argue that the cases evolving from the preliminary reference procedure are of a distinct character. Scharpf argues that the preliminary ruling system implies that there is an inherent structure for promoting market liberal ide-als in the EU Treaties, in the sense that the cases ending up in the Court through the preliminary reference to a high degree comprise some kind of conflict between market liberal ideals and national constitutional values.[12] This conclusion is relevant to this discussion since it implies that the Court is not given the opportunity to examine the broader spectra of legal acts, but instead primarily those that involve a conflict between more or less legal integration for the benefit of promoting market liberal ideals. *Ultra vires*

---

[8] In the *Da Costa* judgment, C-28-30/62, EU:C:1963:6, and *CILFIT* judgment, C-283/81, EU:C:1982:335, the ECJ developed what is known as the *acte éclairé* and the *acte clair* doctrine which sets the criteria when national courts are not obliged to make a preliminary reference to the ECJ about a matter of EU law.

[9] On this matter, see M Wind, Chapter 11 in this volume.

[10] It should, however, be stressed that although the governments are not obliged under EU law to refer cases to the ECJ, it does not rule that they may be obliged to refer cases under national law.

[11] In the period between 1995 and 2015, Swedish courts, for example, only asked one ques-tion regarding the legality of a European act within the framework of a preliminary ruling, see U Bernitz, *Förhandsavgöranden av EU-domstolen* (Preliminary references by the European Court of Justice) (2016) SIEPS Report (2016:9), p 90. In line with the *Foto-Frost* judgment, C-314/85, EU:C:1987:452, lower national courts are also obliged to request a preliminary reference if questions regarding the legality of a European legal acts are raised.

[12] FW Scharpf, 'The Assymmetry of European Integration, or Why the EU cannot be a Social Market Economy?' (2010) 8(2) *Socio-Economic Review* 211.

concerns may, however, exist in legislative acts that are not in this direct conflict zone. In effect, the role of the ECJ 'shrinks' to safeguarding legal integration. Against this background, it is necessary to distinguish between two functions of the Court: One involves refereeing boundary disputes between the institutions while the other targets the monitoring of individual EU legal rights. This chapter focuses on how boundary disputes are brought to the table of the ECJ.

Now, as mentioned above, when both governments and national courts decide to turn to the ECJ it may be explained as being due to national constitutional traditions, which may be more or less in favour of calling in the judiciary to examine the legality of political choices. Even though it is difficult to draw a parallel between the behaviour of governments and national courts, research points in the direction that such correlation may in fact exist. Marlene Wind has argued that national courts in a majoritarian democracy only reluctantly cooperate with supranational judicial bodies by referring very few cases and that this is due both to little experience with judicial review at the national level but also—and more importantly— to a widespread hostility towards (supranational) judicial review in general.[13] This seems to match the hypothesis tested in this chapter, namely that governments belonging to majoritarian democracies are also more reluctant to refer cases to the ECJ compared to governments belonging to constitutional democracies (see Figures 10.1–10.3 below). In relation to the national courts it has been argued that those operating in majoritarian democracies are less inclined to participate in the legal construction of the EU than others. Research shows, for example, a correlation between the preliminary reference rates and the type of democracy in the Member States, concluding that '(..)the strong negative effect of majoritarian democracy on the preliminary referral rates of individual Member States suggests that the institutional legacy of the type of democracy which continues to emphasise the supremacy of parliament and thereby restrain judicial behaviour may prevail for decades'.[14] It has further been noted that '(..)Majoritarian government and the internal balance of power between different governmental branches in the Member States may affect the extent to which national courts willingly participate in the (judicial) construction of Europe'.[15] At a very general level, we could thus assume that majoritarian democracies will,

---

[13] M Wind,'Who is Afraid of European Constitutionalism? The Nordic Distress with Judicial Review and Constitutional Democracy' (2014) *iCourts Workingpaper* No 12 2014, 2246–4891, pp 1–20 20, 2246–4891.

[14] M Wind, D Sindbjerg Martinsen and GP Rotger, 'The Uneven Legal Push for Europe— Questioning Variation when National Courts go to Europe' (2009) 10(1) *European Union Politics* 63–88.

[15] Ibid.

if they ever refer cases to the ECJ, have special incentives in comparison to constitutional democracies. This is arguably a concern for the entire internal EU legal system for democratic control, since it suggests that some Member States consistently deny the *ex post* review of legal acts, despite the possibility that they have, for example, argued against the lack of legal basis in EU negotiations.

As noted above, previous research focuses on the option of a national court to request a preliminary reference while this chapter instead discusses variations in the possibility of EU governments to turn to the ECJ. This chapter does not claim that the Member States should make frequent use of their right to request a legality review, meaning that the preliminary rulings will always outnumber the actions for annulment by Member States. It is, however, argued that when the Member States find that EU legal acts violate especially the principle of conferred powers, the principle of proportionality or fundamental rights as stipulated in the EU Charter for fundamental rights, they need to seriously consider the *ex post* legal review. If not, they undermine the legitimacy of the EU Polity by avoiding scrutiny of its actions, since the EU decision-making process is subjected to a high degree of secrecy. Thus, it is through judicial review this process is subjected to scrutiny.

Before presenting the data, it should be noted that most Member States have opted for the establishment of a constitutional court to counterbalance the political power whereas the Scandinavian countries, the Netherlands and the United Kingdom (UK) have refrained from this model. Greece and Ireland apply their own systems, which are more difficult to categorise. This implies that the majority of Member States would be best described as constitutional democracies while the Scandinavian countries, the Netherlands and the UK fit better under the category of majoritarian democracies. Having said that, the conclusion is not necessarily that majoritarian democracies do not seek to guarantee that fundamental democratic values are complied with. However, they apply scrutiny mechanisms, which are an alternative way for the judiciary to safeguard such values. One such Scandinavian feature is the presence of strong transparency regimes, enabling a thorough *ex ante* scrutiny of legislative measures.

The figures below reflect the number of actions for annulment referred to the ECJ by the fifteen Member States studied in the period between 1995 and 2016.

Figure 10.1 reflects the number of actions for annulment that imply the legality review of a directive or regulation, referred to above as strong cases. Figure 10.2 reflects the number of cases that instead have subjected decisions to legal review, referred to as weak cases. Finally, Figure 10.3 shows the number of interventions that the Member States have engaged in. This diagram does not distinguish between the types of legal act.

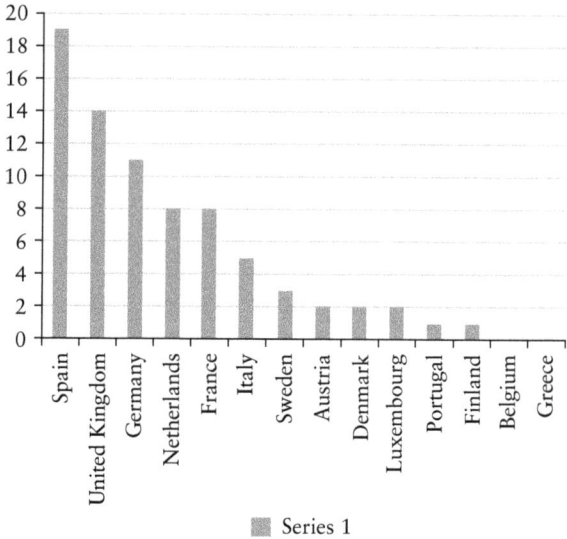

Figure 10.1: Actions for annulment/directives and regulations

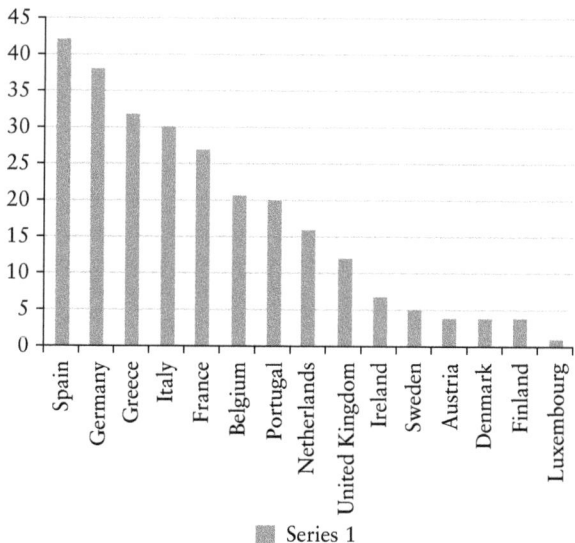

Figure 10.2: Actions for annulment/decisions

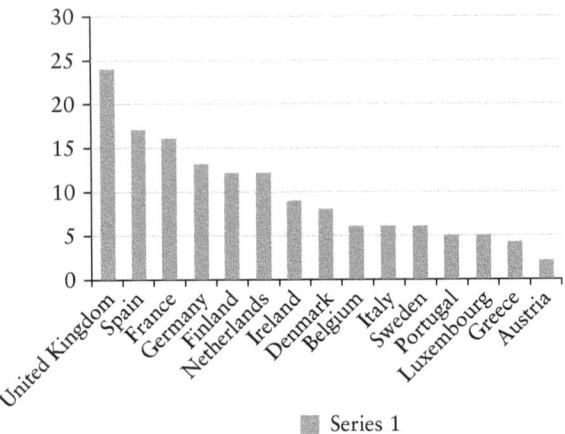

Figure 10.3: Interventions, all legal acts

At first glance, the data does not provide any clear answer to the question of when and why the Member States resort to the legality review option. It can be noted that Spain has the highest record of requesting legal examinations of directives and regulations (strong cases), having referred almost one case per year to the ECJ. The UK, Germany, the Netherlands and France follow Spain. The lowest scoring Member States in this diagram are Italy, Sweden, Austria, Denmark, Luxembourg, Portugal, Finland, Belgium and finally Greece. Belgium and Greece have never referred a case during the period in question.

Moving on to the legality review of EU decisions, Spain again takes the lead, followed by Germany, Greece, Italy, France, Belgium and Portugal. It is noteworthy that the Netherlands and the UK, which were active referees in the cases that examined the legality of directives and regulations, are at the opposite end of this diagram. There we also find Ireland, Sweden, Austria, Finland and Luxembourg. High-scoring Member States also include Greece and Belgium who did not refer any legality reviews of the strong cases.

Finally, the picture changes slightly again when we look at the number of interventions. Again, the UK and Spain are to be found at the upper end of the scale, together with France, Finland (interesting to note), and the Netherlands. At the lower end, we find Ireland, Denmark, Belgium, Italy, Sweden, Portugal, Luxembourg, Greece and Austria.

Now, as noted above, decisions may be looked upon as something distinct from directives and regulations since they are expected to more often represent a concern, which often has direct financial effects for the Member State. 35.5 % of the cases referred by the Member States challenge the legality of decisions in the area of agriculture and fisheries and 42.5 % of these represent cases on state aid and competition. This suggests that some

Member States request judicial reviews of decisions where the decisions made by the Commission have been negative.

When searching for patterns regarding how States interact with the ECJ, it is also interesting to study their voting behaviour in the Council of Ministers. What is interesting to study is whether there is a correlation between the Member States which routinely vote against or abstain from voting in the Council of Ministers (directives and regulations) and their actions for annulment at the ECJ (in a strong case). If such patterns exist, it could indicate that the Member States use the ECJ to obtain a legal examination of a policy preference that they lost during Council negotiations.

This point is, however, very difficult to study due to the tradition of consensus voting combined with shadow votes in the Council.[16] Even when the co-decision procedure is applicable, the Council prefers to reach a consensus and much of the decision making is believed to be conducted before proposals reach the Council (i.e. in the Committee of Permanent Representatives (COREPER) and the Council working groups). In these groups and committees, decision-making is influenced by the preferences of the Presidency, coalition-forming, informal bilateral contracts and 'horse-trading'.

There are, however, a few available sources on Council voting results that can be used to point us to such patterns. Vote Watch reports that governments raise concerns about policy proposals 1.2 times per legislative act adopted by the Council. This implies that they have not been able to resolve their conflicts in the lower Council bodies. In the fields of the environment, regional development, agriculture and the internal market, the number is slightly higher. Vote Watch also reports that in reality, policy proposals may be more contested than it would appear, despite being reported as 'unanimously agreed'.[17] However, it cannot be concluded from this that the reason for the concerns raised by the Member States had to do with the legality of the proposed legislative acts.

Furthermore, a SIEPS report notes that in the period between 2005 and 2010, it was primarily the older Member States that tended to use 'no votes' whereas newer Member States preferred to cast abstentions. Germany, the UK, Sweden, the Netherlands, Denmark, Poland and Italy respectively contested more and were regularly outvoted in the Council. Two larger Member States (Spain and France) and 18 smaller Member States contested occasionally and supported EU legislation more often. In terms of size and geographical location, the data demonstrates that larger and more northern Member States contested more often and with 'no votes'—Italy being the only southern Member State to do so. In contrast, smaller Member

---

[16] V Miller, 'Voting Behaviour in the EU Council' (2013) *Commons Briefing Papers*, SN06646.

[17] 'Agreeing to Disagree: The Voting Records of Member States in the Council since 2009' (2012) *Vote Watch Europe*, Annual Report.

States from the South and the East opposed EU legislation less frequently. The latter group usually made up the majority in the Council and preferred abstentions to 'no votes'. France and Spain were the only two larger EU countries that shared this type of voting behaviour.[18]

To sum up, accessing Council votes is problematic since there is a tradition of consensus voting. Furthermore, the actual negotiation process is to a certain extent protected by EU law. In effect, the studies on the Council votes reflect primarily the clear cases, where the policy choices or the *ultra vires* concerns of the Member States have been so strong that they have defended them openly by voting no or abstaining from voting. This implies that it is impossible to know all the cases where the Member States have objected to the legal basis, proportionality and compliance with fundamental rights in EU legislative proposals during the Council negotiations.

4. CONSTITUTIONAL REVIEW IN THE MEMBER STATES

This part of the chapter looks at whether the interaction or lack of interaction between the Member States and the ECJ can be explained by the constitutional traditions in each particular Member State.

The centralised model for constitutional review, which empowers a special constitutional court to annul legislation that runs counter to the State constitution, was introduced in the European countries after the First World War. The movement started in the former Czechoslovakia in 1920, Lichtenstein 1921 and Spain 1931. Hans Kelsen, being the brain behind the proliferation of constitutional courts in Europe, argued that a system of legislative supremacy would be logically incomplete. He proposed that any given act could only be considered valid if it was compatible with a higher norm, a *Grundnorm*.[19] The presence of a constitutional court in the European countries is today the prevailing model in the Member States. There are constitutional courts in Austria, Belgium, France, Germany, Italy, Luxembourg and Spain. In Austria, Germany and Spain (as well as in the Czech Republic, Slovenia and Slovakia, however, these countries are not included in this chapter) a constitutional complaint can also be raised by individuals who may submit an application to the constitutional court if they consider that their fundamental rights or freedoms have been violated.

The most common alternative to a constitutional court is the American system, providing all courts with the authority to adjudicate constitutional issues during the course of deciding legal cases and controversies. American-style

---

[18] W Van Aaken, 'Voting in the Council of the European Union: Contested Decision-Making in the EU Council of Ministers (1995–2010)', SIEPS Report (2012:2).

[19] H Kelsen, *General Theory of Law and State*, translation by A Wedberg, *Twentieth-century Legal Philosophy Series*: Volume I, (Cambridge MA, Harvard University Press, 1945).

judicial review builds instead on the premise that it may only interfere with the legislature when legislative supremacy has been rejected among co-equal branches of government, thus denying the opportunity of abstract legal review. This system is applied by Denmark, Sweden and Finland. The remaining four countries (i.e. Ireland, Greece, the Netherlands and the UK (soon to leave the EU)) have systems that are difficult to characterise. The Dutch system is worth highlighting as it explicitly prohibits judges from setting aside legislation on constitutional grounds. The same goes for the UK. These two examples deserve particular attention in this chapter considering that their activity in the European Court of Justice is relatively high. My assumption would imply that it should be less so since they do not have a tradition of either abstract or concrete legal review.[20]

As shown above, the majority of Member States have opted for the system of a constitutional court although this choice did not come easy in any European state. On the contrary, before the introduction of the constitutional courts in European states, it was widely held that constitutional review was incompatible with parliamentary governance and the unitary state. It was a strong concern that the acceptance of judicial review challenged the idea of majority rule, which is manifested through legislative supremacy and its corollaries.

Despite the lack of knowledge of what goes on in the Council negotiations, it is at least possible to study whether there is a quantitative correlation between those Member States that apply constitutional review in their national legal orders and their interaction with the ECJ. The test departs from the hypothesis that Member States that take an active part in the *ex ante* review, would be less inclined to get involved in *ex post* review. However, if a Member State has a low profile in the *ex ante* review (e.g. not using the no-vote or abstaining from voting) it would be more inclined to request a legal review. The hypothesis will be further developed below but departs from the categorisation of Member States into majoritarian or constitutional democracies. It should be added that there is, of course, also the possibility that a Member State which is active in the *ex ante* review, using all of its opportunities to vote no or abstain from voting would also wish to test the legality of the legislation that went against it, *ex post*. In such a scenario, I would argue that the interaction with the ECJ is less influenced by national legal cultures.

It is important to stress that the aggregate level of actions for annulment by the Member States shows *some* variations, but that these variations are not really distinct. None of the fifteen Member States turn to the action for annulment in a routine-like way, implying that they all seem to exercise

---

[20] As regards the states that became Members of the EU through the 2004 enlargement, nine out of ten apply the centralised system for constitutional review (i.e. all except Estonia).

their right with some kind of caution.[21] The relatively small number of actions, ranging from 0 to 28 per Member State over the period in question, confirms this. Nonetheless, patterns in the behaviour of the Member States begin to emerge if you study these figures in parallel with additional data on the Member States' use of the ECJ, for example, their submissions of observations and interventions. Furthermore, their internal transparency regimes may cast further light on their behaviour.

First, the data shows that what the UK and Germany have in common is that they are both major Member States, taking active part at all levels (with the exception of the UK that does not request the legality review of decisions in that many cases). This involves expressing their position in the Council *ex ante* adoption and then challenging the legality of the EU legal acts *ex post* in the Court. Spain and France represent another set of major Member States, but which do not frequently vote no or abstain from voting. They, however, use the Court to request legality reviews. Spain is the most active Member State in the ECJ. The Netherlands seems to act in a similar manner to the UK, although it represents a smaller country. The Scandinavian countries (i.e. Denmark and Sweden) seem to share behaviour in both the Council and in the ECJ, while Finland is a consensus voter in the Council and initiates very few actions for annulment in the ECJ. Finland, however, has a higher record of interventions compared to its Scandinavian neighbours.

At most, a Member State may request one action for the annulment of legislative acts per year (Spain) but most of these are found in policy areas where there are strong national interests, suggesting that these cases do not cover questions on the legality of acts in view of the *ultra vires* test. The data indicates that the Member States do not regularly resort to the ECJ in order to have the legal basis, the principles of proportionality or subsidiarity examined. The UK is most inclined to request a legality review on these grounds.[22]

The data also indicates that Member States with the character of a constitutional democracy are slightly more likely to ask the ECJ for an action of annulment compared to Member States whose constitutional systems would be better described as majoritarian democracies. As background information it should be noted that Sweden, Finland and Denmark most frequently dispute legal acts on the grounds that they breach the EU's transparency regimes. This might suggest that they prefer strengthening the regime for the access to the decision-making process to the alternative of subjecting a political decision to judicial review. This would be in line with their national constitutional traditions.

The clearest conclusion that can be identified in the data is, however, that the Member States do not make very frequent use of the action for annulment in comparison to the number of cases when they request an

---

[21] Whether this caution is political or resource-saving is, however, not known.
[22] SIEPS 2017:1op, *Brexit: Consequences for the EU and Sweden*, p. 39, (2017:op1).

interpretation of EU law. Further, when the Member States interact with the ECJ, they all seem to use the Court as a political arena, defending their political positions in a particular case. This suggests that they do not frequently resort to judicial examination for the purpose of safeguarding the control of EU power.

5. THE FUNCTION OF THE *ULTRA VIRES* TEST

Today, it is a widely held ideal that the multidimensional quality of democracy represents both government on majoritarian principles as well as the realisation of certain fundamental rights.[23] Moreover, in many states where there is a constitution establishing a balance between majority rule and certain fundamental values, it is an accepted premise that there must be a court to guarantee that balance. Some view this constitutional architecture as a system of mutual policing in the sense that the court enforces legislative respect for fundamental democratic values, while the legislature retains the ability to re-establish the balance. In this way, the Polity remains in power but will at the same time have to exercise some self-restraint. I will now move the focus to discuss the need for *ex post* constitutional review in the EU. To frame this discussion, I will draw on Kelsen's theory on the 'grundnorm' or basic norm.

Kelsen's model of the juridical state may be translated into a delegation theory.[24] The distinguishing feature of the Principal–Agent models is that they link, as in a chain, authoritative acts of delegation from one constitutionally recognised authority to another. The idea is that the people represent the Principal (sovereign) and that they may ratify a constitution which delegates power to the legislature. The legislature, in turn, delegates power to the executive. Principles can thus be identified by virtue of the constitutional authority they possess to delegate powers through a specific type of normative instrument.[25] In this system the ultimate source of authority is the constitution, which is assumed to express the will of the sovereign people. This model helps to visualise the importance of gluing together the delegation chain. The legitimacy of EU norms strongly depends on the presence of glue binding together EU norms with the conferred powers.

In Kelsen's view, democracy is the realisation of liberty understood as autonomy, in a situation where each person is subject to only norms that the person has established or at least consented to.[26] Although the political system should seek for a maximum level of autonomy, it has been admitted

---

[23] A Stone Sweet, *Constitutional Courts and Parliamentary Democracy* (Special Issue on Delegation), Faculty Scholarship Series, Paper 84, 2002.

[24] Ibid.

[25] Ibid.

[26] M Troper, 'The Logic of Justification of Judicial Review' (2003) 1(1) *I.CON* 99–121.

unattainable. Furthermore, the majority system is commonly accepted as the best choice, although it is widely recognised that the concept of majority could easily be misused to discriminate the minority. Kelsen's compromise for this dilemma is to use a limited judicial review aimed at safeguarding the use of the majority's power including the protection of some fundamental rights. By concentrating on the procedural laws which control the decision-making process, the court may help ensure that the autonomy of the people is kept at a maximum level. Kelsen identifies the *grundnorm or basic norm* as the norm, which confers power on the government. The purpose of the court is to ensure that delegated power remains in compliance with the basic norm.

By arguing in favour of a limited judicial review, Kelsen acknowledges that judicial examination of the content of norms to some extent challenges the premise for a democratic regime, since it may replace political choice with a judicial decision. However, if there are no guarantees for ensuring that the representatives of the people respect the powers conferred upon them, the democratic premise will nonetheless be at stake. This implies that there is no perfect solution but rather that the best balance between safe-guarding political power and ensuring that it respects certain fundamental rights is something to strive for. Kelsen's theory is particularly interesting when you study the power delegated to the EU by the people as the delega-tion chain is further blurred by global governance. This is due to the fact that it is claimed that EU decision-making power demands more secrecy to enhance efficiency in the decision-making process, thus making *ex ante* citizen control more difficult.

So far, to my knowledge, no one has convincingly been able to argue in favour of both democracy and judicial review due to the contradictions inherent in the nature of, on the one hand, political autonomy and, on the other, subjecting it to the legal examination of the judiciary. In this chapter, however, I argue that despite this, Kelsen and Esenmann's way of delimiting the court review to the examination of the conditions for the creation of the law, constitutes a reasonable compromise for the purpose of control-ling that the EU legislature respects the democratic prerequisites of its own power being laid down in the principle of conferred powers. In this context, it is necessary to point out that there are various criticisms of the view that legitimacy is achieved through an unbroken 'delegation chain'.[27]

---

[27] For a thorough analysis, see L Besselink (2017) 'Talking About European Democracy' 13(2) *European Constitutional Law Review* 1–14. As pointed out by the author, one weakness of the 'unbroken delegation chain theory' is that it tends to produce a mechanical perspective on how democracy is attained. As also pointed out in the editorial, democracy may also be achieved from broad public acceptance of acts to which one is subjected, without having had an actual opportunity to influence those acts or measures. But this alternative form is only acceptable if there is some form of influence ('input') possible that could change those acts and measures in the future. The argument made in this chapter is that the European citizens' input is currently so weak that this alternative form is not available.

This means, however, that the ECJ must avoid expressing an opinion on the law, restricting itself to ensuring that the limits of EU power have been respected. The strongest argument for subjecting the EU Polity to more judicial review, compared to its 'counterpart'—the national Polity—is that citizen representation is weaker at the EU level. This also makes it more difficult for voters to pass judgments on the governments' EU policies, endorsing what it has done, or rejecting it in favour of the opposition. Citizen control is aggravated by global governance, which amongst other things weakens citizen control of the decision-making process.

Even though I find the option of a limited judicial review to be a good compromise, having balanced the cons in both options against each other, it cannot be ignored that an enhanced judicial review, even though it is limited to procedural examination, creates new challenges for democracy. Robert Dahl used the example of the US already in 1957 to stress that there is a potential for conflict between the legislature and constitutional jurisdiction inherent in the model of constitutionalism.[28] Despite the fact that this article favours enhanced constitutional *ex post* control, it has to be acknowledged that this system comes at a price; a price far too complex to fully cover in this chapter. The price that comes with a system for constitutional 'law-checking' is that a certain amount of lawmaking must be acknowledged and accepted. This follows from the admitted fact in modern jurisprudence that all legal practice implies a dimension of interpretation.

Some voices have claimed that the problem of democracy and judicial review is not a problem until constitutional courts become 'too successful'.[29] So, how can the ECJ be held back from engaging in too much lawmaking? Even though the ECJ cannot formally be categorised as a constitutional court, due to the *sui generis* character of the EU legal system, including the EU's lack of *kompetenz-kompetenz*, it is still often labelled as a constitutional court. It is further claimed that the Court has been successful in giving itself a constitutional role.[30]

The ECJ's interpretative method has been criticised for being blind to the political and economic EU context. While the judges of the ECJ like to discuss their approach regarding how their judgments respect both the EU legal order and the national legal order, they rarely enter into a discussion on whether they acknowledge the political and economic EU context of any specific situation. A limited constitutional review, focusing on the *ultra vires* test, aiming to safeguard respect for Kelsen's basic norm and at the same time locating the examination in political fact, would arguably constrain

---

[28] R Dahl, 'The Decision-making in Democracy: The Supreme Court as a National Policy-maker' (1957) 6 *Journal of Public Law* 279.

[29] See M Shapiro, 'The European Court of Justice: Of Institutions and Democracy' (1998) 32(1) *Israel Law Review* 3–50.

[30] Ibid.

this dilemma. The ultimate aim in this examination is not to review the policy choices but rather to secure that power resides ultimately where there is political accountability, in other words in the legislature. This is important to ensure that the assertion of final political authority is daunting for a constitutional order to force upon its political actors the importance of introspection and self-justification to their respective constituencies. When most European countries introduced the constitutional order after the First World War, a common argument was that without it, the Polity would be freed from judicial constraint and unburdened with a culture of self-restraint, which could nourish totalitarian regimes.[31]

6. THE WAY FORWARD: *ACTIO POPULARIS*

The data in this chapter suggests that there is a general reluctance at Member State level to turn to the Court for a legal examination of a political decision, although the level of it varies among the Member States. Since this chapter argues in favour of an increased use of the ECJ to rule upon the *ultra vires* question, it has to be acknowledged that more research is needed for the purpose of digging deeper into how often *ultra vires* concerns are raised in, for example, Council meetings. In my view, in order to secure effective accountability of the EU legislature, every such serious concern raised by a Member State (or the European Parliament), should lead to a constitutional examination by the court. Our data indicates that, although there are some variations in the Member States, very few actions for annulment end up in the ECJ through a referral issued by a Member State.

However, it is not difficult to understand why the Member States do not turn to the ECJ for a legal examination of a political decision that they have spent years negotiating. The political bargaining system works in a way that makes most Member States certain that they will profit from accepting the game if they respect the informal negotiation premise. This line of reasoning could be used to argue that the Member States should not turn to the ECJ for a legal examination after all. Nonetheless, I argue that the trend towards less transparency in the EU decision-making process implies that the delegation chain is being resolved. This trend arguably imposes more demands on the *ultra vires* examination to control that the delegation chain is kept together.

As noted above, the ECJ referral grounds are limited to ensure that most legal disputes are digested in the national courts. This also manifests a

---

[31] A Barak, *Judicial Discretion*, trans Yadin Kaufmann (New Haven, Yale University Press, 1989).

national sovereignty (and saves EU resources). Another delimitation is that the ECJ lacks power to examine legislative proposals *ex ante* implying that it can only examine legal acts *ex post* their adoption.[32] This makes perfect sense, since it boosts the authority of the EU Polity to allow political and economic decisions without having to listen to the ECJ. Another delimitation of the ECJ's power is that citizens and legal entities can only turn to the Court in a concrete case (under a very restricted premise). As noted above, research has shown that national courts have their own incentives for avoiding an ECJ ruling, thus making it even harder for individuals and legal entities to obtain a ruling from the ECJ.

The seemingly lack of incentive for both governments and national courts to turn to the ECJ, along with the restricted possibilities for EU citizens to turn to the Court leaves the EU institutions to call in the ECJ should they deem it to be necessary. In my opinion, relying on the EU institutions for this matter does not provide sufficient guarantees for citizen control. This is most probably due to the nature of the political dynamics of the EU, that tend towards the institutions sharing a view on a final piece of legislation and thus finding no reason to turn to the Court for an examination of their own judgments. This, in turn, is the result of the political bargaining process that is taking place behind increasingly closed doors.

What remains to be done in this chapter is to propose a way forward taking into consideration the democratic concerns raised by enhanced citizen control through judicial review. My suggestion tries to balance the considerations raised in this chapter and it departs from the notion that what is missing is primarily the possibility for citizens to directly hold the EU Polity accountable for its actions. Against this background, and especially bearing in mind the lack of transparency in the EU decision-making process, combined with the need for ascertaining respect for the conferral of powers, it is reasonable to institute an *acte popularis* in the EU Treaties.

Needless to say, such an act would have to be conditioned in view of the heavy burden already imposed on the ECJ. I propose a model following the same construction as the citizens' initiative, enabling at least one million EU citizens from at least seven EU Member States to make an *ultra vires* complaint to the ECJ.[33] In this manner, there would be a formal way to expose a political choice to a legal examination, focusing on the procedural requirements for the adoption of EU legal acts in the event the political power refrains from initiating such a review.

---

[32] An exception is found in Art 218(11) stipulating a right for a Member State, the European Parliament, the Council or the Commission to obtain the opinion of the Court of Justice as to whether an international agreement envisaged is compatible with the Treaties.

[33] This proposal was initially made in my dissertation, A Wetter, *Making EU Legislation in the Area of Criminal Law—A Swedish Perspective* (Uppsala University, 2013).

7. SUMMARY

This study does not provide any clear evidence explaining the asymmetries in the Member States' use of the ECJ. This implies that more research is needed to establish whether there is correlation between, on the one hand the Member State with a constitutional democracy label and its use of the ECJ to annul EU legislation and on the other hand, the Member States which fits better under the label of a majoritarian democracy. It does, however, indicate that the Member States' reasons for referring a matter to the Court are heavily influenced by their policy preferences, rarely departing from their interests to ensure compliance with the principle of the conferral of powers, but rather reflecting their distributive policy preferences within the framework of the action for annulment. Considering the limited referral grounds available for EU citizens to promote a constitutional review of the EU Polity, combined with the lack of transparency in the decision-making process, an *act popularis* ground seems to be a reasonable compromise to allow for more citizen control. It is also important to remember that despite the fact that the ECJ has the authority to interpret the EU Treaties, the right to revise the Treaties still lies in the hands of the Member States.

It should finally be noted that this chapter has been drafted against the background of the current political situation in the EU. The upswing of populist nationalist parties in the Member States is a threat to the basic values of EU cooperation.[34] These parties tend to feed on claims that the EU legislator misuses its powers. Furthermore, should they gain power in the Member States, they will be the future negotiators of European legislation. In effect, even the strongest protagonist of the European integration project, who supports democratic values, should be interested in finding ways to secure that there are sufficient checks and balances in the EU legal order. This includes ensuring that the European Polity does not exceed its powers, conferred on it by the European people through the approval of their national parliaments. The ECJ has a treaty-based role in examining the legality of European acts but cannot do so on its own initiative. When EU governments hesitate to react and fall into the general acceptance of the political bargaining game, the *act popularis* may offer the EU citizens a chance to react on their own, holding the EU Polity accountable for its actions. I believe that this is a fair compromise and is also a way of protecting the legitimacy of EU cooperation.

---

[34] Populism in this chapter is defined as a 'thin ideology', one that merely sets up a framework: that of a pure people versus a corrupt elite. This definition draws on the writings of the political scientist Cas Mudde at the University of Georgia.

11

The Scandinavians

The Foot-dragging supporters of European Law?

MARLENE WIND

A LTHOUGH SCANDINAVIANS ARE often celebrated as top compliers with European Union (EU) law, until recently we have known very little about whether courts and judges in these countries have, in fact, embraced the Court of Justice of the European Union (CJEU) by forwarding cases to it. This chapter summarises recent research explaining the variance in reference patterns focusing on the Scandinavian reluctance to forward cases. It is argued that legal and political culture together with Scandinavian legal positivism, may have influenced a much more reticent approach to EU law and to the European Court of Justice than would normally be expected from this region of the world.

1. INTRODUCTION[1]

The Nordic countries have always been portrayed as 'obedient compliers with EU law'. When you look at the statistics measuring the cases before the court there are few violations and directives are mostly implemented on time. In sum, the Scandinavian EU members come out as top compliers. However, looking at these formal indicators is not always enough. Formal statistics tell us very little about what happens behind the scenes and at the national level. Do the Scandinavians engage with the European Court by frequently referring cases? How is the decision-making process

---

[1] This chapter borrows from my previous work on law and courts in the EU. In terms of the summarising argument, it builds on a piece published in a 'Fest-schrift' to Professor Hjalte Rasmussen co-authored with my colleague Professor Sindbjerg Martinsen. See DS Martinsen and M Wind 'When National Courts Go To Europe. Reluctant or Active Players in the Integration Process?' in H Koch, K Hagel-Sørensen, U Haltern and JHH Weiler (eds), *Europe: The New Legal Realism*, (Copenhagen, Djøf, 2010).

preceding a referral set up? Are judges alone in making the decisions and how do litigators experience the process? Is it easy to draw on EU law in court or something national judges prefer not to talk too much about? And what actually happens after cases have been decided? How and when is law adjusted in accordance with the case law emanating from the Court? What kind of barriers do we find and is it possible to distinguish between the cases that are referred to the CJEU through the preliminary reference system and those that are not? Are the ministries part of the process or do the judges refer cases without consulting the ministries (directly or indirectly) who are responsible for the implementation of EU law and proceedings before the CJEU? Just by looking at the numbers, you can glean that the Scandinavian courts in Denmark and Sweden have in fact been very reluctant to interact with the European Court of Justice. But the question is why and how can it be explained? Does it have to do with learning, inexperience or outright opposition to supranational European law? These are some of the questions that my research over the past ten years has tried to address. I will here try to summarise some of these findings with a primary focus on the referral of preliminary references. While my previous work has focused on the functioning of the preliminary reference system, my recent research has documented that Scandinavians have managed to keep a low profile when it comes to international judicial cooperation in general while simultaneously selling themselves as vanguards of international rules and norms. Their reluctance is thus not only reserved for EU law but also applies to international law and the willingness to cite international case law in the national courts.[2] This is despite the fact that since the Second World War, the Nordic States have been portrayed as 'champions of international law and human rights'.[3] What has not been discussed, much less researched in either legal or political science literature is precisely the fact that the Scandinavians have displayed extensive reluctance and enormous hesitance when it comes to the frequency in which they have domesticated the values they themselves officially stand for. For instance, by citing the case law of those international courts they helped set up after the Second World War.[4]

My overall argument explaining this rather counterintuitive finding is broadly speaking that the Scandinavian countries' conception of democracy and the role of (national) courts in society have influenced their dealings

---

[2] M Wind 'Do Scandinavians Care about International Law? A Study of Scandinavian Judges Citation Practice to International Law and Courts' (2016) 85 *NJIL* 281.

[3] J Christoffersen and MR Madsen, 'The End of Virtue? Denmark and the Boomerang of the Internationalisation of Human Rights' (2011) 80(3) *Nordic Journal of International Law* 259. A Brysk, *Global Good Samaritans. Human Rights as Foreign Policy* (New York, Oxford University Press, 2009).

[4] On the theoretical link between citations to international law and these bodies perceived legitimacy see Wind above n 2.

and dialogue with supranational courts. Most Scandinavian countries are what we may call *majoritarian democracies* following the legal philosopher Ronald Dworkin,[5] which means that they have very little experience of and appreciation for judicial review at the national level. This applies specifically to Denmark and Sweden (and Finland). Norway is different having established rather strong review powers and a powerful constitutional court in 1815. Most other European countries became constitutional democracies after the Second World War, which according to Dworkin emphasises a tradition for strong national courts with the power and willingness to overrule the majorities in parliament to protect minorities and basic principles of law. This development towards the spread of constitutionalism—almost world wide—has, however, escaped our Nordic region almost entirely.

My focus in this summarising essay will, however, be on the relationship that the national courts have with the CJEU. For those who are interested in dealings with international law, see Wind[6] where it is shown that Swedish and Danish judges—as opposed to their Norwegian counterparts—very rarely cite international treaty law and the case law emanating from international judicial bodies.

2. STUDYING COURTS AND SOCIETY: THE THEORETICAL APPROACH

The point of departure for this research is neither legal dogmatics nor black-letter law. It is probably closer to empirical legal realism[7] in the sense that the scope of interest of this research is to understand and explain the behaviour and motives of actors around and among courts and judges rather than 'to find the law'. It is thus equally close to political science and sociology where 'interests' and the study of power are central.

From this perspective, courts not only transmit what has been decided in parliament but are seen as powerful societal actors in their own right. Or to put it differently, according to this view, whether courts and judges *decide* to refer a case to a supranational court and also when they choose *not* to do so, they make a *political choice*. Not in the party-political sense of course, but they take part in a political 'power game' or manoeuvring which is far from innocent and which deserves serious scientific scrutiny.

In other words, when a Danish, Swedish or any other European court decides *not* to forward a case to the CJEU through the preliminary ruling procedure where it would have been relevant or has been asked for by the

---

[5] R Dworkin, *Freedom's Law: The Moral Reading of the American Constitution* (Cambridge, Mass, Harvard University Press, 1996).
[6] See Wind above n 2.
[7] J Holtemann and M Rask Madsen, 'European New Legal Realism and International Law: How to Make International Law Intelligible' (2015) 28 *Leiden Journal of International Law* 211.

parties to the case, it is a decision often influenced by factors other than a simple legal analysis. Several considerations and not least several actors are involved. Also the political actors in the ministries, who will often be defending the government's position at the European Court, play a crucial role and—at least in the case of Denmark—influence the decision to refer cases. Recent research[8] also shows that judges are often influenced by other factors even at a subconscious level that are reflected in a society's legal and political culture. For anyone who sees courts as a mere reflection of what is decided by a majority in parliament—a mere *'bouche de la loi'* of what politicians have decided—this is clearly thought provoking. In order to uncover these features, it will be necessary not only to employ statistical analysis but equally, institutional studies, interviews and surveys apart from more ordinary doctrinal analysis.

While a legal dogmatic perspective would argue that only narrow legal doctrine influences the decision of whether or not a national court should refer a case to the CJEU, my work shows that looking at other intervening variables and dependents are essential. This in order to understand the variance that clearly exists when, for instance, you compare two countries of a similar size and with a similar number of citizens but also to understand the broader societal context. Put differently, if the driving force behind a court's decision to ask the CJEU for help when interpreting EU law rested on narrow legal doctrine alone, the variance in reference patterns in the courts of the Member States would be insignificant. However, as research has shown, *variance does exist* and deserves—at least from a social science perspective—to be explained.[9]

Before I present a summary of the findings in my research, it is important to briefly look at the underlying and much broader question of the role that courts play (and ought to play) in society and democracy in general. This debate is far from new, but has influenced legal philosophy and political theory for centuries. It is, however, essential to rehearse the competing views again here, firstly because much legal scholarship on EU law is incredibly under-theorised; secondly, fundamental discussions are necessary to understand 'the politics of law' when discussing the relationship between national and European courts.[10] Lastly, it is important in order to avoid a simplistic criticism of court activism and judicial review while uncritically celebrating

---

[8] See JE Rytter and M Wind, 'In Need of Juristocracy? The Silence of Denmark in the Development of European Legal Norms' (2011) 9(2) *International Journal of Constitutional Law* 470–504.

[9] M Wind, DS Martinsen and GP Rotger, 'The Uneven Legal Push for Europe: Questioning Variation When National Courts go to Europe' (2009) 10(1) *European Union Politics* 63 and M Wind, 'The Nordics, the EU and the Reluctance towards Supranational Judicial Review' (2010) 48(4) *Journal of Common Market Studies* 1048.

[10] J Christoffersen and M Rask Madsen, *Menneskerettighedsdomstolen—50 års samspil med dansk ret og politik*, (Copenhagen, Karnov Group, 2009).

unconstrained majoritarian democracy and black-letter law, which has been dominant in a Nordic context.

2.1. Law, Courts and Democracy

How should you describe the role of courts in a democratic society? Do they—as unelected bodies—fit in at all? The classical question of the legitimacy of unelected judges conducting judicial review over an elected political majority dates back to the earliest writers on democracy.[11] The basic question, even today and certainly also in relation to the CJEU and other international courts, is: should the parliament be sovereign in the sense of being without limits (i.e. not having to subject itself to a form of review mechanism by a court)? Should politicians themselves be trusted to protect fundamental rights as some theorists[12] (and certainly politicians) claim, or do we need independent courts for that? Are courts better than politicians at the job?[13] In this context, it may also be highly relevant to ask whether there is (or should be) a difference between the review power of national and supranational/international courts. To put it differently, if we—which is the case in most of the Nordic countries—have no tradition of *national* judicial review, can we then accept judicial review of national legislation by an international court? This is the dilemma in a nutshell—but interestingly, it is rarely discussed. In Denmark, we have no—or very little—experience of letting our own national courts set aside national legislation (it has only happened once in almost 170 years in the so-called *Tvind* case), but by being part of both the EU and the ECHR, we have *de facto* subjected ourselves to judicial review by two strong international courts.

Though this discussion may seem trivial to some, it is certainly vibrant when you look at the Danish debate in recent years,[14] where not only the role of international courts, but also the role of national courts has been hotly debated. The still unsettled issue of the judicial dialogue between the courts in the Member States and the European Court of Justice (as well as other international courts and conventions) illustrates and underscores the continuing relevance of this philosophical discussion. Looking at this from a theoretical perspective, not only lawyers and legal philosophers have taken an interest in the debate. An important voice in the discussion has been that of the prominent and highly influential American political scientist

---

[11] R Bellamy, *Political Constitutionalism: A Republican Defense of the Constitutionality of Democracy* (Cambridge, Cambridge University Press, 2007).

[12] R Dahl, *Democracy and its Critics* (New Haven, Yale University Press, 1989) 154–59.

[13] See 'Symposium Roundtable: An Exchange with Jeremy Waldron' (2009) 7(14) *International Journal of Constitutional Law*.

[14] See Rytter and Wind above n 8 at 470.

Robert Dahl. In his view, a true democracy should, as a principle, *not* subject itself to any kind of judicial review by the courts. As he boldly puts it: 'No one has shown that countries ... which lack judicial review ... are less democratic ...'.[15] This also applies to the protection of fundamental rights, which, of course, has been the most prominent reason for having courts with strong review powers. In fact, according to Dahl, majoritarian democracies are perfectly capable of protecting fundamental rights *without* the help of judges. As he argues, democracies with judicial review to protect minorities and fundamental rights often get lazy: 'Over time, the political culture may come to incorporate the expectation that the judicial guardians can be counted on to fend off violations of fundamental rights'.[16] According to Dahl, this will make politicians less attentive to their own responsibilities. To summarise, in Dahl's view, elected politicians are better than judges when it comes to protecting fundamental rights.

Though Dahl's faith in politicians to protect fundamental rights seems fragile, it represents the dominant view among most Scandinavian lawyers, judges and politicians. In fact, this understanding has been part and parcel of a common Nordic[17] heritage for at least two centuries—more specifically, since these modern democracies acquired their formal democratic constitutions.[18] In Denmark, Sweden and Finland, judicial review has either been forbidden until recently or rarely practised.[19] In this sense the *parliament has always come first*[20]—elevated above the other branches of governing powers like the courts. More or less unconstrained majority rule (even in its formal minority government version)[21] has thus been the closest you could get to an ideal type of democracy in this part of the world.[22] As Jens Elo Rytter has suggested:

Common to the constitutional tradition of the Nordic countries ... there is an emphasis on the preferred position of Parliament in the constitutional power structure, based on its democratic mandate through elections. The courts have

---

[15] See Dahl above n 12 at 189.

[16] Ibid; see also R Hirschl, *Towards Juristocracy: The Origins and Consequences of the New Constitutionalism'* (Cambridge MA, Harvard University Press, 2004) 3–5; Bellamy above n 11 145–76.

[17] Again, Norway may be seen as an exception, but as described above, in the past decade, the democracy debate in Norway has been centered exactly on the role and excessive power of (international) courts.

[18] H Palmer Olsen, *Magtfordeling: En analyse af magtfordelingslæren med særligt henblik på den lovgivende magt* (DJØF Forlag, Copenhagen, 2005).

[19] M Scheinin, *The Welfare State and Constitutionalism in the Nordic Countries* (Copenhagen, Nordic Council of Ministers, 2001).

[20] M Wind, 'When Parliament Comes First—The Danish Concept of Democracy meets the European Union' (2009) 27(2) *Nordic Journal of Human Rights* 272.

[21] In order to have majority rule, you do not need to have a majority government as long as you have a majority in parliament.

[22] T Knudsen, *Dansk Statsbygning* [Danish State-Building] (DJØF, Copenhagen, 1995).

no similar democratic mandate and therefore, the judicial review of legislation is either problematic in principle or should at least be kept within rather narrow limits[23]

Thus, when the Danish Supreme Court in 1921[24] applied its version of 'judicial self-restraint', it underscored a constitutional need for the courts to refer to the legislator. In this manner it legitimised that in a democracy, it is the majority in parliament which prevails over the judiciary both due to its lack of democratic mandate but also due to the deep-seated anti-rights sentiments found in legal thinking within Scandinavian legal realism.[25] With this understanding, judges should not 'invent the law' on their own from basic natural law principles, but instead should stick to the 'hard' positive law coming out of parliament. Danish courts have no doubt conducted self-restraint over the years and continue to do so. The same can, according to Joakim Nergelius, be said of Swedish courts and judges.[26] As Rytter and Wind writes:

> Generally speaking, it (self-restraint) means that whenever judicial review is undertaken on the basis of broad and imprecise constitutional provisions like for instance human rights, which often have this character of being broad legal principles, the courts should give significant leeway or margin to the assessment of the legislator, recognising the direct democratic mandate of the latter. More precisely, judicial self-restraint means that, vis-à-vis the legislator, a court should not insist in every detail on its own final say as to the specific contents of broad constitutional norms.[27]

The idea of self-restraint thus corresponds well with the dominance of Scandinavian legal positivism/realism and its antipathy for any kind of natural law elements as legal sources.[28] The important point here is the positivist idea—also incredibly strong in Scandinavian political science—that one should always separate 'is' from 'ought'. And since positive law (that comes out of the parliament but which is also found in treaties) is

---

[23] J E Rytter, 'Grundrettigheder som almene retsprincipper' (2001) 83(4) *Juristen* 138.

[24] Upholding an Act of Parliament concerning landownership reform, the Supreme Court stated that the citizen's claim that the Act had not provided full compensation for his loss of property could not be affirmed: 'with the *certainty* which is required for the courts to set aside an act of Parliament as unconstitutional' (here citing from Rytter and Wind above n 8 at 470–504).

[25] See also H Koch, 'Dansk forfatningsret i transnational belysning' [Danish Constitutional Law in a Transnational perspective] (1999) *Juristen* 217.

[26] J Nergelius, 'North and South: Can the Nordic States and the European Continent Find Each Other in the Constitutional Area—or Are They Too Different?' in M Scheinin (ed) *The Welfare State and Constitutionalism in the Nordic Countries* (Copenhagen, Nordic Council of Ministers, 2001).

[27] See Rytter and Wind above n 8 at 5.

[28] Scheinin above n 19 245–85; J E Rytter, *Grundrettigheder. Domstolenes fortolkning og kontrol med lovgivningsmagten* (Copenhagen, Djøf, 2000); see also Rytter and Wind, above n 8.

positive hard law, this represents the 'is' and leaves little room for the 'ought' that could be developed by the courts for instance though a dynamic court interpretation or by citing less hard human rights principles or even natural law.[29] However, from this perspective it clearly but often only intuitively becomes problematic to engage too closely with supranational courts either by citing them too extensively or by referring cases for them to decide. Both the European Court of Justice and the Strasbourg Court of Human Rights employ a dynamic style of interpretation that develop the law over time. This may of course diverge from the direct or original 'intentions' of the politicians and will thus often end up blurring the 'is' and the 'ought' in their interpretation when seen from a strict Scandinavian positivist perspective.

This explains why the political environment—and in the case of Denmark—even the executive branch have encouraged 'self-restraint' when it comes to referring cases to international courts such as the CJEU.[30] In spite of this, the development of international law and new supranational courts with strong review powers has increasingly challenged this Scandinavian perspective since the Second World War. Few have described the challenge of the Danish courts better than the former Danish President of the Supreme Court, Niels Pontoppidan, who even goes so far as to recommend a move away from the lawmaker and thus positivist legal thinking as the holy grail in Scandinavian legal thinking:

> The development since the Second World War has strongly reduced the importance of the lawmaker as the most important source of law and legitimation. It simply no longer covers legal realities sufficiently[31]

This acknowledgement caused a great stir when it was first uttered and a few constitutional lawyers even thought that the Danish Supreme Court might now gradually transform itself and become more open to the constitutional development in Europe.[32] With an increasingly powerful EU Court and its Strasbourg counterpart, the more-or-less unlimited Scandinavian parliaments thus acquired new rivals. In what follows below, it will become clear, however, that these new developments have been met with great hesitation. Even though Scandinavian courts and judges have started opening up to the world in some areas, huge scepticism prevails.

---

[29] J Murphy Bernard, *The Philosophy of Positive Law* (New Haven, Yale University Press, 2005).

[30] Wind (2010) above n 9 at 1041; see also Rytter and Wind above n 8.

[31] Niels Pontoppidan—then President of the Supreme Court—in an interview in the Danish journal *Weekendavisen* 28 June 1996, p 11.

[32] Rytter and Wind above n 8.

3. WHY DO NATIONAL COURTS HAVE DIFFERENT
REFERENCE PATTERNS?

Due to the Scandinavian embracement of what Ronald Dworkin has named *majoritarian democracy* with the lawmaker (and positive law) at the centre, Danish courts—and indeed the public administration maintaining the Danish relationship with the European Union—have not over the years been too eager to refer cases to the CJEU for interpretation. In 2010, I demonstrated how the Ministry of Justice has played a significant role in consulting with the courts, through the state attorney, and determining which cases ought to be referred and which ought not.[33] Normally, there would be a sharp division between the executive and the judicial branch of government. However, in Denmark there has always been a significant overlap and close recruitment ties between the two institutions.[34] A top civil servant from the Danish Ministry of Justice even emphasised when speaking about this 'problem' that he preferred judges in the Supreme Court who had had a good education *in* and strong ties *with* the ministry when taking up the position as judge.

The preliminary ruling system, embedded in the Community with the Treaty of Rome in 1957 (then Article 177) which requires courts and tribunals to refer cases to the CJEU if there is doubt about the interpretation of EU law, thus introduces a judicial review mechanism fundamentally foreign to most Scandinavian legal and political traditions.[35] Though aware of other explanations, I have elsewhere argued that for a political and legal culture with no tradition of judicial review, it is clearly counterintuitive to ask an international court—with substantial review powers—to evaluate what a lawmaker (and administration) has decided in parliament. The same applies to asking it to judge whether national implementation of EU law has been sufficient, on time, or in direct breach of EU regulations or previous court cases. What makes the relationship even 'worse' is that on top of this we are dealing with a supranational court which does not reveal dissenting votes and which employs a dynamic style of legal interpretation.[36] Hence, the 'political control' of the courts and judges, which of course is implicit and indirect through recruitment systems, common education, consultations, networks etc. and certainly never discussed in a Nordic context, is non-existent or of a completely

---

[33] See Wind (2010) above n 9.

[34] See O Hammerselv 'Independence of the Danish Judiciary' in *Separation of Powers in Theory and Practice: An International Perspective*, LE Groot-van Leuwen and W Rombouts (eds), (Nijmegen Wolf Legal Publishers, 2010).

[35] See Wind, Martinsen and Rotger above n 9; Rytter and Wind above n 8.

[36] H Rasmussen, *On Law and Policy in the European Court of Justice: A Comparative Study in Judicial Policymaking* (Boston, Martinus Nijhoff, 1986).

different character in the European system. In this way, the EU's preliminary ruling mechanism not only introduces judicial review into a Scandinavian legal and political system where judicial review is uncommon, but it also introduces collaboration with a constitutional judicial system that even celebrates legal activism (e.g. a dynamic style of interpretation) and which confronts a philosophy of 'self-restraint' head on.

Referring cases to the CJEU when there is a doubt regarding the interpretation of EU law is, nevertheless, the cornerstone of the EU constitutional order.[37] In order to make sure that the EU's legal system develops in a harmonious and cohesive manner, and to establish legal certainty for companies and citizens, it is (and has always been) essential that national courts willingly engage in an ongoing dialogue with the European Court of Justice. You can also argue that the ability of the European Court to enhance and define the scope of European constitutional law depends on the willingness of the national courts to bring preliminary references before it. In a long-term and overall perspective, national courts—in the EU as a whole—have largely accepted and taken on that role.[38] National courts have become European courts. However, not all courts have collaborated with similar enthusiasm. The German Constitutional Court for one is known for its revolts against the EU system and also other higher European courts have taken a long time to adjust to a new higher constitutional layer. Below we will take a closer look at the long timespan statistics to put the Danish and Swedish cases into perspective. It is important to emphasize, however, that looking at statistics alone will not help us much when it comes to really understanding the cultural and legal-political layer of resistance. Numbers are easy to manipulate and by making all kinds of comparisons, it is easy to simply refuse to enter into any discussion.[39] It is therefore very important to emphasize that a thorough study of legal and political culture and philosophy of science dominating the discipline in question together with interviews with judges and civil servants are absolutely essential to be able to conclude anything meaningful about the dialogue (or lack thereof) between Scandinavian judges and the European court. Now to the statistics: first, the general trends.

Our data below thus confirm that Article 267 (previously Article 234 and Article 177) references continued to increase significantly between 1961,

---

[37] JHH Weiler, 'The Transformation of Europe' (1991) 100 *The Yale Law Journal* 2403.

[38] KJ Alter, 'The European Union's Legal System and Domestic Policy: Spillover or Backlash?' (2000) 54(3) *International Organizations* 489; see also K J Alter, *Establishing the Supremacy of European Law. The Making of an International Rule of Law in Europe* (Oxford, Oxford University Press, 2001).

[39] See, for instance, N Fenger and M Broberg, *Preliminære forelæggelser for EU-domstolen*, (Copenhagen, Djøf, 2008).

when the first preliminary reference was forwarded to the Court, and 2014,[40] the most recent reference point.

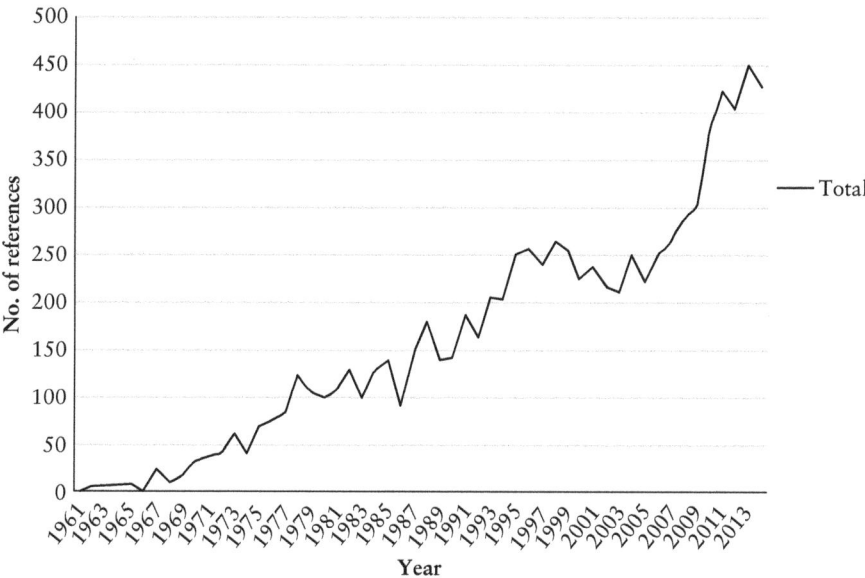

Figure 11.1: Trend in total number of preliminary references (Art 267) 1961–2014[41]

The more recent figures in our data confirm this historical trend. By the end of 2014, 8,710 preliminary references had been made to the European Court. From 1993 onwards, more than 200 references were made annually, with a maximum of 450 references in 2013. The interplay between the national courts and the European Court is indeed a growth factor on its own in the European integration process.

Nonetheless, the data also confirm that national courts do not participate with similar intensity to equal degrees. Some courts appear more reluctant to refer questions to the European judiciary, and one of the most pronounced characteristics behind the aggregated trend illustrated above is the important heterogeneity across Member States (see Figure 11.2).

It is clear that the heterogeneity in the total number of preliminary references per Member State may be attributed to various factors. The length of the membership period seems to play a role, as Belgium, Germany, France, Italy and the Netherlands have had the highest number of references, whereas the later arriving EU-12 Member States for the most part have

---

[40] *The Annual Report 2014*, Court of Justice of the European Communities (2014). The latest report is from 2014.
[41] Own data elaborated on the basis of *The Annual Report*, see above n 40.

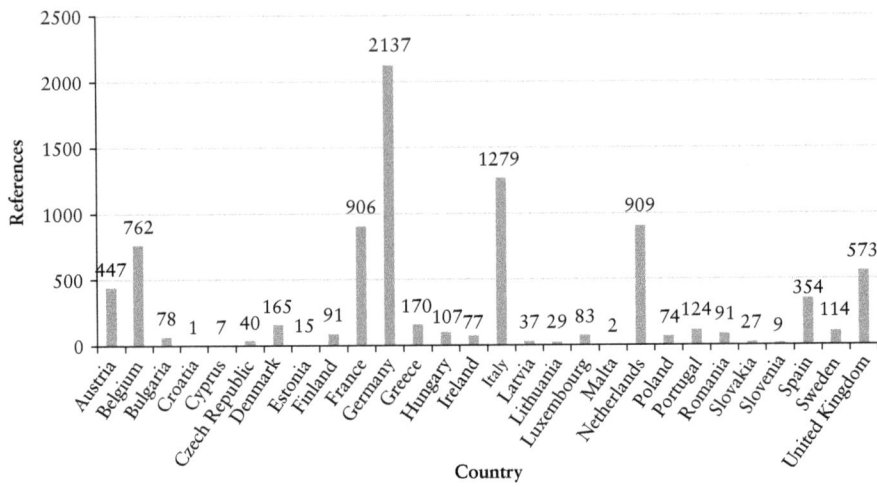

Figure 11.2: Total no. of references pr. country 1961–2014[42]

made much fewer. If we take year of membership into account, heterogeneity is, however, still significant, as Figure 11.3 demonstrates.

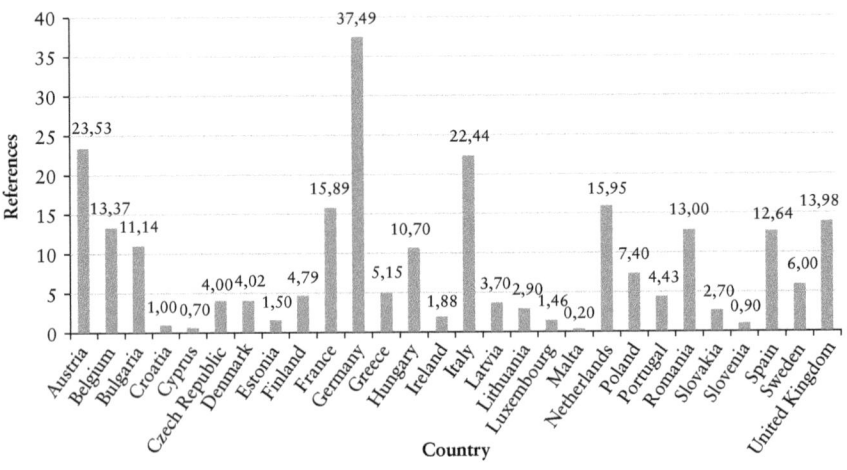

Figure 11.3: Average number of references per country per year of membership 1957–2014[43]

[42] Ibid.
[43] Ibid. Years of membership is calculated between 1957 and 2008.

It has been argued that population size may in part explain the heterogeneity regarding the reference practice of Member States.[44] However, when controlling for the different population sizes, the variance across Member States is still remarkable. Although the picture of the Member States' reference practice is now a different one, Wind et al previously demonstrated that there is *no causality* between population size and preliminary reference practice.[45] In political science terminology, this means that population size cannot *explain* the different number of preliminary references that come from any individual country. This is apparent when we compare Austria and Sweden. Both acceded to the EU in the same year—1995—and have, on average, the same population size. However, from the figures, it is clear that Austria has referred many more cases than Sweden. If you look at the Nordic states, there are also significant differences:

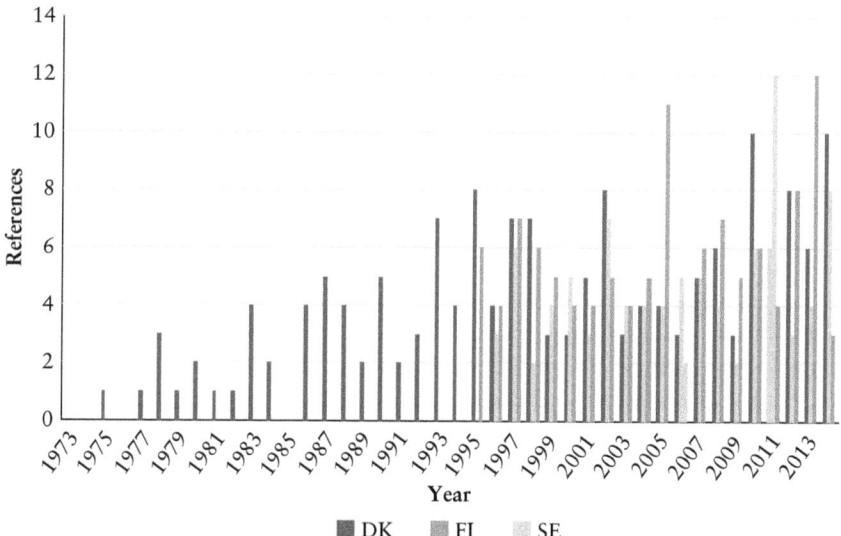

Figure 11.4: Case referred by the Nordic countries (1973–2014)

Source: The Court of Justice of the European Communities (2014), *The Annual Report 2014*: 115–116.

However, if differences in population size do not explain why some Member States refer more cases than others then what does? It is clear that individuals trying to make their case before the European Court have a long, troubled way to go. The absence of causality between population size and

---

[44] N Fenger 'Om danske domstoles relative tilbøjelighed til at forelægge præjudicielle spørgsmål for EU-domstolen', (2009) 91(10) *Juristen* 269.
[45] See Wind, Martinsen and Rotger above n 9 at 79.

preliminary references make it clear that we need to take a closer look at other explanatory factors to make sense of differences and similarities in the interplay between the EU and national courts. Above, we pointed out how legal and democratic cultures might explain this reluctance to make use of the preliminary reference procedure. This study, as the first of its kind, uses democratic traits/characteristics as an explanatory framework when studying divergent preliminary references among Member States. The most influential explanations launched by political scientists studying variance in reference patterns has, however, not been legal and political culture, but rather general theories relating to macro factors, such as the level of trade between countries and court competition.[46]

Let us briefly look at the most common explanations.

3.1. Why go to Europe in the First Place?

Existing studies attempting to explain variance have provided very different narratives about why national courts have participated in the legal constitutionalisation of Europe. One of the explanatory variables suggested in prior studies is whether interest groups are active within a certain policy area, and thus provide the resources to take cases to the CJEU.[47] The litigiousness of individual societies is another explanatory factor. That is, are courts in general used to solving societal conflicts—do citizens regard going to court as something natural?[48] A third explanation concerns national legal education and judicial learning. How well educated are national judges— do they know enough about EU law and the workings of international courts?[49] A fourth (and quite prominent) explanation is judicial competition: It is argued by Alter 2001 that national judges especially from lower courts often see a strategic advantage in addressing the European court level. They bypass their own national legal hierarchy in an attempt to challenge their own top/supreme/highest court.[50] When you look at Sweden and Denmark, however, we demonstrated that it is very rarely the lower

---

[46] A Stone Sweet and T L Brunell, 'Constructing a Supranational Constitution: Dispute Resolution and Governance in the European Community' (1998) 92(1) *American Political Science Review* 63; see also J Golub, 'The Politics of Judicial Discretion: Rethinking the Interaction between National Courts and the European Court of Justice' (1996) 19(2) *West European Politics* 360.

[47] K J Alter and J Vargas, 'Explaining Variation in the Use of European Litigation Strategies' (2000) 33(4) *Comparative Political Studies* 452; see also L Conant (2001), 'Europeanization and the Courts: Variable Patterns of Adaptation among National Judiciaries' in MG Cowles, J Caposaso and T Risse (eds), *Transforming Europe—Europeanization and Domestic Change*, (London, Cornell University Press, 2001); see also Alter (2000) above n 38.

[48] See Alter (2000) above n 38.

[49] J Golub, 'Modelling Judicial Dialogue in the European Community: The Quantitative Basis of Preliminary References to the ECJ', (1996), *EUI Working Paper RSC*, No 96/58; see also Alter (2000) above n 38.

[50] See Golub above n 46; see also Alter (2001) above n 38.

courts which make the referrals. In fact until very recently this almost never happened.[51] Here, it was left to the Supreme courts to interact with the CJEU as it was not something that the lower courts saw themselves as competent enough to do. This was further supported in a survey made with the judges themselves.[52]

Many of the factors presented by in particular American scholars may have been plausible for making sense of the reference practices of individual countries or within different policy sectors. What seems unlikely is that there is one *general theory* or one main cause which can explain all situations. However, grand explanatory frameworks seeking to explain which general mechanisms can foresee reference patterns in all countries, has for a long time been the only commodity on the shelf and this is—I would argue—highly problematic. When Stone Sweet and Brunell, for instance, claim that the rise in preliminary references can be predicted by a rise in transnational activity, measured as intra EC trade,[53] this is far from convincing. They thus argue that the greater the trade between countries the greater the number of cases that will be referred to the CJEU by national courts: more trade implies more conflicts and more EU legal disputes to be solved. My previous work[54] has, however, not found any support for this causal relationship even in Denmark or Sweden, which are small, open economies with a great deal of trade with other states. In Denmark and Sweden, the high trade flow has not led to more preliminary references. The fact that these obvious examples do not fit into Stone Sweet and Brunell's model made us hypothesise that *type of democracy* might be a much more solid explanatory factor.

There is little doubt that the institutional features that structure the relationship between law and politics differ between democratic traditions in the Member States. As already suggested in the introduction, Ronald Dworkin[55] (as well as Richard Bellamy)[56] has, in other contexts not dealing with preliminary references, court behaviour or even Europe for that matter, presented two different democratic traditions which have shaped the role of the courts and democracy in fundamentally different ways; *majoritarian* and *constitutional democracy*.

As mentioned already, the *majoritarian democracy* tradition is known and well established in all of the Nordic countries except perhaps Norway, which was the first European country to have a court with explicit review powers. However, even in Norway criticism of the courts and constitutionalism has been prominent in recent years. The concern here and in

---

[51] See Wind (2010) above n 9 where a schematic overview over which courts actually make the preliminary references is presented.

[52] See Martinsen and Wind, above n 1.

[53] See A Stone Sweet and T Brunell above n 46 at 63.

[54] See Wind, Martinsen and Rotger above n 9.

[55] R Dworkin above n 5.

[56] J Bellamy, 'Adaptive Governance: The Challenge for Regional Natural Resource Management' in AJ Brown and JA Bellamy (eds), *Federalism and Regionalism in Australia: New Approaches, New Institutions?* (Canberra, ANU E Press, 2007).

the Nordic countries over the past decades has been the fear that courts will take over at the expense of political institutions.[57] The United Kingdom, which is also broadly speaking a majoritarian democracy, also falls within this category of court scepticism and has recently voted to leave not only the European Union (in order to get its 'own laws back' as Theresa May put it in a speech in February 2017), but has also threatened to leave both the ECHR and the ECtHR. Since majoritarian democracies rest on the idea of parliamentary supremacy, it is not surprising that the United Kingdom is prominent in the majoritarian camp.[58] For this reason, it has become commonplace to view constitutional and majoritarian democracy as almost incompatible: 'The ideal of limited government, or constitutionalism, is in conflict with the idea of parliamentary sovereignty'.[59] Parliamentary governance systems are, moreover, founded on the notion that parliamentary majorities represent the 'will of the people' and that such majorities should not be subject to judicial review.[60] Courts are, therefore, regarded as a 'counter-majoritarian' force since they place the protection of rights and civil liberties by the courts above 'the will of the people'.[61]

Although most majoritarian democracies have constitutions, laying down the division of power principle (at least formally) and as mentioned above even some kind of weak review, it has not been part of their daily practice for the courts to challenge or actively review that legislation is in accordance with the constitution.[62] As noted, Denmark, Sweden, Finland and the UK, all have roots in this tradition.[63] In the UK, there is no written constitution, and the idea of parliamentary sovereignty has always been extremely strong.[64] Accordingly, the courts have had almost no powers of legislative review and have—as is also the case in the Scandinavian countries—generally regarded themselves as '*la bouche de la loi*'; loyal primarily to the executive and the democratically elected majority.[65] In principle, EU membership

---

[57] See Ø Østerud, F Engelstad and P Selle, *Makten og demokratiet* (Oslo, Gylendal Norsk Forlag, 2006).

[58] T Ginsburg, *Judicial Review in New Democracies* (Cambridge, Cambridge University Press, 2003); see also Dworkin above n 5.

[59] See Ginsburg above n 58 at 2.

[60] See Dworkin above n 5 at 19–20.

[61] A Føllesdal 'Rawls in the Nordic Countries' (2002) 1(2) *European Journal of Political Theory* 181–98.

[62] See Scheinin above n 19.

[63] A Føllesdal and M Wind, 'Introduction to Nordic Reluctance towards Judicial Review under Siege' (2009) 27(2) *Nordic Journal of Human Rights* 131.

[64] D Chalmers, 'The Positioning of EU Judicial Politics within the United Kingdom' in K H Goetz and S Hix (eds) *Europeanised Politics. European Integration and National Political Systems* (London, Frank Cass, 2001); see also Dworkin n 5 above.

[65] ML Volcansek, 'Judges, Courts and Policy-Making in Western Europe' (1992) 15(3) *West European Politics* 109; see also Chalmers above n 64.

challenged the division of labour between law and politics in the UK. However, British courts did not explicitly accept the supremacy of EU law before the *Factortame* judgment in 1990,[66] and preliminary references were simply not made during the first decade of membership.[67] Long-established institutional traditions thus resisted an adaptation to a new supranational context for a long time. As mentioned earlier, we see a similar pattern in the Nordic countries where, in Finland, the judicial review of legislation was directly forbidden until a very recent amendment to the constitution in 2000.[68] In Sweden, the review of legislation has been formally allowed since a change to the constitution in 1979 but it is almost never practised. In Denmark, the constitution is silent on the issue and Danish courts have—as noted above—set aside legislation only once in the past 170 years.[69] Moreover, the majoritarian paradigm in the Nordic countries has cultivated a '... *corps* of judges who are unusually loyal to the legislator, never questioning his wisdom and not perceiving its task as protecting the rights of the individual against the state.'[70] Moreover, as judges perceive themselves as neutral and apolitical 'civil servants' there is little doubt that the entire European development—in the EU as well as the European human rights regime guided by the Court in Strasbourg—has been perceived with great unease and suspicion. These courts are doing everything that a Nordic judge has been taught not to do.

Constitutional democracy takes a different route. It is first and foremost an American invention, which only gradually came to influence a number of European countries after the Second World War. Constitutional democracies generally embrace judicial review and view it as a constitutive aspect of what it means to be a true democracy. Supranational judicial review at the European level is therefore perceived as a natural extension of national practice; not as a threat. Theoretical as well as descriptive literature has recently presented some very general trends characterising constitutional

---

[66] Many other European constitutional and Supreme Courts have had their reservations and can even today be seen as reluctant compliers with the supremacy principle. However, if one looks at the daily practice of law and the lower courts interaction in most European Member States, there is little doubt that they have accepted supremacy. See more on this in B de Witte, J Mayoral, U Jaremba, M Wind and K Podstawa (eds), *National Courts and EU Law: New Issues, Theories and Methods* (Cheltenham, Edward Elgar, 2016).

[67] PP Craig, 'Report on United Kingdom' in AM Slaughter, A Stone Sweet and JHH Weiler (eds) *The European Court and National Courts—Doctrine and Jurisprudence.* (Oxford, Hart Publishing, 1998), 200–205.

[68] See Nergelius above n 26 at 85; see also T Ojanen 'From Constitutional Periphery toward the Centre—Transformations of Judicial Review in Finland' (2009) 27(2) *Nordisk Tidsskrift for Menneskerettigheder* 194–208.

[69] See Nergelius above n 26; Rytter above n 28; Palmer Olsen above n 18; Rytter and Wind above n 8.

[70] See Nergelius above n 26 at 88.

democracies in Europe and elsewhere.[71] These studies often emphasise that judicial review became a reality in Europe after the Second World War when the defeated powers, Germany and Italy, adopted the institution to better protect fundamental rights. In reality, there is, of course, great variation in the manner in which judicial review was institutionalised in different European countries.[72] Research suggests that historical/institutional factors such as court structure, monism/dualism, experiences with dictatorship and/ or communist rule influence the emphasis countries place on judicial review and the need to limit parliamentary power.[73] Moreover, as Martin Shapiro has pointed out, countries which conduct judicial reviews are often (but not always) organised along federalist lines.[74] The US and Germany are good examples of federalist states in this category. However, Australia and Canada are unitary states and they still have a judicial review system,[75] so the emphasis should rather—he argues—be put on the presence of an explicit division of powers element. Having some kind of division of powers system (sometimes combined with federalism) may thus better explain the acceptance of a judicial review system. Another hypothesis is the rights hypothesis, which may supplement the division of powers hypothesis. As Shapiro points out: 'Those polities which first adopted judicial review did so because of the division of powers. Rights concerns engendered recent judicial review … Most probably: a conjunction of division of powers and rights concerns is most likely to generate successful review.'[76] The interesting thing here is that Denmark and indeed the other Nordic countries have traditionally not been very occupied with either the division of powers or with letting courts protect fundamental rights.[77] Rather, *the state* has been regarded as an all-embracing entity protecting the individual from 'cradle to grave'.[78]

---

[71] S Kenny et al, *Constitutional Dialogues in Comparative Perspective*. (London, Macmillan, 1991); see also M. Shapiro and A. Stone (eds), 'Special Issue: The New Constitutional Politics of Europe', (1994) *Comparative Political Studies* 26(4): 397–561; see also A Stone Sweet, 'Constitutional Dialogues: Protecting Rights in France, Germany, Italy and Spain' in S Kenny, W M Reisinger and JC Reitz (eds), *Constitutional Dialogues in Comparative Perspective* (Minnesota, Palgrave, 1999); see also A Stone Sweet (2002), 'Constitutional Courts and Parliamentary Democracy' 25(1) *West European Politics* 77–100; see also SW Sheive, 'Central and Eastern European Constitutional Courts and the Antimajoritarian Objection to Judicial Review' (1995) *Law & Policy International Business*; see also Scheinin above at n 19; see Dworkin above n 5; Ginsburg above at n 58.

[72] See Kenny et al above n 71 at 62.

[73] P Magalhães, 'The Politics of Judicial Reform in Eastern Europe' (1999) 32(1) *Comparative Politics* 43–62; see Sheive above n 71 at 1–25; see also Stone Sweet above n 71 and Ginsburg above n 58.

[74] M Shapiro, 'The Success of Judicial Review' in S Kenny, WM Reisinger and JC Reitz (eds), *Constitutional Dialogues in Comparative Perspective*. (London: Macmillan, 1999), 193–219.

[75] Ibid at 197.

[76] Ibid at 201.

[77] See Rytter above n 28; see Palmer Olsen above n 18; see also Wind, Martinsen and Rotger above n 9.

[78] See Rytter and Wind above n 8.

With little focus on the protection of the basic rights of citizens there has also been little incentive for Danish courts to actively test the Danish state's administration of EU law implementation. Due to the recruitment pattern in the Danish courts where the majority of judges (despite a judicial reform to change this in 2000) are still recruited from the Ministry of Justice, judges will often be more loyal to the state apparatus and to the political establishment than to the EU-generated rights of citizens.[79]

This was also documented in a study by Professor Peter Pagh, who demonstrated that the preliminary reference procedure in Denmark is in part conditioned by an extraordinarily close relationship between the executive branch (the Ministry of Justice and Foreign Affairs) and the Danish courts.[80] Historically, there has always been—as mentioned earlier—a close relationship between the Ministry of Justice and the national courts. Danish judges were, until recently, mainly recruited from the Ministry of Justice, and loyalty to this executive body has remained virtually unchallenged. This, in part, explains why the so-called *Judicial Committee* plays an influential role when it comes to preliminary references. In his study, Pagh demonstrated how the Judicial Committee not only advises the Danish courts on preliminary references through the attorney of the Danish state. The committee also participates in the selection and drafting of 267 questions while many of its members also advise the government in the implementation of EU law.[81]

Joining the findings of Professor Peter Pagh, my research has shown that because of the legal education system, legal and political culture and its many overlapping and occasionally contradictory tasks, the Judicial Committee will, all in all, have very little incentive to suggest to a national court (through the Danish state attorney) that it submit a preliminary reference. A comprehensive survey conducted on this issue among all Danish judges in the winter of 2006 confirmed that one of the main reasons for the low number of preliminary references was discouragement from the legal adviser to the Danish government based on a so-called 'responsa' by the Committee.[82] Asked specifically about their main reasons for not making any (or very few) preliminary references, an overwhelming 69% of the judges (at all levels) referred to discouragement from the state attorney.[83] The involvement of the Judicial Committee is the most convincing single explanatory factor for the low number of referrals from Danish courts since Denmark became a member of the European Community. Pagh's own study shows

---

[79] This was confirmed in interviews with judges.
[80] P Pagh (2004) 'Præjudicielle forelæggelser og Juridisk Specialudvalg' 41 *Ugeskrift for Retsvæsen* 305—13.
[81] Ibid.
[82] Ibid.
[83] Wind, Martinsen and Rotger above n 9.

that from 1986 to 2003, the Judicial Committee has recommended *not* referring a case to the CJEU in 20 out of 26 cases, even though all 26 cases dealt with the interpretation of EU law and at least one of the parties had requested an interpretation by the CJEU.[84] Generally speaking, the Judicial Committee has only recommended Danish courts to make preliminary references in those cases where there is already direct action being taken against Denmark by the Commission.[85] While the Judicial Committee is 'just doing its job'—advising one party—the Danish government– in a case—it is perhaps more puzzling that the Danish courts treat this advice as 'the highest legal expertise' as one of the judges in our interviews put it. However, having been brought up in the Ministry of Justice, most judges may feel inclined to take its advice very seriously.

4. CONCLUSIONS

Martin Shapiro once noted that: 'judges make rather than simply discover law'.[86] While this may be a trivial insight in any constitutional democratic context, it is still a rather provocative statement to make in a Scandinavian political setting. In this part of Europe, there seems to be a wide but subtle consensus holding that a true democracy should elevate parliament above the other branches of government, foster close links between the courts, the legislature and the executive branches of government, and only give courts scarce judicial review powers. Indeed, the successful Nordic welfare states have even regarded their corporatist structure, homogenous culture and more or less unconstrained parliaments as role models for other democracies and as eminent examples of good democratic principles, where 'the will of the people' is reflected in political majority decisions. There is no doubt that 'the will of the people' is here to stay with Trump, 'Brexit' and the 'people-elite' bashing going on in most of the western media. The question raised here is, however, whether the courts may not also be seen as the protective bodies we sometimes need when the majority goes too far?

---

[84] See Pagh above n 80 at 307.

[85] In particular, the infamous '*Can-Case*', case C-246/99, in which Denmark was charged by the Commission for hindering the implementation of Directive 94/62 dealing with the marketing of cans instead of ordinary bottles on the Danish market.

[86] M Shapiro 'Towards a Theory of *Stare Decisive*' in M Shapiro and A Stone Sweet (eds), *On Law, Politics and Judicialization* (Oxford: Oxford University Press, 2002) 20.

12

On Specialisation of Chambers at the General Court

ULF ÖBERG, MOHAMED ALI AND PAULINE SABOURET*

1. INTRODUCTION

S INCE ITS ESTABLISHMENT in 1988, the *raison d'être* of the General
Court has been to improve the judicial protection of individual interests, in particular in proceedings necessitating close examination of
complex facts, while maintaining the quality and effectiveness of judicial
review in the EU legal order.[1]

The General Court has since then expanded in both size and jurisdiction,
as the EU has moved to a Union of 28 Member States, and from covering
only certain competition and civil service cases, to now having a general
jurisdiction of cases in more than 40 areas of law.[2] The growth is also paralleled in the court's caseload, as the increase in the number of cases has created a substantial backlog.[3]

With the considerable expansion in jurisdiction and almost tenfold
increase in cases since its establishment, the main focus of the General Court
in recent years has been on organisational change as a way to increase its

---

* This chapter is based on a panel discussion involving Judge Ulf Öberg and others at
Stockholm University, 9 December 2016, on the theme: 'Understanding The European Court
of Justice: Multidisciplinary Perspectives?'. The authors would like to thank Mattias Derlén,
Johan Lindholm and the people at Hart for providing helpful comments on earlier drafts of the
chapter. The usual disclaimer applies.

[1] Recitals and Article 1 of Council Decision 88/591 of 24 October 1988 establishing a Court
of First Instance of the European Communities (OJ 1988, L 319/1). See also Case C-185/95 P
Baustahlgewebe GmbH v Commission, EU:C:1998:608, para 41.

[2] The areas of law include, e.g., access to documents, agriculture, intellectual and industrial
property, competition, employment, restrictive measures, taxation and environment. For an
overview of the General Court's cases, see the Court of Justice of the European Union, *Annual
Report 2016*, 215.

[3] See, e.g., then CJEU President Vassilios Skouris' Draft amendments to the Statute of
the Court of Justice of the European Union and to Annex I thereto, enclosed in Letter from
the President of the Court of Justice to the President of the European Parliament and to the
President of the Council of the EU, 28 March 2011, 2 ff. Available at: http://curia.europa.eu/
jcms/upload/docs/application/pdf/2011-04/projet_en.pdf (last accessed 1 April 2017).

productivity. In an attempt to remedy the lengthy proceedings considered to be incompatible with the requirements of both the Charter of Fundamental Rights of the EU and the ECHR,[4] the European Parliament and the Council adopted Regulation 2015/2422 (below the 'Regulation') to increase the number of judges of the General Court in three stages, to 56 judges by 2019, or two judges per Member State.[5] More limited suggestions for reform, such as adding fewer additional judges from certain Member States, creating specialised courts, or increasing the number of legal secretaries were discarded in what resulted in the largest reform of the General Court since its inception.[6] The proposal for doubling the number of judges was premised, in particular, on the steady increase of new cases and the excessive duration of proceedings in state aid and competition cases.[7]

The question is whether doubling the number of judges will enable the institution 'to continue to fulfil its task in the interests of European litigants, while meeting the objectives of quality and efficiency of justice',[8] and whether or not the General Court needs further internal reform, including an increased specialisation of its chambers, to enhance both the quality in its adjudication and its legitimacy.

Specialisation could contribute to fulfil the General Court's founding promise of improving the judicial protection of individual interests, in particular in proceedings requiring a close examination of complex facts, and maintaining quality and effectiveness of judicial review in the EU legal order. Part of the realisation of the General Court's objectives should then be to address the concerns raised by the court's different stakeholders, in light also of Article 10 of the Treaty of the European Union (TEU), namely that decisions shall be taken as openly and as closely as possible to the EU citizen.

---

[4] The General Court has, on several occasions, been found to be liable for the excessive length in proceedings before it. See, e.g., Case T-577/14 *Gascogne Sack Deutschland GmbG and Gascogne v European Union*, EU:T:2017:1, according to which the EU was ordered to pay more than €50,000 in damages to companies as a result of breaches of the obligation to adjudicate within a reasonable time in competition cases before the General Court.

[5] Regulation (EU, Euratom) 2015/2422 of the European Parliament and of the Council of 16 December 2015 amending Protocol No 3 on the Statute of the Court of Justice of the European Union [2015], OJ L341/14.

[6] For a description of the background of the reform, see, e.g., F Dehousse, 'The Reform of the EU Courts (II)—Abandoning the Management Approach by Doubling the General Court', 2016 Egmont Paper 83. Available at: http://egmontinstitute.be/wp-content/uploads/2016/03/ep83.pdf.pdf (last accessed 1 April 2017) and A Alemanno and L Pech, 'Thinking Justice Outside the Docket: A Critical Assessment of the Reform of the EU's Court System' (2017) *CMLR* 129–76.

[7] See n 3 above.

[8] President of the Court of Justice, Koen Lenaerts, as quoted in J-C Ernst, 'Koen Lenaerts: Le Tribunal doit prendre au sérieux son rôle de « High Court of the Union »', *Le Jeudi* 27 January 2016. Available at: http://jeudi.lu/koen-lenaerts-le-tribunal-doit-prendre-au-serieux-son-role-de-high-court-of-the-union/ (last accessed 1 April 2017).

2. THE DIFFERENT CALLS FOR SPECIALISED CHAMBERS
AT THE GENERAL COURT

There have been several calls for specialised chambers in the General Court, both internally and externally.

Originally, one of the reasons put forward by the Court of Justice to justify its proposal for the reform of the General Court was that it would allow for allocating judges to the most pressing areas,[9] which may vary over time. This could be taken as a signal of its intention to achieve increased specialisation within the General Court. In its proposal for a reform, the Court of Justice also emphasised that:

> ... an increase in the number of Judges will not, by itself, resolve every problem. It is essential that it be accompanied at the same time by reflection on how to make the best use of all the General Court's resources, perhaps through specialisation by certain chambers and flexible management of cases allocation ...[10]

The Commission argued in favour of the reform, stating that since the nature and volume of litigation before the EU courts has changed radically in recent years, the 'organization, resources and functioning of the courts need to be adapted so that they can cope with all these developments'.[11] According to the Commission, a flexible solution would be to establish specialised chambers within the General Court itself.[12] The current method of organisation where classes of cases are automatically assigned, forces judges to master all areas of law and the President of the General Court can derogate from the current system of rigorous equality between the different Chambers only in exceptional cases.[13] The Commission considered that these features could not be maintained in an enlarged General Court, as the large number of chambers would result in an even more fragmented distribution of the various classes of cases.[14] It therefore took the view that some subject-matter specialisation by several General Court chambers would be necessary to ensure a more efficient and rapid handling of cases, while preserving flexibility in order to adapt to emerging types of disputes.[15]

The European Parliament also outlined, in its report on the draft regulation, that the steady increase in cases lodged with the General Court could

---

[9] See n 3 above at 10.
[10] Ibid.
[11] Commission Opinion of 30 September 2011 on the requests for the amendment of the Statute of the Court of Justice of the European Union, presented by the Court, COM [2011] 596 final, para 8.
[12] Ibid, para 36.
[13] Ibid, para 34.
[14] Ibid, para 35.
[15] Ibid, para 36.

not be sourced back to a single factor, being instead a product of a combination of factors:

(a)   the expansion of the General Court's jurisdiction;
(b)   the increase in litigation after the accession of new Member States in 2004 and 2007;
(c)   the expansion of EU competences since the Single European Act and the increase in the number and variety of EU legal acts; and
(d)   the growth of litigation in traditional areas such as trademarks.[16]

In addition, the Parliament stated that the criteria for the appointment of new judges should be based on suitability and reflect what the citizens want, given that they '... must be able to depend on the fact that their concerns are ruled on by the most suitable judges (and not only by suitable judges)'.[17] This can be interpreted as an argument for having specialised judges.

From the perspective of some practitioners and researchers, as the General Court has moved from being a specialised competition court to being a general administrative court, it has also evolved from exercising a significant disciplinary effect on the Commission's decision-making in the enforcement of competition rules to having a marginalised review in these cases.[18] The General Court has also been criticised in intellectual property cases for incoherence in its case law (e.g. when assessing the likelihood of confusion between trademarks).[19]

Finally, it should be noted that, while calls for more specialisation have emanated from different stakeholders in the context of the reform of the General Court, a thorough consideration of the option of increased specialisation may be considered to constitute the explicit will of the European Union legislator. The Regulation itself provides that, by 26 December 2020, the Court of Justice is expected to have a report 'using an external consultant', focusing on the efficiency of the General Court as well as 'the necessity and effectiveness of the increase to 56 judges, the use of and effectiveness of resources and the further establishment of specialised chambers and/or other structural changes'.[20]

---

[16] See also Alemanno and Pech, above n 7 at 133 based on the Report of 10 July 2013 on the draft regulation of the European Parliament and of the Council amending the Protocol on the Statute of the Court of Justice of the European Union by increasing the number of judges at the General Court (02074/2011—C7-0126/2012—2011/0901B(COD)) para 2 (Explanatory Statement). Available at: www.europarl.europa.eu/sides/getDoc.do?pubRef=-//EP//TEXT+REPORT+A7-2013-0252+0+DOC+XML+V0//EN#title1 (last accessed 1 April 2017).

[17] Ibid, para 8 (Explanatory Statement).

[18] See, e.g., F Montag and F Hoseinian, 'The Forthcoming Reform of the General Court of the European Union—Potential Specialisation within the General Court' (2012) *Fordham Competition Law Institute* 89.

[19] See, e.g., I Fhima and C Denvir, 'An Empirical Analysis of the Likelihood of Confusion Factors in European Trade Mark Law' (2015) *International Review of Intellectual Property and Competition Law* 310–39.

[20] See above n 3, Art 3(1).

The different stakeholders' arguments for specialisation of the General Court's chambers, both pre- and post-reform, have therefore focused not only on increased litigation, which was the main cause of the reform, but also on the quality of its adjudication.

3. INCREASED SPECIALISATION: A WAY FORWARD TO DEAL WITH COMPLEX CASES?

As mentioned above, competition and civil service cases were the first cases transferred to the General Court by Council Decision no 88/591, and were used as a justification for the court's creation with regard to the cases factual complexities.[21]

Yet, the conclusions that can be drawn from comparing the ways that the General Court has dealt with civil service and competition cases and past experiences with specialisation, is that a certain degree of specialisation may be beneficial in addressing such cases, the treatment of which lay at the heart of the creation of the General Court.

When it comes to past experiences with specialisation, the former Civil Service Tribunal, which consisted of seven judges specialised in EU civil service cases, has arguably been an overall positive experience, not only in terms of its productivity—as it relieved the General Court of between 150 to 200 cases a year to become the most productive court of the EU system— but also in terms of the quality of its judgments, as the procedures of the Civil Service Tribunal could be adapted to the nature of cases before it.[22]

In the discussions pre-reform, certain judges at the General Court argued that the creation of a specialised court for trademarks, designs and models would facilitate the rationalisation of the General Court's jurisdiction, allow the recruitment of judges specialised in intellectual property and ensure a greater coherence in the case law on the subject. They pointed out that specialised courts not only have fewer judges, but also fewer legal secretaries and assistants; consequently, they would be cheaper to operate than non-specialised courts.[23]

The challenge for the General Court in the current phase of the reform is to assess whether or not the same arguments hold true for the creation of specialised chambers within the court.

---

[21] See above n 1. See also M Prek and S Lefèvre, 'Competition Litigation before the General Court: Quality if not Quantity?' (2016) *CMLR* 65.

[22] See, e.g., 'Doubling the General Court's Judges: Why Progressive, Reversible and More Economic Solutions are Far Better' as cited in F Dehousse, above n 6, at fn 77. Available at: http://egmontinstitute.be/wp-content/uploads/2016/03/ep83.pdf.pdf (last accessed 1 June 2017). See also I Pelikánova, 'The Advantages of Creating a Specialised Court'. Available at: http://g8fip1kplyr33r3krz5b97d1.wpengine.netdna-cdn.com/wp-content/uploads/2015/04/28April2015-EP-Strasbourg-specialised-courts.pdf (last accessed 1 April 2017).

[23] Ibid.

As to the General Court's handling of competition cases some critics have argued that the review is not thorough enough and that the Court's current standard of review leaves too large of a 'margin of appraisal' to the Commission.[24] The trend over time has also seen a relative decline in the number of new state aid and competition cases in the General Court's docket, with 148 new state aid cases lodged in 2014 compared to 73 in 2015 and 76 in 2016.[25] There were 41 new competition cases lodged in 2014, 17 in 2015 and 18 in 2016.[26]

One of several plausible explanations for this development could be that an increased marginalised judicial review by the General Court in complex cases leads to a decrease in the number of applications lodged.[27] Should there be any merit to this theory, which admittedly would require further in-depth examination, it would reinforce the need for the General Court to fully assume its stated original role of improving the judicial protection of individual interests, in particular in proceedings necessitating a closer examination of complex facts.

On several appeals over the last years, the Court of Justice has addressed this issue stating that the EU courts cannot rely on the Commission's margin of appraisal 'as a basis for dispensing with the conduct of an in-depth review of the law and of the facts'.[28] In state aid cases, the Court of Justice has recently reiterated that 'the EU Courts must in principle, having regard both to the specific features of the case before them and to the technical or complex nature of the Commission's assessments, carry out a comprehensive review as to whether a measure falls within the scope of Article 107(1) TFEU'.[29]

In other words, the General Court is faced with the task of showing that it has the ability not only to decide cases efficiently according to the aim of the reform, but also ensure that it upholds a rigorous standard of quality

---

[24] See Montag and Hoseinian above n 19. For a contrasting view, see M Jaeger, 'The Standard of Review in Competition Cases Involving Complex Economic Assessments: Towards the Marginalisation of the Marginal Review?' (2011) *JECL & Pract* 295 ff.

[25] See n 2 above.

[26] Ibid.

[27] See, for other explanations, such as shrinking EU enforcement with deference to the Member States under Regulation 1/2003, the success of the settlement procedure in this area, or that cartel deterrence is working. See Prek and Lefèvre above n 21 and M van der Woude 'Competition Law and the Reform of the General Court of the European Union'. Presentation 31 March 2017, Washington DC.

[28] Case C-389/10 P, *KME Germany and others v Commission*, EU:C:2011:816, para 129; Case C-386/10 P, *Chalkor v Commission*, EU:C:2011:815, para 62; Case C-199/11, *Otis and others*, EU: C:2012:684, paras 59 and 61.

[29] Case C-486/15 P *Commission v France and Orange*, EU:C:2016:912, para 87. See also Case C-73/11 P, *Frucona Košice/Commission*, EU:C:2013:32, paras 75–76, which points out that the EU courts must establish not only whether the evidence relied on is factually accurate, reliable and consistent but also whether that 'evidence contains all the relevant information which must be taken into account in order to assess a complex situation and whether it is capable of substantiating the conclusions drawn from it'.

in its judicial review that can sustain an increased control by the Court of Justice on appeal. Specialisation could be a means to such an end, enabling the General Court to invest more resources into complex cases and ensuring that such cases are given appropriate attention through a formal and open system, while at the same time relieving the Court of Justice in certain areas of law and/or types of proceedings.

Indeed, at the heart of the debates on the reform and the future judicial architecture of the EU, also lies the question of whether a transfer of competences from the Court of Justice to the General Court should follow.[30] Article 256(3) of the Treaty on the Functioning of the European Union (TFEU) provides that the General Court shall rule on preliminary references in specific areas of law laid down by the statute.[31] To date however, preliminary references remain within the Court of Justice's exclusive competences. If the General Court's docket were to be opened to national judges enquiring about the interpretation or the application of EU law, the General Court would act more as a constitutional court, at least in those areas devolved to it, and may, for the sake of its legitimacy, have to convince that it holds the proposer expertise to add on to its current fact-based reviews.

A number of questions linked to the institutional architecture of the EU courts would then need to be resolved, such as whether a two-tier judicial system remains relevant in those areas of law.[32] Because of the difference in judicial treatment between preliminary rulings and other cases and considering that the preliminary rulings by the General Court would be limited to certain areas of law (e.g. intellectual property, customs or public procurement), specialisation at the General Court's level would also likely be a prerequisite to that end.

Therefore, the increased specialisation of chambers as a way to deal with complex cases not only has a basis in past experiences within the General Court (e.g. relating to intellectual property and civil service cases) but may also prove necessary to address concerns raised about its current limited review and to allow potential further expansion in its jurisdiction.

---

[30] See above n 3 at 9–10. See also, Art 3(2) of Regulation 2015/2422 (above n 6), which provides that by 26 December 2017, the Court of Justice should draw up a report to address 'possible changes to the distribution of competence for preliminary rulings under Article 267 TFEU'.

[31] Article 256(3) of the consolidated version of the Treaty on the Functioning of the European Union [2012] OJ C 326/47 (TFEU) provides that '[t]he General Court shall have jurisdiction to hear and determine questions referred for a preliminary ruling under Article 267, in specific areas laid down by the Statute.

Where the General Court considers that the case requires a decision of principle likely to affect the unity or consistency of Union law, it may refer the case to the Court of Justice for a ruling.

Decisions given by the General Court on questions referred for a preliminary ruling may exceptionally be subject to review by the Court of Justice, under the conditions and within the limits laid down by the Statute, where there is a serious risk of the unity or consistency of Union law being affected.'

[32] Ibid.

4. INCREASED SPECIALISATION: A WAY TO INCREASE THE QUALITY IN JUDICIAL DECISION MAKING

As already highlighted by various stakeholders, increasing the number of judges in a vacuum, without additional structural reform, does not sufficiently address the changing nature of litigation before the General Court and its increased level of complexity, both of which require a focus on the quality of its decision making.

The notion of quality has already been evoked by Koen Lenaerts who has suggested allocating a larger number of cases to five-judge chambers rather than three-judge chambers, after the reform.[33] Such a change would, in his view, lead to better quality judgments and, in turn, further enhance the legitimacy of the General Court's decision making.

To date, the General Court has not yet given heed to its stakeholders' calls for increased specialisation, instead opting for maintaining a high level of generalisation at the court, as evidenced both by its new rules on allocation of new cases and its judicial activity.

On 11 May 2016, shortly before the arrival of new judges as a result of the second phase of the reform, the then members of the plenum of the General Court decided that new cases, as a default position, should continue to be attributed to chambers sitting with three judges and that all chambers should in principle hear all types of cases.[34] The General Court is currently composed of nine chambers of five judges, meaning that annually, about 1,000 new cases are, by this default rule, attributed to 18 different three-judge constellations.

Looking to the initial statistics of the reform, the General Court is still deciding cases mostly in three-judge constellations, as was the case pre-reform. Cases decided in three-judge formations accounted for 80 per cent of the General Court's judgments and orders in 2007, compared to about 87 per cent in 2016.[35]

With more specialised chambers, a flexible management and a thorough review, particularly of difficult and lengthy cases, would be facilitated for several reasons:

(a) reporting judges would have more resources within their chambers to allocate to such cases, since their attention would be divided across fewer areas of law. For example, under a governance model focused on a moderate degree of specialisation, a chamber would presumably not be specialised in both state aid and competition cases; rather the

---

[33] See Ernst above n 8.
[34] General Court, Criteria for the assignment of cases to Chambers (2016/C 296/04), para 2.
[35] Greffe du Tribunal, Statistiques judiciaires état au 31 décembre 2016, document interne, 16.

workload caused by specialisation in one of these areas would be compensated by additional specialisation in areas where cases are typically dealt with faster, such as staff cases or intellectual property cases;

(b) increased specialisation of chambers could help avoid 'high entry costs' in particular for new judges in certain areas of law where the jurisprudence is both technical and voluminous, with greater efficiency as a consequence; and

(c) increased specialisation of chambers could also lead to the improved collective participation of all the judges specialised in any given area of law, with increased collegiality as a consequence and more cases dealt with by five-judge formations

One of the main arguments against specialisation has been the assumption that judges dealing with mostly one area of law could lose sight of a more systemic perspective which would be necessary to ensure the uniform interpretation and application of EU law across the board, and not just in one area alone.

However, the increased specialisation of chambers provides an example of the type of internal structural measures that should be considered to counterbalance the inherent risks of maintaining the status quo. It has been argued that the reform, underpinned by statistics-driven justifications premised upon the backlog of cases, currently places a premium on efficiency and speedy handling over other values typifying the quality of the judicial process.[36] The same critics allege that it is through a narrow, input-output metric that human resources have been mobilised within the General Court.[37]

Productivity constituted an appropriate goal at a time when the increasing workload of the General Court was paralleled with significant delays causing it liability. However, going forward, the balancing of the General Court's scorecard should concentrate on designing criteria aimed at evaluating the quality of the judicial activity and its accessibility to the European citizenry.

Indeed, it is generally admitted that 'quality' of justice should not be subsumed within 'productivity',[38] but measured and defined in relation to 'the ability of the system to match the demand of justice in conformity with the general goals of the legal system'.[39] Pursuant to this approach, the quality of

---

[36] See Alemanno and Pech above n 6 at 163.
[37] Ibid.
[38] Consultative Council of European Judges (CCJE), 'On fair trial within a reasonable time and judge's rule in trials taking into account alternative means of dispute settlements', Opinion No 6 2004, para 42. Available at: https://wcd.coe.int/ViewDoc.jsp?p=&Ref=CCJE%282004%29OP6&Sector=secDGHL&Language=lanEnglish&direct=true (last accessed 1 April 2017).
[39] Ibid.

justice at the General Court should, in a not too distant future, be measured in its wider context by taking into account the external web of relationships established with different stakeholders.[40]

Thus, in order to guide its forthcoming internal reforms, the General Court would benefit from conducting a comprehensive external stakeholders analysis and measuring the quality of its judicial decision-making in the eyes of the EU institutions, agencies and bodies whose decisions are contested before the General Court; the EU citizens or private parties whose interests are directly affected by judicial review; and the Court of Justice itself. As outlined above, since several of these stakeholders have already called for increased specialisation, it is an issue which the General Court will have to address sooner or later.

5. INCREASED SPECIALISATION: A WAY TO INCREASE LEGAL COHERENCE AND OPENNESS IN JUDICIAL DECISION MAKING

It may be recalled that two specialised chambers for intellectual property cases were operational between 1998 and 2003 and a specialised *chambre des pourvois* was created to deal with appeals against decisions of the Civil Services Tribunal. These specialised chambers were set up in accordance with Article 25(1) of the Rules of Procedure of the General Court (corresponding to Article 12(1) of the then 1991 Rules of Procedure) which provides that the court can make one or more chambers responsible for hearing and determining cases in specific matters. In particular, the chambers specialised in intellectual property were set up to lay the foundations of the case law in this field and ensure legal coherence.[41]

The task of ensuring legal coherence may become overly burdensome after the reform as it entails monitoring what is approaching 800 annual judgments and orders and 1,000 annual new cases produced by 56 judges sitting by default in 18 different chambers of three judges. Diverging legal approaches along with the erosion of quality in decision making could be possible collateral and unintended consequences of the reform, as has already

---

[40] That criteria's should be designed to evaluate whether the judicial architecture reflects the expectations of the different stakeholders of a given court, see, e.g., a study on the French legal system: Centre d'Etudes et de Recherches de Science Administrative—CERSA et Observatoire des mutations institutionnelles et juridiques—OMIJ, 'La prise en compte de la notion de qualité de la justice dans la mesure de la performance judiciaire, Appel à projet de la Mission de recherche Droit et Justice' (2016) *Revue française d'administration publique*, 1. Available at: www.gip-recherche-justice.fr/wp-content/uploads/2016/01/Synthèse-QUALIJUS-JA2.pdf (last accessed 1 April 2017). See also: 'Actualités de la Recherche—Interview croisée sur la notion de qualité dans la mesure de la performance judiciaire'. Available at: https://mrdj.hypotheses.org/362 (last accessed 1 April 2017).

[41] See, e.g,. E Coulon, 'Le Tribunal de l'Union européenne à l'épreuve du temps, (2009–2010) *Law & European Affairs*, 411.

been argued by outside stakeholders and commentators. Legal debates and attempts to seek clarification or improvement of the jurisprudence are likely to prove more difficult, when the judicial decision-making process at the General Court leaves no room for dissent and little room for individual voices to be heard.

The principal solution chosen so far by the plenum of General Court in view of the reform has been to entrust its Vice-President with this difficult mission of ensuring legal coherence. Arguably however, with more specialised chambers, debates about legal coherence or reform could be initiated by the judges sitting on cases, rather than by external intervention or a hierarchical approach pursuant to General Court's judicial activities. Legal coherence would be guaranteed on the basis of a more collegial approach and expertise, rather than a 'one-size fits all' solution.

To some extent, Article 30 of the Rules of Procedure of the General Court, which provides for the appointment of an Advocate General in specific cases, if it considers that the legal difficulty or the factual complexity of the case so requires, shows that the aim of relying on experts is a common objective for the Court of Justice and the General Court. Being a specialist in the designated area of law, the Advocate General may adopt a transversal approach and help the judges, who are deciding a case, to ensure legal coherence with previous case law, particularly where the General Court finds itself confronted with unprecedented legal issues, or conflicting case law. However, this provision has yet to be used in the General Court in a post-reform context. The use of this provision could be facilitated by the introduction of formal specialisation which would highlight the respective areas of expertise of judges at the General Court.

Just as legal coherence is essential to the so called *rayonnement* or *visibilité* (i.e. the external outreach) of the General Court's jurisprudence, so is openness about the functioning of the General Court. Currently, a degree of specialisation already exists at the General Court, albeit at an informal level. Pursuant to a decision of the General Court adopted at its plenum on 11 May 2016,[42] the default position is that cases should be attributed to the chambers following four separate rotas:

— for cases concerning the application of the competition rules applicable to undertakings, the rules on State aid and the rules on trade protection measures;
— for cases concerning intellectual property rights referred to in Title IV of the Rules of Procedure;
— for civil service cases; and
— for all other cases.

---

[42] See General Court above n 34. See also Arts 26– 28 of the Rules of Procedure of the General Court [2015], OJ L 105/1.

These four separate rotas reflect the fact that at least three distinct pools of cases can be identified, with the rest of the jurisdictional activity of the General Court accounting for the 'other cases'.

Derogation from these rotas is possible at the initiative of the President of the General Court, in order to take account of a connection between cases or with a view of ensuring an even spread of the workload.[43] What the 'connection between cases' actually means in practice is not further explained and has been left at the discretion of the President. This has, however, become the steering device pursuant to which cases are attributed, as the President of the Court of Justice has himself stated.[44]

The increased specialisation of chambers, which is formally recognised on the basis of Article 25(1) of the Procedural Rules of the General Court, would provide greater openness and legal certainty by avoiding attributions on a case-by-case basis. This, in turn, could contribute to fulfilling the expectations of litigants to have their cases tried by a 'deeply committed' bench.[45]

6. CONCLUSIONS

Since the aim of the General Court, as of any court, is to achieve a balance between quality, quantity and speed in delivering justice, the question is whether doubling the number of judges in a vacuum provides an adequate means to this end.

It is important that measures are put in place not only to impact positively on the timeframe over which cases are dealt with, but also to allocate more resources to more complex cases and to ensure legal coherence and greater openness in the eyes of litigants.

If anything, this should call for more cases to be dealt with by more specialised chambers. There is perhaps a risk that judges develop a judicial 'tunnel vision' or impose excessive judicial policy-making[46] in areas in which they feel familiar, or that the EU judiciary would become captured by special interests. However, such a risk, which is inherent to any jurisdiction, is largely outweighed by the benefits where parties will at times see their highly technical or complex cases dealt with by specialised chambers and

---

[43] Ibid.

[44] See Ernst above n 8.

[45] President Koen Lenaerts, as cited in Alemanno and Pech, above n 7 at 159. On the issue of transparency of cases, note that currently, the majority of the General Court's judgments and orders are not published, as the court publishes about 23 per cent of its judgments and orders in their entirety in 2016. Greffe du Tribunal, Statistiques relatives à la publication au Recueil général, état au 31 décembre 2016, document interne, 1.

[46] See, e.g. S V Damle, 'Specialize the Judge, not the Court: A Lesson from the German Constitutional Court' (2005) *Virginia Law Review* 1281; and W Hellerstein, 'Specialized Tax Courts in Multijurisdictional Systems: An American Perspective, in M Lang *et al* (eds), *CJEU— Recent Developments in Value Added Tax* (Wien, Linde, 2015) 107.

the judicial protection of individual interests will be enhanced. The reform on specialisation is particularly timely considering the difficulties the EU is facing with its legitimacy in question and a gap between the EU institutions and EU citizens.[47]

Finally, given that the reform of the General Court has increased the number of judges and not legal secretaries in each chamber, one of the main benefits of the increased specialisation of chambers should ultimately be to engage the expertise of the judges themselves, as opposed to that of their legal secretaries. The logic behind the reform creates an impetus for the General Court to embrace to a greater extent a 'writer' model of internal judicial organisation, where the legal secretary's work is to improve the draft which originates from the judge himself, as opposed to a 'manager' model, where the system relies on the abilities of the legal secretaries.[48]

The 'writer' model pushes for the expertise of judges to be more utilised. Specialisation would then guard against a persistent emphasis on productivity and generalisation, which may lead Member States appointing judges to treat them as interchangeable since there is no 'premium' on their expertise or level of specialisation.

---

[47] On the issue that both generalist courts and specialist tribunals may lack the requisite institutional legitimacy to address cases involving broad policy considerations, see D Mantzari, 'Economic Evidence in Regulatory Disputes: Revisiting the Court-Regulatory Agency Relationship in the US and the UK' (2016) *Oxford Journal of Legal Studies* 585.

[48] R A Posner, *Reflections on Judging* (Cambridge MA, Harvard University Press, 2013) 238–45. See also S Kenney, 'Beyond Principals and Agents Seeing Courts As Organizations By Comparing Référendaires at the European Court of Justice and Law Clerks at the U.S. Supreme Court' (2000) *Comparative Political Studies* 614. Available at: www.researchgate. net/publication/258130329_Beyond_Principals_and_Agents_Seeing_Courts_As_Organizations_By_Comparing_Referendaires_at_the_European_Court_of_Justice_and_Law_Clerks_at_the_US_Supreme_Court (last accessed 1 April 2017).

Index

Lightning Source UK Ltd.
Milton Keynes UK
UKHW021431280520
363987UK00006B/332